My Dear Wife,

My Dear Wife,

The Letters of a British Airman and Soldier
Written During the First World War

My Airman Over There
His Wife
(Aimée Bond)

and

Letters to His Wife
R. E. Vernède

My Dear Wife,
The Letters of a British Airman and Soldier Written During the First World War
My Airman Over There
by His Wife (Aimée Bond)
and
Letters to His Wife
by R. E. Vernède

First published under the titles
My Airman Over There
and
Letters to His Wife

Leonaur is an imprint
of Oakpast Ltd

Copyright in this form © 2013 Oakpast Ltd

ISBN: 978-1-78282-064-2 (hardcover)
ISBN: 978-1-78282-065-9 (softcover)

http://www.leonaur.com

Publisher's Notes
The views expressed in this book are not necessarily
those of the publisher.

Contents

My Airman Over There   7

Letters to His Wife   205

My Airman Over There

Contents

Chapter 1	13
Chapter 2	16
Chapter 3	20
Chapter 4	23
Chapter 5	27
Chapter 6	29
Chapter 7	33
Chapter 8	36
Chapter 9	39
Chapter 10	42
Chapter 11	44
Chapter 12	47
Chapter 13	51
Chapter 14	53
Chapter 15	56
Chapter 16	58
Chapter 17	61
Chapter 18	64
Chapter 19	66
Chapter 20	67
Chapter 21	70
Chapter 22	72
Chapter 23	74
Chapter 24	80
Chapter 25	85
Chapter 26	88
Chapter 27	92
Chapter 28	95
Chapter 29	100

Chapter 30	104
Chapter 31	107
Chapter 32	112
Chapter 33	120
Chapter 34	123
Chapter 35	126
Chapter 36	129
Chapter 37	131
Chapter 38	133
Chapter 39	136
Chapter 40	139
Chapter 41	141
Chapter 42	143
Chapter 43	145
Chapter 44	147
Chapter 45	149
Chapter 46	151
Chapter 47	153
Chapter 48	156
Chapter 49	158
Chapter 50	162
Chapter 51	164
Chapter 52	167
Chapter 53	169
Chapter 54	174
Chapter 55	176
Chapter 56	178
Chapter 57	180
Chapter 58	182
Chapter 59	184
Chapter 60	186
Chapter 61	188
Chapter 62	190
Chapter 63	192
Chapter 64	198
Chapter 65	200
Chapter 66	202

TO THE SQUADRON

Chapter 1

On Wednesday, very early in the morning, Bill went to France.

"Can I go too—to Folkestone, I mean?" I said to the officer person who stood just inside the platform gates beside a sort of desk where they all had to sign their names.

"I'm sorry—if you were the wife of a brigadier-general you couldn't," he replied very kindly, adding, "One tried last week, and she was brought back under arrest."

I smiled back at him, but I had to bite my lip.

Bill appeared just then. He had been seeing about his baggage and things.

"Have you asked?" he questioned, and his face was quite stolid.

"Yes, . . . I can't come," I told him.

We walked along the platform. It was crowded with those who were going, like Bill; and those who were being left behind, like me.

There were a few moments only. We stood by the carriage door and didn't say anything. I felt I couldn't begin because there would be no time to finish. I daresay Bill felt the same.

Anyway my throat was funny and I didn't want him to know.

They began to bang the doors. Suddenly I had to speak. It was urgent.

"Don't kiss me here," I whispered in a panic; but after all he couldn't have heard for he bent down.

"If the boat is delayed I'll wire and you'll come at once, won't you?" he said, and kissed my mouth.

I nodded my head: the train moved.

"Goodbye, old boy," I managed quite clearly, and smiled.

He smiled too.

"Goodbye," he answered.

I don't know if he hung out of the window, for I walked away and never looked round. Outside, although it was spring-time, the rain and the snow came down together.

I wondered what to do, and as it didn't seem to matter much I got into a bus that no one appeared to want. When it had been going for some time, I got out and went in an underground.

Then I remembered that I'd left all our luggage at the hotel.

"But I'll go home first," I thought

"Home" meant the place I lived in before I married Bill. No one bothers about you there. You can stow yourself away and arrange all your things for as long as you like—that is if you can find an empty place.

When Purcell opened the door she looked surprised first, then understood.

"Oh, Miss, has he gone?" she said.

"Yes," I answered, and ran upstairs as fast as I could.

In my old room was the victrola and I recalled how Bill had wound it up the night we slept there. It was when we came to town unexpectedly once and couldn't get in at the hotel, where we stay for sentimental reasons, that wouldn't appeal to anyone but ourselves.

We had danced to a ragtime tune—he in his blue *crêpe-de-chine* pyjamas and me in the stage of undress that makes him call me his "*Kirchner*" girl. Now I put on the same record and watched it while it solidly ground away. Just as it finished with a horrid scrape, and I was wondering what to do to make it stop, Purcell came in with a tray, holding steaming coffee, and bread and honey and the morning newspaper.

"There you are, Miss," she said, placing it on another small table and dragging it over to the fire to which she set a match.

I don't know whether it was her tone, or the scent of the coffee, or the sight of the newspaper, or the crackle of the flames—but all at once something cleared away the cloud that had swallowed me up ever since the night before when Bill had come back from Adastral House and announced:

"They won't give any leave—I am to go in the morning."

Those words had bothered me ever since, but now I remembered something else.

In the night he had spoken.

"You must be happy," he had said. "I'll come back to you, I know. . . All our life together, our wonderful adventures and our work . . . all is so clearly mapped out . . . . I feel I'm coming back to you. . . . You're to be happy."

"Yes," I answered—whispered, you know, like you do in bed because your faces are close to each other's. There was a pause. I knew something waited. I scarcely breathed, and it came at last.

"And if I shouldn't come," . . . he went on. . . . "If I shouldn't come, you're to be happy even then," he said.

Chapter 2

And I *have* been happy—ever since.

It is as though a presence is with me; the embodiment perhaps of Bill's philosophy.

He believes, you know, that we make our own light or darkness as we go, and his refusal to be baffled by circumstance is not merely the outcome of good health and a man's more sweeping outlook, as I told myself at first it must be.

Now, sometimes, I wonder at my calm. I wonder how other wives feel, and I recall some I have known during these years of war. Those who have loved their men have been feverish all the while—aching with loneliness—adrift—forlorn.

In spite of work, or perhaps because the labour they have chosen has been too strenuous or too unusual, their health seems to have suffered; and husbands, returning, have found what I think soldier men have no right to expect—wives more in need of doctors than husbands.

And so I—who have rebelled always, who have, until now, refused to accept even the inevitable—am glad of, while I marvel at my calm.

The first letter was written before he crossed. I knew it was meant just to greet me when I wakened because he would not be with me to kiss me before we spoke.

When Purcell had gone, with my head still on the pillow, I read:

Ma Bien Aimée,

I discovered that, because I was 'O. C. train,' I had to wait for the second boat.

Immediately I looked up the guide but found you could not reach me before it left.

It will be very rough crossing—a sort of switch-back one that

would make you giddy even to contemplate.
I hope you are feeling as cheery as I am. I find myself in excellent spirits—not excited, you know, but buoyed up by interest. I am longing to know my address though, so that I can begin to hear from you.

All love, my darling wife,

Bill.

I pressed my face against the join of the pillows, for that is where our lips always met instinctively almost before sleep had unclosed our eyes.

At lunch time a telegram came from France, giving me the address, so that immediately after I was able to send all that I'd talked of on paper since he went. Then I had to wait until Saturday morning for all that he had spoken on Thursday.

Doesn't it seem absurd—and yet so amazing!

This is what he said:

My darling wife.

My luck's all in as usual, for I have come to one of the best squadrons in a good part of the line. The machines are things of beauty and the mess is splendid. What more could a flying man want? I am to fly a—scout, which is, if anything, better than the one I flew at home. They dive faster and fly and climb quite as well.

You'd go into an ecstasy if you saw one.

I am longing to try one, but shall have to wait a day or two when I shall have a new one: all mine, like you.

The weather is very wild and there is little doing.

I reached here last night. On landing I was put on a tender and had a three hours' ride over the hills through the rain. And when I went to the orderly room to report I found myself reporting to Hyatt. I was awfully pleased. He arrived four days ago. It's great luck, I think, and further, I've been posted to the same flight.

I know lots of the fellows here; for in the same aerodrome is the squadron to which Fitz-Garrick came; but I learn that he went down behind the Hun lines a few days ago—under control, so it is presumed that he is a prisoner. Engine failure must have caused it.

I'm sorry I took such trouble to keep down my kit, for travelling

was so easy that I could have brought three times as much.
But I can't think of anything I want you to send me except your letters and your love.
It is so much sweeter to be out here knowing that I have someone who matters so enormously to me. I am very happy, *ma bien Aimée*.
When I was in the train and leaving London I thought for the first time of your precious tears. It thrilled me, darling, to think of them—to remember you lying in my arms making my face all wet.
I realized that I couldn't realize how much I love you.
Darling wife, I am so glad you wept in my arms. I treasure the memory of it intensely.
   All My Love,

                  Bill.

P.S.—I came across a topping book at Folkestone—a quaint yarn about the Latin quarter—by a young Canadian officer, who also has written some quite good verse.
It's 'racy' and therefore not flawless, but his pictures of the quarter are lovely, I think.
By the way, my next letter will be addressed to the country, for I don't want to think of you in town.

Isn't it remarkable! Hyatt and Bill were at Suvla together and, later, in the trenches in France, where each won his "little bit of ribbon." Then, when both volunteered for the Flying Corps, they met at the same aerodrome in England; and both, having married in the same week, brought wives who called each of them "Bill" to the same cottage on the edge of Salisbury Plain—all by chance—without prearrangement!

The wives were different though. Hyatt chose a lovely woman—fair and with perfect features. Her blue eyes gazed from dark lashes too, and her brows were dark.

Usually I can admire impersonally, but after looking at her I said to Bill:

"I wish I were beautiful also."

He turned from the glass where the important business of hairbrushing was taking place. His tone was awfully serious.

"You're not to wish that—you mustn't wish that—tell me you don't wish it," he said.

"I don't wish it," I answered, "but why?"

"Because we're so happy—so content.... Because I love your face just as it is.... I wouldn't have it altered the tiniest little bit!"

Isn't he rather satisfactory?

It was so amusing to talk to the other Mrs. Bill. She and her Bill looked forward to a house in Kensington or Hampstead and they had the furniture all arranged. She was sorry for me, I think, when I told her we don't mean to have a house at all because we want to explore so much of the world.

Soon I realized that we spoke a different language, so I didn't say much about the studio in the *Quartier Latin*, or the cottage of Madame Champigny on the Seine, or our winters in Switzerland where the hot sun glints on the snow.

She is no vagabond—the other Mrs. Bill—but she has a lovely face.

Chapter 3

An old man is cutting the hedge. Every minute he takes several steps backward and stares at what he has done.

The air is soft and damp from yesterday's rain, but the sky is blue except for the fluffiest white eiderdown clouds.

I wonder if the sky is blue in France?

The old man who cuts the hedge has three sons there—one buried: one in hospital: and one in the big new Advance.

I daresay his thoughts are with them when he steps backward and stares, instead of with the bare places from which the branches have been clipped.

Most of the gardens we attend to ourselves. I'm the "Handy Andy" one. You remember how, at the circus, he always trod on everything and got in every one's way! A row of peas and one bean have peeped out of the earth.

Now Irene, that sister of mine, fills me with wonderment. Before breakfast she grooms Joey; and if anything goes wrong with Polly Blue she just takes off her bonnet and pulls her engine to bits—and puts it together again.

Then, without neglecting the family in the least, she writes an article on a topical subject just at the most topical moment; and in the evening she looks as feminine as a woman who has done nothing except care for herself all day.

Besides all this she interests herself in the welfare of the village, and when the tractor plough has convalesced she means to help to plough the fields.

The "County" who called on Tuesday—a nice, large woman, unconsciously humorous—suggested that she also might undertake the job of Agricultural Registrar, as the vicar doesn't seem too enthusiastic about the work. Irene pointed out that the need is small in a village like this, where the few women there are labour on the land of their own accord—of necessity, you know, to take the place of their men; but if, as a matter of form, it has to be done, so that every village is accounted for, she will add that to her routine and never turn a hair.

As for me—it takes me all my time to get up and to do my exercises and dress before my tray comes.

Irene likes to breakfast alone with her family; and so do I, with my casement window opened wide, eating my porridge looking beyond the trees of the garden and the dull red roofs of the barns, and beyond the windmill too, on to the Downs from which comes the breath of a far-off sea.

And I have my letter from Bill to read!

No wonder I feel content.

Of course some there are who think it unbecoming to be happy now when so many suffer and are sad, but I say that there is enough sorrow. I, too, have had some and imagined more, but now I will be glad while I may; and if it should happen that sorrow comes again I hope I still have courage to be glad.

My letter on Monday said:

Bien Aimée,
This morning I made my first trip on this machine.
It was quite successful, and I found it, if anything, easier to take off the ground and to land than the one at home; but it was very different in the air, much heavier and trickier on the steep turns.
I did two spins but did not loop. Then later I went up again for a machine-gun practice, which consists of diving at a target on the ground and firing at it.
The weather has been very much better today, though now it is getting squally again.
But I'm forgetting the news. Hyatt went over the lines on patrol this morning for the first time and got a Hun!
It was quite comical too. He was out with two others and when over the lines got lost in the clouds. He searched around for some time, not knowing at all where he was, and then suddenly a Hun two-seater came out of a cloud and flew at him. Hyatt fired promptly and saw the Hun turn over, go down spinning and crash to the ground.
Then he got 'Archied' and climbed out of it, guessed his way

and landed an hour overdue.

How are you? I send all my love.

Bill.

As I owed the other Mrs. Bill a letter, after breakfast I wrote to tell her the news in case her husband, man-like, forgot to mention it. But I know her pleasure at his feat will be counterbalanced, as mine would be, by the thought that some woman suffers through it.

Later we tramped through the fields and into the woods.

An old man worked in a clearing making hurdles. The sun, unwilling that day for the rest of us, was pleased to shine on him. Tall and erect he stood. His earth-stained clothes seemed a part of him and he seemed a part of the land.

Gaiters held together by string, corduroy breeches whose patches even had worn through, a coat out at elbows and a ragged cowboy hat over his tawny hair—such clothes in town would seem inadequate, but here, where the dirt is Nature's own, they made the picture more complete.

A pile of hurdles were stacked; another was being added to with easy speed. A blade, strong-handled, an upright block, and a curved bar upon the ground, were all the tools he used as he cut and split and bent the supple wood.

On we went—Irene and I and her family of one, for Nanny chose to be busy at home and Joey ran wild in his field.

Garry spied the primroses first and the violets, too, but for the daffodils we hunted in vain.

Chapter 4

In today's paper there is an account of a divorce case.

Both letters are dignified. The happiness they gave to one another; the years of congenial work together; the understanding and sympathy are not denied. Each is grateful to the other, but, as the man says, "Things change!"

Now this is a prospect Bill and I have discussed. It comes as a shock, in the midst of perfect agreement, to recall that nothing remains just as it is; that two human beings seldom develop equally; that chance may bring another woman—another man.

In reason can one hope to be more than a very precious part of another's sum total of living?

Bill and I have made no vows to one another beyond the formal words spoken at the marriage office.

Yet we set out with brighter prospects than most. Our outlook is the same, our work is the same, our desires too, for both are vagabonds! And what one lacks the other seems able to supply. Indeed our chances are fair—yet we have made no vows.

Tuesday's letter said:

Ma Bien Aimée,
Tonight I hope to get your first letter, darling.
I did no more flying yesterday than the two trips I told you of. In the evening, rather to my surprise, I was told to go out on a line patrol with two others. I was much pleased because it was a perfect evening, and I should have got a good idea of the line without going over it. However, when we were already in the machines, it was all washed out, and the others—the experienced ones—were sent to convoy a bombing raid.
This morning, however, I was put on the first offensive patrol and went over with two others.

I thoroughly enjoyed it. We started at 6.45 in triangular formation and worked down on our side of the line, crossed it at 12,000 feet, and worked back north about eight miles the other side. We saw five Hun machines which kept a long way clear and were 'Archied' nearly all the time. I saw a good deal of the line though I was busy mostly trying to keep my place in the formation.

We were out one hour and forty-five minutes, and I was told that I had flown quite well. And so to breakfast.

Have you any of my towels? I need another as I brought only two. Another khaki shirt too, if you please.

The weather is very fine but rough.

All my love,

Bill.

I'm sure I don't know where the towels are—or the shirt. The only shirt I have is the one his mother sent to Suvla. Thinking it a happy inspiration she gathered some apples from the garden and wrapped them in it, and, when after months of travel to the Dardanelles and back again, the parcel came to be opened it simply knocked them down.

The apples were no more, and the tail of the shirt had rotted into holes

After it had been scalded and hung out in the air for days, Bill—home on sick leave—commandeered it for a relic. He wore it on his marriage day—holes and all.

We're rather fond of that shirt

But I must write to town and order what he needs.

I'm sure he must have gone without lots of things, for his packing appears to be the most casual affair.

Smokes and hair lotion seem to be the only things that matter; and I'm afraid I like too much to sit and watch him mix tobacco on a newspaper to do my wifely bit.

Besides I don't want to get into a habit of bothering him with small inquiries. I think wives begin to be a burden when they go into detail too much.

Wednesday's letter was simply a scrawl to say nothing had arrived from me. It was written on Sunday and my first letter was posted from town on Thursday afternoon, so I suppose the boat must have been delayed. Thursday brought a lovely budget, though.

Darling,

At last I have your letters. There are two of them, the first two. It is so thrilling to hear about you. By this time you will have had several letters from me, so many of your questions are answered.

To what I have told you I can only add that I am more than content to be in this squadron. There are some awfully good fellows in it: good fellows both as pilots and personally.

My flight commander. Captain Romney, came out eight months ago and is a great *Hun Strafer*. Several years before the war he was an art student in the *Quartier*.

He leads our patrol, and I need not assure you how closely I follow his lead. We have tremendous confidence in him.

Incidentally he formed a good opinion of me, which may explain why he took me over the lines so soon.

Today is a 'dud' day so everything is washed out. The same thing happened yesterday afternoon, but I was up for fifteen minutes in the gale to try my new machine. It is splendid. It climbed incredibly fast and flew level at a topping speed.

All the gun-fittings are being finished today, and tomorrow I shall take it over the lines.

I haven't said much about going over the lines—about my impressions, I mean. Well, really, I didn't have any very pronounced ones. The principal thing I felt was that comical sort of detachment I have had in other things—as if someone else were doing the show and I were looking on. But I was elated to be so high above the clouds looking down through the holes on towns and villages eight or ten miles behind the German lines.

It was thrilling but not exciting. It was thrilling to be all alone in my machine, depending on myself and good luck. (I'm thankful I'm not responsible for an observer.) And yet I could not help being astonished at the absolute absence of emotion—no anxiety, no fear, no care—except one, to stick close to the patrol leader.

As we were crossing the lines initially we had one burst of anti-aircraft shells put up against us, but it was very wide and we did not change our course. The German A.-A. shells burst in black woolly balls and they generally put up about a dozen all round one at once.

I told you I could hear nothing in the air. I was wrong. I can hear 'Archie' bursts, when they are near me. The noise is curious. Something like: '*Woof! Brupp!*' and if the burst is quite near, the machine rocks about.

On our return, however, while we were up over 15,000, the Boche gunners got us very well, and then for ten minutes we dived and zoomed to throw his ranging out and came through untouched.

Then the leader dived into the clouds, which had gathered thickly and risen to the height of about 9,000 feet. After him we all dived, and then for nearly five minutes I saw nothing but thick fog all around me. I looked frequently at my Pitot, which was registering a steady 120 miles an hour, and kept hoping I wouldn't run into the leader or into Hyatt, who was just on my right.

At last I came out at about 3,000 feet and just over our side of the trenches; and, looking round, found the formation about 500 yards away on my right. Except for being more widely apart than when we started we were still in formation.

With the mail, bringing your letters, came my new tunic and breeches. They are topping. I wish you could see them. The stream-line cap is quite all right too.

Yesterday afternoon, after testing my 'bus, I went out for a ride with Hyatt. I struck a most lively mount who tried hard for ten minutes to get rid of me before he yielded to coercion. Then my stirrup leather broke and I had to return.

As the weather is so bad today we may have a tender to go to the Vimy ridge for a look round the captured trenches.

Darling wife, I have so many sweet memories of you in my mind, I am loving you just all the time.

Bill.

Chapter 5

Today no letter has come from my love. I want one. I want him to fly over the edge of the Downs and in at my bedroom window. I want to kiss his mouth.

Irene has taken her family to find chalk to burn on the fire.

Miss Kerr-Kerr told us about it yesterday when she came to tea. You put a few lumps on with the coal and apparently it stays red-hot. We hope it does, for the coal cellar is getting rather empty and no one for miles around seems to have any to supply.

Thank goodness the summer is coming and not a long chilly winter like the one that is loth to leave us now.

Today we feel dissipated. Last night a concert was held at the next village inn and we sat for three hours without ventilation, breathing hot humanity.

The village children, wearing their starched white frocks with bright blue and pink ribbons, did nursery rhymes and *tableaux*.

Their faces shone and their hands, too, and their hair was crimped until it stuck out from their heads.

We had a song, about the boys coming home, by a very thin woman with a very large mouth; and another song, about a diver who slept at the bottom of the sea, by one of the old men who seem to blossom here. He twitched a lot, but valiantly went through it twice like everyone else.

Then came revue songs of the season before last and one doubtful joke by an experienced labourer of sixteen.

There were piano solos and dialogues and a speech by the preacher man, who has here such a priceless opportunity for simplicity.

At ten o'clock we came out into the clean night air, glancing, now and then, as we strolled along, into the ditch on either side of the road; for Nanny, having driven us in Polly Blue, backed up by Irene's support, had raced back home alone.

The most unforeseen things happen to Polly's mechanism, but somehow she manages always to do what is asked of her. We found Nanny in the nursery, and there was a jug of hot coffee in the grate. We sat round on low stools and drank while we told each other all the news.

Chapter 6

This morning when Mabel pulled back the chintz curtains from my casement window the brightest day poured in. It was all so fresh and clean that I might have been wakened out of doors. Then later when my breakfast tray came up, on it were two letters and a book from France.

Is it any wonder that I paid no attention whatever to the long envelope!

The writing of the returned pot-boiler it contained had amused *us* for an evening in our cottage parlour on the slope of Salisbury Plain—so it had served its turn.

Yesterday's letter was short—just a note to say that only two of mine had reached my Bill, so today's I opened avariciously to read that still no more news had found its way to him.

But he understands that the post, not I, is to blame. He says:

Ma Bien Aimée,"
"There has been no mail again since the day before yesterday (Tuesday), but I hope to hear from you today.
The mail is much worse than it used to be; it is taking a minimum of four days to get a letter from home now.
Yesterday afternoon I went with Hyatt on a tender to S——and had a bath—a very hot one. Needless to say it was most refreshing and I gloried in its cleansing and invigorating virtues.
This morning I was out on early patrol with Hyatt and another fellow. We were across the lines at 7 a. m., but saw nothing. The wily Hun was under cover. The clouds had gathered below us and we finished our patrol flying over the trenches at 1,000 feet.
After breakfast I was up for half an hour on target practice.
A remarkable incident happened just after I came down. An-

other fellow on target practice was diving vertically at the target from 1,500 feet when his right-hand lower wing came off. He heeled over to the right but managed to get her level with his aileron controls, shut off his engine and glided down slowly and crashed in a ploughed field without being hurt. It was a splendid effort. I saw the whole thing happen.

I haven't done any work. I'm busy reading *The Opium Eater*. Yesterday, though, I did a cheap parody on the *jabberwock*. A few days ago one of the much despised quirks brought down a new fast Hun scout, quite to our disgust. *Voilà*—The Jabberwock and the Quirk.

'Twas brillig and the Slithy Quirk
Did drone and burble in the blue,
All floppy were his wing controls
(And his Observer too).

'Beware the wicked Albatross,'
The 'O.C. quirks' had told him flat;
'Beware the Hun-Hun bird and shun
'The frumious Halberstadt.'

But while through uffsh bumps he ploughed,
The Albatross, with tail on high,
Came diving out the tulgey cloud
And let his bullets fly.

One, two; one, two, and through and through,
The Lewis gun went tick-a-tack,
The Hun was floored, the Quirk had scored,
And came galumpling back.

'Oh, hast thou slain the Albatross?
'Split one, with me, my beamish boy,
'Our R.A,F.-ish scout has found them out.'
The C.O. wept for joy.

(R.A.F.— Royal Aircraft Factory.)

You'll find, if it's worth looking at so closely, that the system of rhyming isn't regular, but neither is it in the original. *After Lunch.*

I have just got your note written on Sunday morning!

By the same post came one from mother. She gave me tons of good advice. She says: 'Be calm, careful and contented, and last,

but not least, steady!' Oh, Fids! Isn't she delicious!
All my love, darling,
Bill.

I think Bill and I are especially lucky in our choice of mothers.

Sometimes you scarcely could believe that anyone living on this planet should remain so unworldly as Bill's mother, but he vows she has a little spice of "*La Diable*" (The French one) in her veins. It has been discouraged, of course—by Dad and her environment; but it's there and shows itself in a few saucy ways.

"I get it all from her," Bill said once, and of course I understood what he meant—but *she* wouldn't!

The other letter, which had been opened by the base censor, had been posted three days before. The brand new machine he speaks of must be the same he wrote of since, in the letter that came several days ago. But here is the whole:

> *Ma Bien Aimée,*
> I did a big escort and patrol this morning. There were seven of us escorting six two-seater machines and we went about nine miles over the lines at 15,000 feet. I found that the height didn't affect me in the least.
> A brand new machine has just arrived for me and is being fitted for a trial test this afternoon.
> By the way, I forgot to tell you more about FitzGarrick. I asked particularly how he got on out here and was told that the Fitz-Garrick here was entirely different from the FitzGarrick at the home aerodrome. He was much more lively and agreeable in mess and quite eager and steady as a pilot. Incidentally he was called 'Iolanthe.'
> I am still waiting to hear from you. The post has been very much delayed, during the present push.
> Poor Cotton, who is in the other squadron of our aerodrome, looks very miserable. I feel I ought to conceal my own good spirits when I talk to him. You see he crashed so many scouts at home that he was sent out on a two-seater and he doesn't like it at all.
> All my love, *ma bébé*,
> Bill.

The book was *The Pretender*, by Robert W. Service. I shall read it in bed tonight for now Irene and I and her family of one are going on to the Downs to catch the sun and play with the wind.

I forgot to tell you that we went to church—except Irene, who stayed to finish an article. I disgraced myself several times. First of all I went without my collection and had to run back, then I led Garry into the wrong pew, and he followed, thinking "The Aunt" could do no wrong.

When we had been hauled out by Nanny and things had gone smoothly for a while I knocked Garry's penny out of his hand as we both tried to reach the bag at the same moment.

Then to prove that we don't always get our deserts a most unexpected release occurred.

The family and Nanny having disappeared discreetly during the end of the hymn, I had collected all the prayer mats together with my feet preparatory to listening to "Horace's" oration in comparative comfort, when the whole thing was, as Bill would say, "washed out."

That happens sometimes. You have something tacked on to service and you do without a sermon. My joy was improper. I hastened home to my writing table, but paused on the way to have a word with the old lady at whose house we drank tea some days ago.

Her head nods all the time as though it were fixed to a spring, and her eyes must be as old as the pyramids.

I wonder what thoughts pass through her brain.

Chapter 7

My wife—dearest,
I'm so happy to read of your contentment and comfort. I have just got your letter—the first real one from the country—telling me of your room into which I fit so unobtrusively.
By the same post I had a letter from Cox's saying they have sent you a cheque book. They did not tell me how my account stood. When I left there wasn't much in credit, but there were many payments overdue, and when I am gazetted there will be 8/6 a day in arrears from last month to go in. However, in any case I shall not be drawing on the account until about the end of the month, so any small cheques you draw will be all right.
I was over the lines for about two hours this morning. We went out at 7 a.m. and saw nothing. This afternoon Hyatt and I may get permission to fly over to another squadron to see various people.
I have forgotten to mention that my ideas of saving have been modified slightly. I told you it was a good mess—really it is much more; it is a wonderful mess. But it is not cheap. However, I don't complain a scrap because it is so lovely to have the comfort and excellent food on active service.
That's all. Remember me, please, to Irene and Garry.
All my love,
Bill.

Neither do I complain a scrap.
"My gracious no!" as *Madame* used to say.
Indeed I find it is most essential to a wife to know that her man is well nourished, otherwise the maternal instinct would be perplexed dreadfully.

They amused Bill—my spasms of looking after him.

Once, when he was springing from a taxi, carelessly, before it had stopped, I cried: "Be careful."

"I've been doing it for quite a number of years," he said as he held out his hand to help me—and we both laughed.

Yet they love to be spoiled—just enough and not too much—but that's the secret of everything, isn't it? Just enough and not too much.

Today on our way through the fields up to the Downs we met old Witchell, wearing his best black clothes and a new pale green satin spotted tie.

"That's to show he's on his club, and for the time being not a working man," explained Irene in an undertone.

"And how's your lumbago today, Witchell?" she asked aloud.

"Not so bad and not so good," he beamed, his round, red face creased with smiles—"and how be you. Master Garry?" he added, looking down upon the small shrimp who gazed up with wide eyes.

"Ve'ey well, fank you, Wit-fel—an' how be Jack and Jim?"

With this opening old Witchell began. Many times already had Garry heard the recital of Jack, who is with the Marines: and of Jim, who has been with his battalion in the East "these two year past cum May," but the spratling, all eagerness, breathed it in once more; for he is of that priceless specie—the ardent listener.

"And you be goin' to be a sailor lad yourself. Master Garry—maybe an admiral an' all!" finished the old man at length.

"Yeth—I do be," agreed Garry, blandly, taking his rank as a matter of course.

Then it was that the so unreasonable momentary depression came down upon me.

Perhaps Irene felt it too. Garry an admiral! By that day old Witchell would have gone; by that time Witchell's sons and Irene and I would be as old as he is now; and the small spratling whose small tongue can't yet command his words would have seen much water; would have sailed far from his world, bounded now by the tall hedge that hides it from the road.

Indeed things change!

But have we learned anything at all if that truth hurts us one little bit? *Mon Dieu*, we unlearn our lessons as fast as we take them in!

On and upward we tramped—our admiral keeping pace; and soon, high on the level of the Downs, we came to the sign of a more immediate change.

"Those are the jumps Curtis spoke of—you remember?" Irene said.

My thoughts retraced themselves to an afternoon last week when walking to "Rutham's Folly"—that weird tower on the hill on the other side of the Vale—we came across a woman who, till then, I had thought of only as the manipulator of the harmonium in the village church. Soon it was arranged that we should go back to the farm for tea.

There the pictures first attracted my attention. They were a queer mixture—old prints—sets of them—mellow and quaintly designed; and beside them crude modern pages torn from journals, and drawings and etchings and paintings in oil and wash. One and all included those long sleek horses that seem to slip through the air rather than run on legs.

Round the parlour table—eating maize bread and homemade butter and drinking cup after cup of tea—I began to comprehend. The talk, too, was of horses and nothing else. Even the war was mentioned from their point of view: races were re-run and each animal was spoken of as though it were a loved child—since gone out into the world.

"Prince now—that day he walked his eighteen miles to the course; won his two races and walked all the way home again, for he didn't like to sleep away from his bed. Once there, though, he lay down and for the first time in his life admitted he was tired."

As he spoke the meagre young old man gazed at each of us in turn. Irene rose to the occasion.

"A wonderful horse!" she said.

"Yes, and he had the pluck of twelve, had old Prince—the beauty. You should have seen him take those jumps on the Downs! His grave is out there in the field—a proper one he has!"

The harmonium lady spoke with wistful tears in her eyes, and even I understood.

These were people I never before had come in contact with. Somehow I had thought of them as gamblers only; but now I realized that they had lived *for* their horses rather than *by* them.

War has changed their mode of life, and agriculture and farm produce now occupy their time. The steeplechasers are scattered, the riders scattered too—and the unused jumps on the Downs stand as monuments.

Chapter 8

Ma Bien Aimée,
After the big budget of yesterday I had only one letter this morning—from father. Mother enclosed a note in which she addresses me as 'My Dear Boy,' the result, I suppose, of your rallying her. You remember how we puzzled about her meaning in the letter that came on our marriage day, 'My Dear Boy—I suppose this is the last day I can call you that—!'
If she's not careful she will provoke me into marrying you again or doing something reckless.
After writing to you yesterday I was sent up at 6.30, and during an hour and a half we saw one Hun. This morning we did not see any. I suppose I'll come across swarms at once. I expect there will be much more doing shortly. Today it is cloudy, but one can get up through the gaps and it is perfectly clear above. Last night I lay awake a long time thinking of you. It was so wonderfully sweet.
  My darling wife, I love you.
                                        All yours,
                                                    Bill

I am so glad I am his wife; I am so glad he stayed awake in the night thinking of me: and that the thought of me is sweet.
But women have to be made of wood and iron now-a-days, I think.
Listen to this:

Darling,
I told you that when we did see Huns, we'd see a whole lot. We did!
Our repeated failure to see them was annoying, as other patrols

came in and reported the sky thick with them. Messages came from the infantry and artillery stating that Huns were about in hundreds.

But our patrol—Duff, leader; Hyatt on the left, and Your Husband on the right—never saw one within ten miles and just said so. The temptation to see them at all costs was growing, however, and when we were getting ready to start again last night—Sunday evening—Duff said:

'It's no use; we've just *got* to see Huns, so take it from me we're going to see five at least—in our report'

So we crossed the lines 8,000 feet and climbed steadily, going due east. For nearly half an hour we had the sky to ourselves; then we saw Duff whip round to the left and dive. Looking down in his direction, we saw Huns. Real Huns! Four big, fat ones!

Two were painted a vivid red; the others were a nasty mottled yellow and green. But we didn't mind. They could have had blue hair and scarlet eyes for all we cared.

Now, when you're on patrol and the leader dives on a Hun, the other scouts have to search the sky above and behind them for other Huns before following. It is a favourite trick of the Boche to plant a couple of machines below you as bait, and then wait above until you go down. Then they dive on you when your attention is occupied.

Neither Hyatt nor I overlooked this, and before we had dived far we saw that this had happened. Five Huns were on our tail!

We opened out, and went past Duff. Duff looked round and saw the Huns, and started to climb dead into the sun and forward the five.

They turned off at this, and passed us about 2,000 yards away.

We continued to climb and circle, so that we got the sun behind us.

Then we began to see Huns in earnest. From every one of the 360 degrees of the compass they came. Still we climbed and circled, waiting for their attack. Gradually they gathered together, until we could count fourteen. Some could outclimb us we could see; but they stayed together, and when we were as high as they. Duff headed straight for them.

Immediately they split into parties, left and right; while two dived underneath us. This was the bait trick again, and we refused it. Again we circled back into the sun and awaited their attack. It never came; but all the time the west wind was drifting us further over Hun land.

The finish was a comedy. Duff made a quick left turn, and Hyatt, on the inside, tried a vertical bank; but so absorbed was he in watching the rainbow formation in front of us that he turned right over and went down in a spin. I thought, perhaps, he had been hit, and looked behind. Three more Huns on our tail!

Hyatt had gone right down into the clouds. I looked for Duff and could not see him. I was alone against the whole Hunnish Flying Corps!

When I stopped spinning, I was just above the clouds at 7,000 feet. My spin had started at 13,000.

******

I headed carefully for the sun, due west, and home. Then I looked back. The Huns were still there—just a few dots in infinite distance.

Sometime afterwards I picked up Hyatt, and together we tootled home. Duff landed a few minutes later.

In our report we mentioned that we had seen *a* Hun!

I find the pen excellent. Thanks. Your letter of Thursday has just arrived.

      All my love, dearest,

                                                  Bill.

P.S.—This morning we went out and saw another Hun—and got him. Will tell you about it tonight. Just going out again.

Chapter 9

My breakfast tray has come. On it, in blue and white cottage china, are porridge and coffee and some homemade maize cakes that are eaten with syrup.

These things are pleasant to contemplate! But the pleasantest of all is my letter with the postmark, "Passed Field Censor."

It is a thick budget that I tear open and read:

Ma Bien Aimée,
To continue the tale of ourselves and the Huns:—
Neither Hyatt nor Duff nor I were feeling absolutely full of confidence, nor pleased with life, last night. The idea of Huns jostling each other in the sky like that was not nice to think about. Hyatt and I thought we'd dream of Huns—pink ones and red and green—but we didn't.
This morning I started right away to get back my confidence by going up after breakfast for half an hour's joy-ride. I climbed to 7,000, and then looped three times, did about a dozen violent vertical bank turns left and right, a vertical spiral, and a spinning nose dive of 2,000 feet. I felt enormously better for it.
At 11 a. m. we went over the lines. We crossed at 9,000, and almost immediately saw one Hun. With last night fresh in our minds we looked for others, but they were not there. It seemed too easy.
When we first saw him we were above him and a long way to his north—all going east. We climbed behind him, and got right around to the east of him and dived. Duff fired first and passed under him, and I then went all out for him. I got him dead in the sights, and when less than 100 yards away I fired. One shot answered, and then the gun stopped. I steered away and climbed, trying desperately to clear the gun which had

jammed. I cocked it as I thought, and went in again down on his tail. At not more than 50 yards' range I fired again—at least I pulled the lever—but nothing happened. Still sighting dead on, I cocked the gun twice more. It was hopelessly jammed.

The Hun had turned on me now. I spun in the approved C. F. S. way. When I turned level, Hyatt was diving on him, and I saw him going down, turning over slowly until he fell into the clouds.

We came home fearfully bucked; but I pulled down my gun—it is mounted over the top plane above my head—and found a hellish jam. I blasphemed and yelled to myself all alone!

"It was just this I was going to tell you about just before going out, but there was no time.

This morning's exploit was eclipsed this afternoon.

We went out in the same way, and after going about 5 miles over the lines turned and spotted two Huns about 2,000 feet below us. Duff dived on one and I on the other. I went down nearly vertically, sighting on. (Incidentally I glanced at the Pitot which was showing 160 miles an hour.)

I fired a burst at 150 yards' range and felt sure I had hit the machine near the observer's seat. I passed right underneath him, pulled up quickly, turned, and found myself facing him broadside on. I fired two more bursts. I wondered why the observer did not fire at me, and concluded I had put him out.

Then my gun stopped, and at the same moment the Hun turned and got his forward gun on me. I heard and thought I saw about 20 shots come my way and decided it was enough. Out came the spinning trick once more, and when I came out and looked round, the sky was bare.

The rest of the story I learned at the aerodrome. Hyatt and Duff landed ten minutes after me.

Hyatt had been watching me tackling my Hun, and when I suddenly steered off he saw the Hun dive also. Hyatt followed him down nearly 5,000 feet through the clouds and fired a burst at him. Then he found himself 800 feet off the ground and decided to leave it at that, and climbed above the clouds again and came home. He, too, thought that the observer must have been done in as he (Hyatt) was not fired on.

Duff's experience was different. After getting off one short burst at his Hun he turned round just in time to see another

Hun dive past him firing, and three others above him.
So he came home!

Half an hour later the artillery people reported that a Hun two-seater had nose-dived through the clouds and was believed to have crashed. Our Hun!

If my gun hadn't jammed this morning I'd have had one off my own bat. However our patrol—which simply couldn't see a Hun before—has driven two down today.

Your letters are so sweet. I do love you. I got your lovely long one of the 19th just after I got back this morning. It was so perfect to read what you are doing and to know you're so happy. I, too, am very happy—in the knowledge of your love for me and mine for you; it is still quite wonderful, more wonderful, in fact, every day. Darling Aimée, all my wife. (I like writing it.)

Well, about the book; Irene's criticism of the diary used as it is, was mine, you will recall: I thought it abrupt, too. Besides, it is called *Ad Astra*; and the Suvla and Ypres diary *have* nothing to do with my being an airman. However, I agree with your idea of trying it as it is, and in the meantime I may develop some material for its reconstruction, to fit the title idea better.

All my love,

Bill.

Chapter 10

From where I sit in the garden under the trees I can see the ridge of the Downs against the sky—and all is radiant with sunshine.

I think of my Love, and my heart is full of joy because he is mine. He is like sunshine in my life. I seem to bask in the most glowing memories of him; and not in memories only, but in the knowledge that we are with each other all the time.

I think of our wonderful understanding, and again I read the letter of today:

My dearest,

Yesterday we had lots of excitement. It didn't happen to me, though—my two patrols were quite uneventful, except that I was once just on the point of strafing an observation balloon, when I discovered that it was one of ours!

The excitement was over the exploit of two others—one of them a fellow who was in the tender that night when Hyatt left.

A Hun two-seater was met just over the lines at 17,000 feet. The pilot was heading east and our two were going west, so they attacked him and forced him down. His machine was faster than ours, but by manoeuvring they always kept to the east of him and made him lose height gradually.

The fight went on for forty-five minutes, and finally ended on the ground ten miles this side of our lines.

The Hun landed, and our people landed with him. A brand new machine, undamaged, and pilot and observer!

We collected the machine and it arrived on our aerodrome just before dinner.

By coincidence the C.O. had invited the Marine Light Infantry Band to give a concert in the squadron, and so we had them playing in the mess during dinner. It made a celebration.

Today is rather unpleasant. We left the old aerodrome for another nearer the line and everything is upset and uncomfortable at present

We had breakfast at 6 a. m., and had to have everything packed by 7 a. m. Then the pilots flew their machines here and had to wait in cheerless wooden huts until the lorries with kit and furniture arrived.

Another fellow and I, however, cleared away early and explored the new district; finally coming to anchor in a very pleasant cafe-restaurant, where we had omelette, bread and cheese, red wine and coffee. When we got back here and found no lunch going we felt we had scored.

The weather is too bad for patrols; the clouds are thick and low.

I am looking at your photograph as I write. I love it. I love you. Darling, you matter so very much to me and I am so glad. Dear, dear Aimée.

I found myself wishing you were having that quaint lunch with me this morning. You would have thought it quite thrilling. That is what we will do often. Isn't it?

        All my love to you, my wife,

                                        Bill.

The tenderest wind rustles the trees and sways the daffodil stems. I don't feel it, yet the air is buoyant.

Between here and the rising slope a man, clad in earth-coloured clothes, is sowing a field. I see the even semi-circular movement of his arm and the shower as it falls. He tramps steadily, there and back and there again once more.

I wonder what the sunshine means to him.

Chapter 11

What do you think we are doing this morning? Why—sitting on the sea shore, staring out to seal

Where the ripples break they make white surf—"wild white horses" tamed by the sun.

I have taken off my dress and shoes and stockings. What remains is a pair of Wedgewood blue "pantaloons," a blue jersey, and an enormous battered straw hat with a blue ribbon swathed round the crown to hold it together.

Irene wants to take a photograph to send to Bill.

I would love to have him here at this moment, but instead there is his letter, which the postman brought just as we started away in Polly Blue. I have kept it until now to read.

Down there Garry is up to his knees in water. He is like a white spot in the big ocean. Near him Nanny, holding her skirts high with one hand, and unconscious of the tail of soaked petticoat at the back, is searching the shingle—for something that may be turned into food or medicine or healing balm, I'm certain.

Further along the bank Irene is scribbling. The sky is blue. It is a perfect day.

I read:—

My darling,

I had a most lovely letter from you yesterday.

Last night I read it again and thrilled with joy. My heart said he had something most important to say to you, but he would not tell me what. He insisted that he preferred to deliver the message himself and, though he didn't like waiting, he said it was more than worth it.

'It's a Wise Heart,' I answered, 'that knows his own love!'

I'm frightfully interested to hear of your idea for work.

With regard to what you speak of, don't you think the material might be used to make *Ad Astra* more complete?

Yesterday afternoon I did two patrols, one was for balloon strafing, but the balloons would not wait to be strafed. On the second one, however, Hyatt lost the patrol, was attacked by Huns, shot one down and got away.

Today is dud—for the lines at least. I was up this morning for a joy ride and to practice 'stunting.' This afternoon Hyatt and I are going to ride into L—— to get a bath.

A new flight commander has just arrived. He was my instructor at home. Two of the present flight commanders are about due to go home for three months' rest, as they have been out nine months.

I've only eight months and a bit longer to go. Hooray!

We are not staying at this aerodrome for long; but when we move again it should be final,

I knew you'd hate the slip-shod flippancy of *The Pretender*. I didn't read critically, but was just ready to be pleased with the '*Quartier*' bits.

I think I understand perfectly and appreciate what you say about my being 'free.' But I find that I am not free—not while I love you. Oh, darling, it is the most enchanting bondage; the most perfect happiness to feel that I am not free because I love you so utterly. I adore you.

Bill.

That being so, the day is more perfect; the sun god more passionate! . . . I thank him for my lover and his love.

Now where do you think we have been? Why, in the sea, of course.

The cold water stung our bodies and caused us to shriek aloud. Then, while Nanny scrubbed away at Garry's skin with a prickly towel—standing herself in a, mackintosh with her hair hanging in dripping streaks—Irene and I lighted cigarettes and leisurely slipped on just enough in the way of garments to spare Nanny's blushes.

The shore is deserted. Tamarisk trees make a screen from the fields, and from Polly Blue who brought us here before the morning was awake.

Through several villages she ran, then down a long, long country lane, ending suddenly right on to the sea. The others had been before, but to me it was a revelation.

Wouldn't all the small children from all the big towns just revel in this place!

Almost I could be futile and persuade myself that it is callous to enjoy such tranquillity while others live in the turmoil of war. Yet sanely I know that my spell of leisure hurts no one, and adds greatly to my Bill's ease of mind.

I recall the munition factory with its ceaseless activity. With horror I again realise the mechanism and inhumanity of industrial life; for many there are unacquainted with leisure—and by leisure may be counted only the time when one is alert in mind and body and has no task that must be done.

But war is not responsible.

The toilers must toil in any event. Work without contrast is an abomination!

But that's ancient history, isn't it?

Nanny has builded a fire—of stones and tin cans and sticks—against a bank. On it the kettle whistles—literally, for there's an invention in its make up to enable it to call attention to its state. Our rations are spread—pheasants' eggs taken from their preserving jars, war-bread, and Nanny's best friend, a teapot full of tea. Garry is to drink creamy milk instead, but of solid food he will stow away in his small interior as much as any of us, and at the same time he will gaze upon the ocean and seem to ponder with complete detachment. So, I suppose, are admirals reared!

Chapter 12

From the garden I hear the mingled voices of the lawn mower and Irene and her family of one—and less obviously the song of the birds and the whisper of the trees.

The chintz curtains, drawn away on either side of the widely opened window, frame a picture at which I never weary of gazing.

Inside, too, there is nothing that does not please. It is so chaste.

Imagine plain cream walls and a darkly polished floor; and against these a single bed, of Jacobean design, and of dark wood, spread with a coverlet of blue-green chintz.

Imagine then an easy chair, a small bookcase, and a table on which may remain, undisturbed, a medley of writing materials, letters, books, and cigarettes.

A narrow full-length mirror reflects a part of the scheme. Two candlesticks complete it, except for a photograph of my Bill who—though he may seem just like other men to the uninitiated,—to me has the most beautiful face in the whole world.

His letter brings the contrast of excitement to this perfect calm. The first sentence, though, adds a touch of domesticity:—

My darling,
You will be glad to hear that yesterday I succeeded in getting a very hot bath. It was at a hospital, for aged men and women, run by nuns.
This morning the weather is good for flying, and I did an O.P. at 8 a. m.
There was another big push on, and I was able to look down at it, but couldn't see much beyond the constant explosions of our artillery barrage, and in a few places the bits of trenches where our men were making a new line after this successful advance.
You will have missed a letter from me on the 29th. We were

moving again and had a very uncomfortable day.

At 6.30 a. m. I was out of an O.P. with another fellow. I was leading, and after we had been over the lines half an hour, getting 'Archied' very badly, we lost each other in the mist which was very thick.

There were no Huns about, so at the end of an hour I started to return to the new aerodrome and, through carelessness, took the wrong direction and went south. After twenty minutes I failed to recognize the country and turned north on chance, struck an aerodrome, and found I was nearly forty miles away from here. The fellow who went out with me is posted as 'missing.' He must have had engine trouble or lost his way and been taken prisoner.

During the morning two Huns came over our aerodrome at an enormous height and I was sent up to chase them.

It was quite absurd, as they had only to put their noses down and glide home while I was climbing up. When I got to 19,000 feet, they were no longer in the sky.

The day before yesterday I had a quaint experience in firing on the range.

As I told you before, we put a target sheet, 6 ft. square, on the ground, and then go up and dive on it, firing short bursts with the Lewis gun.

It is rather trying, because you get so keen to sight properly on to the target, when you are coming down almost vertically, that you forget the ground is coming near.

Anyhow I dived six times altogether and emptied one dram of ammunition—97 rounds (bullets).

Then I asked on coming down if I had hit the target at all.

'Oh, yes!' the gun-room man said quite eagerly; 'there's one shot on the target.'

'One hit out of ninety-seven shots,' I gasped.

'Yes, sir,' he replied, 'but you're the first to hit the target at all. It's been out five days too.'

I feel I would like to write down to the bottom of the page, just saying: 'I love you, Aimée,' many, many times. But if I did it would not convey my love for you.

I am thrilled anew every time I look at your face. My darling, I adore you.

                All yours,   Bill.

By the same post came another letter.

Bien, bien—Aimée,
Since writing to you before lunch a letter from you has arrived.
I read it and then came to my hut to look at your face again, and so now I will talk to you a little, more.
The weather is very hot, and I am sitting in a deck chair outside my door.
A few moments ago an old thought struck me afresh and much more strongly.
I thought, suddenly, as I looked round our little camp, of in how many camps I had sat just like that—writing and smoking—during the last three years.
First there was the Northern Cavalry Depot, where I felt a foreigner in England, besides a stranger to soldiering; then there were the moors in Yorkshire, where I was pleased enough with my surroundings but impatient to see the war; then not long afterwards, sitting in the sweltering Gallipoli heat on a high ridge north of Suvla Bay, depressed and disgusted, I longed for France and the 'civilization' of the Western front.
Another five months and I was squatting on the muddy floor of a tiny dugout north of Ypres, with my knees up to the level of my chin and my spirits higher than that; then again, as the summer came round, outside in the sun once more, but this time on a Bairnsfather farm just behind the Belgian frontier.
There were the aerodromes in England, and now finally here I am, an airman on active service. Ahead of me I see a neat row of shining silvered machines—and the third from this end is mine, my fighting scout.
Last night I learned the greatest cure for war pessimism.
It is to dine with an R.F.C. mess in France.
The general commanding our brigade and a colonel from the brigade were dining with us. Combine the ages of our C.O. (a major) and that of our two guests and the average is about 26 years.
And hear them talk and laugh. They do it, roughly in equal parts. Of course it is almost entirely shop talk, but it is the comical and quaint side of 'shop.'
I looked on as an impartial spectator. The picture was one of

youth not sobered, but stimulated, by responsibility: graced, not by a heroic air, but by one of serenity; endowed with unfailing optimism and avowing but one object of hate—not the Hun but the perpetrator, whoever he may happen to be, of 'hot air.'
"Nearly thirty people under twenty-five years old doing a vital part of the work on which a whole army may depend!
The lesson of optimism hit one most fully when one realized that this was but a tiny part of the great mobilization of youth. I'm getting horribly heavy, darling. The only way to retrieve this letter is to tell you I love you. But I was going to do that anyway and I was dying to get to it.
    I love you,
                      Bill.

Chapter 13

A moment ago the postman with the ginger beard that sticks out at right angles from his chin, stopped his absurd donkey at the gate and clambered down from the queerest, most imbecile cart. It is so miniature, seeming to have a spring inside for a seat. The old man looks like a "Jack-in-the-box" when the lid has been opened suddenly.

But between them they bring my letters from over the sea.

Was there ever, since the beginning, so beautiful a postman or donkey or cart?

I read:

My wife,
I wrote last night describing a great and successful exploit of the squadron yesterday morning. But on consideration I found that it would be unwise to send it through the post.
When the wheeze is no longer new I will describe it.
It was an experiment in balloon strafing and it came off. Six of us attacked six balloons and we destroyed five. One fellow failed because his gun jammed like mine did that day, you remember?
I had eleven bullet holes in my machine and some of the others were nearly as bad.
This morning we got up against the whole Hun flying corps again.
We crossed the lines at 12,000 and saw two quirks trying to crawl away from a large formation of Hun Scouts—all red ones. We cut in between and stood over the Huns, who turned east again. We counted nine. They went out of sight, climbing, and reappeared to the south obviously trying to get between us and the sun. We defeated them in that and outclimbed them too and then went straight at them—three of us.

They promptly turned east again and we never got within range. They are faster than us on the level.

This business went on for nearly an hour. The nine red Huns came back four times, heading for us very bravely, but every time we got into the sun and then went for them. They never stayed, and ultimately went away for good.

There was no mail yesterday and therefore I expect two letters from you today.

Later,

They have come—two lovely letters!

When you tell me how happy you are, darling, I am thrilled every time. My heart, as yours, is full of joy. All the time I have a glow of content I never knew before.

A few sentences in a letter from home increased my happiness. I think they will increase yours. Joan says 'Aimée seems to like to have mother's letters. Sometimes, when I come to think of it, it seems strange how much she is one of us. I think we all love her more the more we know her.'

Writing since to Joan I said how I value her words and asked: 'Wasn't our instinct right?'

Was it, *bien-Aimée?*

Yes, I really love the photograph. I look at it many times a day, and when I look I think of many wonderful and delicious things, and I tell it how I love you.

All yours, dearest one,

Bill.

Chapter 14

Down in the valley the tiny dull red village seems to be asleep. Except for the ploughmen who harrow the patchwork fields there is no sign of life—and none of war.

Yet from every cottage almost a husband or sons have gone to the fight—sailors mostly, for the road, when it branches off, leads directly to our most special navy port.

I think the Vale is like the calm face of a woman who hides in her breast the woe anxiety breeds.

I will read my letter again. I feel rather alone up here.

My dearest one,
We are having things a good deal easier just now for some unknown reason. I really think that the period during which the Huns very seriously were threatening to be top dog in the air is at an end.
But the weather has been unspeakably fine since we changed our quarters, and we are all praying for a 'dud' day, so that we may feel free from flying for twenty-four hours.
I have just recalled something the Odd Man was telling us. He was saying how much his wife was learning of flying corps slang, and instanced her letter of the previous day, in which she said that the nurse was ill in bed, but added, 'However, the devil has had a "dud" day with the children'!
Hurrah! . . . It has started to peal with thunder, and we are all delighted, I especially, for I can go on talking to you.
Nothing very thrilling has happened. I did a patrol last evening and another this morning, and saw no Huns on the first, but today there were quite a number about. I was up alone and saw two formations—one of three and another of four. I outclimbed them and headed for them, but they went away east

✶✶✶✶✶✶

Ball's latest exploit is delicious.

About ten days ago, when the clouds were down to 2,000 feet, he went and 'sat over' the Hun aerodrome. Five Hun machines came up to strafe him, and he shot three down and made the other two crash on their own aerodrome.

The Odd Man has asked me to write an article for his magazine!

Really, I could do quite an interesting one on 'The vicar as his parishioners do *not* know him.'

He is a wonderful person; a raconteur, a sportsman and a tomboy. Just now he is working hard trying to level the ground in the middle of our huts to make a tennis court.

On Sunday night I went to a service. There were about thirty of us in the ante-room of the —th Squadron Mess. The walls were thickly decorated with Kirchner and Pinot studies—of what I call the sublime sacred—and cards were strewn on the tables. Before the service could start we had to cut off George Robey—in the middle of a doubtful song—on the phonograph.

The Odd Man explained that he wanted to make it a meeting rather than a service; therefore after prayers and a few hymns he proposed we should smoke while he gave us an address.

It stimulated thought, he said.

✶✶✶✶✶✶

It is worth a good deal to see him at the aerodrome when any big stunt is going forward.

He was down there to watch us start for the balloon strafe. He was fearfully grave and just walked around the machines—hardly saying a word. I don't think he expected any of us to return.

I was the second to get back. The first was the one whose gun had jammed. I lost my engine on landing and stopped on the far side. The Odd Man sprinted out, beating the '*accemmas*' (mechanics) by yards.

'Any luck?' he shouted. He was fearfully excited.

'Yes, it's all right,' I said.

'Oh, damn good!' he exclaimed. 'Damn good. . . . Absolutely topping!'

The others came in at intervals, and he beat the C.O. and every

one in welcoming them. He ran about from pilot to pilot, saying 'Damn good! ... How completely splendid!'
The C.O. joined him in a duet of jubilation and supplemented his 'damn good' by extracts from the new vocabulary.

★★★★★★

I have just had instructions to go by tender to —— to fly back a new machine. So I will finish this and post it without waiting to see if there is a letter from you.

        All my most passionate love,

                                            Bill

Chapter 15

There are times when I long, beyond reasoning, for a sight of my beloved—to hear his voice, too; to touch his mouth, to lie with his arms wound about my body. It was so last night, and I wept. Today I am a philosopher again. My letter brings me nothing but joy:—

My darling wife,
I got your letter before lunch. It thrilled me more than any. I want you, I love you intensely—oh, so much! I dare not think of our next meeting. It is too—too wonderful to contemplate!

******

The trip to X—— to fetch the new machine did not turn out as I expected, but very much better.

When I arrived at the sheds there and was almost ready to start, the C.O. turned up, with the Odd Man, in his own car and said he would fly back, as he wished to get home immediately. We could return together he said.

So we watched him start away. In the meantime the weather had picked up and was gorgeous, so I had a good idea that there would be work going about.

But the Odd Man said that was all right. He had seen to it for me and we could stay and have dinner at X—— .

First we had tea at the Pool, where one meets everyone one ever knew in the Flying Corps—and then motored into the town with much dignity; I with my streamline fittings and the Odd Man with his dark blue, and light blue and red brassard on his sleeve bearing the letters R.F.C.

We drew up at the big French *café* in the square, and there 'degusted' each two *Dubonnets*; and then went to the Restaurant V—— for a perfect little dinner.

Having been happy in our choice of a white wine we allowed it to circulate well and came out to the big green car behind our cigars, feeling that for one night at least nothing could interrupt our tranquillity.

★★★★★★

This morning we—the C.O. and your husband—left the aerodrome at 4.45 in semi-darkness. It was an early bird effort to catch the Hun worm, but the sky was empty, so about a mile over the German side of the trenches the C.O., who is a stunt pilot, did a few turns.

He started by a loop. I promptly followed. He 'chucked' two more and so did I. Then he did a series of 'Immelmann turns' so quickly that, watching him from the ground, you would have sworn he was flying upside down most of the time.

A few hundred yards away I was hard at the same thing.

The Huns down below must have wondered.

I wound up the show by two of my best spins of 1,000 feet each.

★★★★★★

The Odd Man has finished the tennis court and we have started a tournament. I am down with him, and while he is easily one of the best players I am easily the worst. I have been sent for, so—*Au Revoir, ma bien-Aimée*. I love you.

Bill.

P.S.—I forgot to say that the cheques you have written will be all right.

As for it being a strain—why I am intensely happy and amazingly content.

It is first because of our love and then because I know you, too, are happy and contented in your surroundings.

A strain! My darling, even if it *were*—but it is a delight. It is wonderful to feel that I am making some one happy because I was afraid I might never be able to do that. It is lovely to know I can—and yet it is so little I do.

Bill.

I, also, find it wonderful to be able to make someone happy.

I think most of us have it in our power to do so only if we are met half way, and I can make Bill glad because he wants me to, and because he gives all of himself in response.

One feels so powerful—and yet so humble, too.

Chapter 16

Today we passed along a roadway cut through a wood and then, at the other end, came upon a village apparently composed of a few cottages, several houses standing in acres of ground, and a church.

It was the most fascinating church I have ever seen. The inside was white-washed and the oak beams were black and uneven with age. There was brass exquisitely designed, and lilac and wild apple-blossom stood upon the altar. A list of vicars from the 14th century hung outside the studded door.

Leading to it, of course, were the inevitable tombstones, some so ancient that the moss completely covered them.

One grave was quite new.

I hated to think of the decaying body under the earth.

Two old men hobbled past us as we restarted Polly Blue. They were all we saw of human life.

"How do they manage to live so long?" I asked of Irene, as though she should know.

"Why not? . . . There's nothing to make them die here, is there?" she said.

We heard the boom of a gun practicing at the naval port across the hills.

Nothing to make them die,—and so much death not far away!

Soon we returned to our glorious circle of the Downs. Our village is like a plainer woman with a subtle imagination—a much more enticing companion!

A letter from Bill had arrived by the afternoon post I ran up here, to my own den, to read:—

My sweet wife,
Nearly a month has gone already!
Yesterday was Sunday and a day of 'hate' as usual.

I was on the mid-day patrol with my flight commander. Captain Romney, and about half way through we spotted two Hun scouts a good way over the other side. We climbed round them and dived.

Romney, who goes in for getting right up to his Hun before firing, approached to within 40 yards of the first one and then fired ten rounds.

The Hun did an Immelmann turn and came out on Romney's tail. Romney did the same, got off another burst and the Hun dived away. I saw only the first manoeuvre, for I was diving on the second one. But mine didn't wait to do any Immelmann turns. I started firing at about 100 yards, and put 3 rounds into him. The Hun went on diving, and so fast that I could not gain any more.

The artillery people on the ground reported one of the Huns crashed! They had watched the fight. We don't know whose it was but think mine.

In the afternoon Romney got one again. There were four of us out, but he got so close to the Hun—a two-seater—and sat so persistently under his tail that we could not get near and dare not fire. Ultimately the Hun went down burning, and that was confirmed from the ground.

★★★★★★

This morning when we returned from early morning patrol there was a new balloon strafe on the *tapis*.

I was sitting opposite the C.O. at breakfast—imagine a tousle-headed youth in pyjamas and a flying coat, for he had been called up early to organise the raid—and he asked me if I would go again. I said 'yes.'

Romney, however, intervened, and said he was entirely against anyone doing it twice. He proposed, however, that the remainder of the squadron should be sent up to 'demonstrate' over the balloons and distract attention from the 'contour chasers.'

★★★★★★

I was late in getting off the aerodrome and the raiders had got over the lines before I was in a position to see them. I had to climb, you see.

However, from miles away I watched three balloons start burning and collapse.

Tootling round I spotted three more balloons a good deal south of the ones we had to attack, and went over to investigate. Three machines were flying behind them—Hun two-seaters.

I spiralled down above them to have a nearer view and when at about 1,200 yards' range, I heard one of them firing. So I changed my spiral into a dive on to the nearest one and heard the gun going again. Then they dived too and eastward. Next moment I knew the reason, for five of our new scouts came tearing past taking up the chase.

Soon the whole eight were out of sight.

I turned round, and being now only a couple of thousand feet above the balloons I thought I'd have a go at one.

I didn't get far. They had been watching me too long from the ground and immediately I was greeted with machine guns. The tracer bullets came up in silver streaks and the next minute there was a nasty cough behind as their anti-aircraft fired its ranging shot.

I didn't wait, but tootled home.

The second raid was quite a success. Six balloons were destroyed, but one of our fellows is missing.

★★★★★★

Last night we had an officer from the Army Headquarters to mess. He came to tell us how bucked the infantry people were with what our squadron had done in the first balloon strafe.

I hear that the post is just going out. I loved your letter this morning.

I love you,

Bill.

Chapter 17

Last night propped up against my pillows reading Bill's thrilling experiences over again, I came to this, which at breakfast time seemed quite unimportant.

Two letters have come from Greta de Jeunaisse.
You remember—I told you how kind she and her mother were to me in Paris? ... She writes from there telling me all the latest news, and she finishes:—
'Your greeting, and above all your portrait, have given me great delight.... You do not tell me when you are coming to Paris. I am impatient to see you once more.'

It was midnight—a time when things come to us poignantly—and I began to wonder if this Greta holds the very French notion that Bill's marriage is one of convenience and that—having written and sent his photograph in answer to the letters which followed him about and reached him only after his marriage—he is eager for an "*affaire*."

Although I want him to feel free as the wind, I couldn't help writing to point out that Latin women have the foresight not to believe in so-called platonic friendship. As a matter of fact I scarcely can imagine even an Englishwoman expressing her impatience to see again the man who had told her of his wife.

In theory it sounds ridiculous, but practically it is impossible for any man—unless he wishes to be taken seriously—to show appreciation of any feminine human being who is not old enough to be his mother or young enough to be his child.

It is true—and the reverse is true also. Almost any woman could, with the opportunity, make any man who is not blindly loving some other woman, think lovingly of her.

Today's letter is so thrilling that my thoughts seem trivial.

Dearest one,

I got a Hun yesterday afternoon. It was a great scrap and I was fearfully pleased, because for the first time in a scrap I tried a pukka Immelmann turn and brought it off. I was with Romney and when we were at 16,500, about five miles over the lines, he dived on two Hun two-seaters at about 14,000.

I saw him go down and pass right underneath and then I went for the other.

It was a big bus with polished yellow wooden body and green wings. At about 100 yards I started firing, and the Hun, who was going across me, turned and climbed round as if to get on my tail.

Then came my Immelmann! With engine full on, I pulled the machine up hard and nearly vertical. When she was almost stalling I kicked her left hand rudder hard and the machine whipped over on one wing, turned her nose down, and came out exactly in the opposite direction.

The Hun was now dead in front of my gun about 200 feet below me. I opened on him again and almost immediately he started diving and slowly spinning.

To keep my gun on him I had to go down absolutely vertical, and eventually went beyond vertical and found myself on my back with the engine stopped through choking.

When at length I fell into a normal attitude again, the Hun had disappeared. One of our patrols which had come over in time to see the scrap says he went down spinning and crashed.

★★★★★★

This morning I was detailed to lead a patrol—my first.

It might have been a success but for 'Archie.'

I headed over the lines and crossed at 10,000 feet. Then war broke out and for several minutes I couldn't see the two fellows who were following, for the black shell bursts all around us.

To put the A-A gunners off their range I side-slipped and stunted and then climbed above a cloud. The others did the same.

It was only a small cloud, however, and soon came to an end. Promptly on reappearing we got another salvo and I felt a violent shock on the 'joy-stick.' The whole machine shuddered, but before I had begun to wonder what had been hit I stuck my nose down hard and due west. Everything looked all right.

Leaning out and peering round the engine cowling I found

the under carriage was still there. I waggled the 'joy-stick.' The tail controls were all right. Again I waggled the 'joy-stick.' Wing controls all right. But no, nothing happened. I looked at the ailerons. The left one moved, but the right one did not move. Then I glanced at the aileron controls. Just against my screen the right aileron control had been shot away!

I kept my nose down, heading for home, and found that I could still get a sufficient amount of wing controls to make slow turns. Landing became a problem, as the moment I switched off the engine the right wing dropped. I flew right on to the ground, though, without smashing anything.

I have the broken parts of the rod and the armourer is going to produce some souvenir from it for you.

******

I have read and read again your last few letters. They made me feel so wonderfully happy, longing for you ever so impatiently, yet curiously content to wait; just loving you, darling, with all the passion I own.

All yours,

Bill.

After reading that I wonder if it would be dreadfully foolish of me to post my misgivings about Greta.

Somehow I feel I want him to share all that passes through my mind. He deserves the truth.

Some men would dismiss this, thinking it to be the sort of jealousy by which married people are supposed to make life a burden to one another.

There *is* a tinge of jealousy of course—but it is something deeper which makes me want to speak. I can't express what I think. It is very difficult.

Chapter 18

All my own darling.
I am in the orderly room relieving the orderly officer for dinner, and I want to talk to you.
Every day I am more staggered by this amazing life. It is the contrasts in it, the abrupt changes that make it so astounding.
Before lunch I was sitting in a cosy mess writing to my wife. At teatime I was fifteen miles over the lines, flying over Hun land, aiming my gun, and shooting to kill. And then, later, changed into clean clothes, I dined in comfort unsurpassed even in England just now.
Yesterday we went over to another squadron, where the C.O. was to fly a Hun machine—an Albatross Scout—against one of ours. The idea was to test them for speed level, climbing, diving, and turning, and then to have a scrap. We expected some good flying, but the whole was a washout as the engine went dud.
It is to be tried again tomorrow, and I am to fly one of our machines against the C.O.
Captain Kyle crashed this morning in the trenches. His engine stopped and he turned upside down about 500 yards behind the front line. A big artillery strafe was going on at the time, and he couldn't get out of the machine, but just had to hang there head first, by his belt, listening to the big shells crumpling all around.
At last some Canadians managed to run out and release him from the wreckage. They took him into their dugout, and when things got quieter he came away.
There's a hell of a lot of strafing every day, and the sky in the east is vivid all night through.
The weather refuses to break, and it is oppressively hot. You

would love it, I know. But we are longing for a real break. We want a rest from patrols for a day or two.

I quite forgot to tell you about Hyatt. He had claimed three Huns, and a fortnight ago was put on a roving commission—that is to say he was left to fly when he liked and where he liked, provided he got Huns.

One day he went up late and came back at dusk. He said he had been a long way over the lines and had met three Huns. Two he shot down on their own aerodrome and the third dived away.

Going along further south he picked up a single machine and later saw five Huns. Thinking he had the assistance of the scout he had picked up he dived at the five. Hardly had he started than the scout fired at him from behind. He turned round and climbed and discovered black crosses on the scout.

It was a Hun!

Getting under this Hun he put his gun up, emptied his drum, and saw the Hun dive down and into a pond!

Then Hyatt came home.

Two days later—that is three days ago—he crashed on landing. He was not damaged, but said he had hurt his head. He is now at the hospital here and says he can't remember anything.

He had to be informed that there is a war on and that the French are fighting with us. He recalls London vaguely. Fortunately he recognizes his wife's photograph.

So Hyatt may be home with her shortly.

Later.

The post has come bringing the lovely letter you wrote in bed.

Your doubt about Greta's attitude brought doubt to me for the first time. In any event there will be no chance of my going to Paris at present.

Tuesday Evening.

The post is going now. I send you all my love.
My wife!

Bill.

Chapter 19

I have climbed to the highest point of the Downs to let the wind blow through and round me.

So many thoughts have tangled themselves in my brain and now that they are weeded out I want to tell of them.

It all started, of course, with Bill's remark:

In any event there will be no chance of my going to Paris at present.

"That means," I said to myself, "that *were* there a chance he would go without me! ...Why then did I not go to Italy with Desirée instead of refusing because I knew he wanted us to go together afterwards... . And he would see his Greta! ...Why then have I made a resolve not even to write to any of those men who easily might persuade themselves that he—although my husband—is not my dearest love?"

Then I was aghast.

"What," I exclaimed. "Have I descended to this?"

My dear and I have discovered that we are able to accompany one another into our most intimate thought gardens; and I know he will understand that, afterwards, I tried to pull the weeds—that's all.

So I reasoned.

"Bill's and my marriage has in it the possibilities of perfect romance. He is most beloved of me; yet if, now or at any time, he lightly should appreciate our romance—and with so fragile a flower to be careless and to kill were the same—then which should I regret? Him or romance?

Why romance, of course; for there are other men and other interests, but seldom the possibility of pure romance!

Now the garden is clear once more.

I love him this dear, dear lover of mine.

Chapter 20

My darling Aimée,
After writing you yesterday I found that I was due out on the next patrol.
It was the most uncomfortable patrol I have ever had. Romney led and a new pilot—an excellent one—made the third.
We climbed all out and when a good way over saw a Hun two-seater. Romney gave chase and it headed northeast.
I don't know for how long we followed, but we gained slowly, and at last Romney dived.
As he did so the Hun fired three rockets, evidently a signal.
Romney fired at close range and sheered off. The Hun observer fired back at him as the pilot dived. I then went down vertically after him firing dead on and did not stop until my drum was empty.
The Hun was still going down—falling. He had not fired at me and we believe both pilot and observer had been hit.
I started climbing while changing my empty drum for a full one, and, looking around, saw two scout machines above me.
'Romney and Grahaeme' I thought; and proceeded leisurely, climbing up to them.
One of the pilots put his nose down and came towards me, and next moment I heard the familiar and horrid '*Pop-pop-pop.*'
They were firing at me. It certainly was neither Romney nor Grahaeme.
As I had feared all through the chase the Hun two-seater had been a lure and now I was in a trap. They had a thousand feet of height on me, so I put my nose westward and downward, and, glancing round, saw they were doing the same.
By losing height steadily I was able to keep up speed, but I

hadn't realized how far east we had come. It seemed hours before I saw the trenches in the distance—actually it was fifteen minutes before I reached them.

All the time the Huns were firing short bursts, but I was never going straight for three seconds together. I kicked the rudder and slid flat from one side to another, and at last as I crossed the reserve Hun trenches—now at less than 3,000 feet—I saw the Hun machines turn away.

It wasn't all over, though, for first, tracer bullets came up from the ground and, after I had dived and side-slipped to avoid them, the anti-aircraft guns put up a barrage in front of me. For five minutes I turned and twisted to throw them off and finally got over our trenches at 1,000 feet.

Later I heard that when Romney had stood off after he too had been attacked by two Hun scouts, but being on their level he had climbed away from them. One of his planes had been badly ripped by the fire from the first Hun we attacked.

The third fellow had seen us diving and looking around saw four Hun scouts coming out of the clouds. He went to have a look at them and then got lost in the clouds. It was half an hour before he found his way back to the lines.

******

I haven't told you about the Air Hog! He is an excellent fellow really, but he takes things frightfully seriously and is simply crazy to get Huns. His air-hoggishness was revealed early—when he came into the mess announcing that he was going on a 'jolly old patrol.'

It was the first time we had ever heard it so called. Most of us use something much more sanguinary.

However, he went out a few times and then developed a habit of going up and tearing about the sky all alone.

He went Hun-strafing mad. If he saw a Hun five miles away and chased it for ten minutes he hardly would be able to contain himself, and would talk about what 'a jolly old patrol' it had been.

At last he was put on the roving commission game and since then has spent eight hours a day at least in the air.

When it is not fit for patrol he mopes and frets, and worries everybody about the weather; and doesn't improve because he fails to get any sympathy from us.

Later.

Two letters from you, glowing about your work—the revision of the play and the articles—and smelling of your lovely perfume.

It is brilliantly fine again. I'll be flipping soon.

Dear, dear wife, I love you.

Bill.

Bill, couldn't you just managed to "flip" over the edge of the Downs? You are so near, really. If you were to go up into the sky with the wind behind, you could be here with me, in this room, in one little hour. Think what it would mean to me. And I'd let you go back again after I had given you my kisses and listened to your voice, telling me of your love!

Chapter 21

Bien Aimée,
The squadron did a thrilling exploit last night. It went bathing at midnight. The Odd Man, of course, was the leader.
Some miles away there is a most topping valley occupied by a *château* and its grounds. A river runs through it and about a week ago the C.O. and the Odd Man got permission from the people at the *château* to dam the stream—or, as the Odd Man prefers to put it, 'to erect an artificial barrier across the stream—in order to form a swimming pool.'
The squadron did the work and it was finished yesterday. After dinner the C.O. suggested that we should all go and bathe in the pool. We had a tender and fifteen of us went—some of us armed with pocket lamps and all attired in pyjamas, towels and flying coats.
The water was beautifully deep and clean; and it was eerie to see the naked bodies scrambling about the barrier of tree trunks amongst the shadows thrown by the huge monsters on the bank.
The Odd Man was the noisiest of the crowd.
He did high dives into the black pool, shouting and splashing like a water baby.
Today four of the fellows have developed colds, and even the Odd Man is a little off colour. I tell him that midnight revels with water nymphs do not suit him.
But I haven't told you of my expedition!
Yesterday, with the C.O.'s permission, I travelled for many hours on a motor-bicycle—seeing the war. I had tea with a general, and supper with a sergeant.
The sergeant was Dick. Supper consisted of bottled Bass and a

cake from home.

It was a frantic business, finding where his brigade was. After touring the larger part of Northern France I entered Z——, and ran into a fellow I knew, who is now C.R.E.—that is to say officer in charge of works.

He took me along to H.Q., and there I found where the division and the brigade were. Then I went to the town commandant's billet with my pal, and had tea with General ——, to whom I hot-aired about flying for half an hour.

At last I got out of town and found Dick at the wagon lines. To get there I had to pass through a belt of most amazing country—the piece of ground that for two years until last month held our own trenches, the Hun trenches, and no man's land.

The sight cannot be described.

It is as if roads and villages and woods and fields suddenly had become liquid like a sea, and had rolled themselves over and over in huge waves—stopping abruptly at their most fantastic moment.

I found Dick in a little tin hut with his sergt-major, Q.M.S., and the other sergeants—all good fellows.

He was looking wonderfully fit and was in excellent spirits.

I went to the officer's mess also and was awfully well received. They spoke glowingly and quite spontaneously of Dick.

Writing home I have told mother that they have described him as a 'damned good lad with lots of guts.'

They told me about the military medal exploit. It was during the bombardment prior to the advance.

The Huns barraged the road on which the ammunition teams were working between the dump and the batteries, and smashed up several teams. Just when everything was horribly confused, Dick came along and, irrespective of who was who, and in the thick of the shelling, organised some order out of chaos and blood.

A few days ago he was congratulated personally by the divisional G.O.C.

I gather that his C.O. is quite keen on Dick's prospects for a commission. And so am I. It has been good for him to start from the beginning, but now it is time for him to move on.

I got home at 10 a. m, It was a topping experience.

    Most happily yours,   Bill.

Chapter 22

Could a woman know greater joy than this? Listen:

For whom I live.

Your long letter of Monday night has come.

I love your idea of Romance.... It is all mine. I will treasure and guard Romance, embodying you, so jealously. But you have made me realize how it may be destroyed by the merest want of thought and in spite of the most sincere loyalty.

This letter thrills me more than any. I have read it many times. Darling Aimee, I love you! I love you! I am all yours. It makes me deliriously happy to know we are so much to each other that is satisfying and more than that.

Since you mention it, I may as well refer again to my remark about going to Paris. You never could believe to yourself that I would choose to go on leave anywhere without you.

Dear, I am living for you: I want you,—I can't tell you how I love you!

I have told you often that I am curiously content. But it is not complacency, and I know you know that. My contentment is made up of the most wonderful memories and the most wonderful promises—and of your and my own happy philosophy of life. Oh, *bien-Aimée!*

And yet I may go to Paris and alone! Until quite recently pilots used to be sent there for new machines and maybe, this will happen again. It is not likely, however, that I should go, and if I did I would not visit Greta.

In this case and in any case, I not only see your point but agree with you. I must admit I had not seen the danger of it as applying to myself, but already I had made up my mind neither to write to, nor to see her, for a long time.

Darling Aimée, I love you. I love you to the exclusion of everything in life but your happiness; and that is my happiness, too. I love you beyond all measure.
It is ecstasy to say 'My wife.'
      And I am all yours.
                Bill.

 Bill, you are perfect. You make me your slave—no, more than that, your friend—when you understand like that!

Chapter 23

Purcell has borrowed my favourite weapon to write the laundry list.

She came in and said:

"I'm sure. Miss, you must have collected all the pencils in the kitchen last night."

I don't know why she wants to write a laundry list on Whit-Sunday; but it never would do for me to say so. Certainly if I tried to prevent her she would go and "munition," and then this household would tumble to pieces altogether.

The window is opened wide; but outside there are no Downs, no trees, no distance—only a "thin piece of sky" and dozens and dozens of chimney pots and the two top storeys of a building, loftier than the rest.

I can't see the street, for I am too high above it and too far back in the room; but the whirr of traffic is unavoidable. An instant ago there was a pause like the quiet at a table where every- one has been talking: but already a motor-lorry—the boisterous one of the party—flings itself into the vacancy.

This is town!

So much has happened that I can't recall why I decided—originally—to come here. Oh, yes, I do remember. Irene's parents wrote. They wished to visit her for a week if arrangements would allow for their entertainment. Of course that was as a royal command.

Immediately Nanny looked for finger-marks, Irene stowed cigarettes at the bottom of the trunk which holds her out-of-use riding habits—"to keep the moths away"—and I looked up the best through train for London.

It's safer to be a myth to the parents of one's friends. They have too much eye for detail, and the very ideas which attract us to each other to them would seem revolutionary. After all Irene is their ewe lamb, and I stand for the enemy outside the gates.

It needn't be, but, like lots of things that needn't be, it is.

And now, having come to town, I seem to be involved in the most thrilling episodes.

Really they all, indirectly, are the outcome of a sisterly letter which arrived a week or two ago from Maisie:—

"Dear Amy," she wrote—and that's the sisterly touch in chief, for she refuses to recognise the picturesque translation of my name—

> I've read a thing of yours that I found lying about the house. I know you'll be wild, for you're such an ass about anyone seeing anything; but anyway I don't see why you shouldn't pull yourself together and be businesslike and try to make some money for a change. I'm sure you've cost mother enough one way and another.
>
> I'm glad to say you write better than I expected, though I think you ramble on a bit too much. You should come to the point quicker. We're in a hurry nowadays, and much too tired to wonder what it's all about.
>
> Anyway don't trouble to alter what you've done. I'll bring it up-to-date myself if necessary. I've given this thing to a man who knows the editor of the *Philanderer*, which is decidedly the smartest magazine of the moment. Now don't get into a temper about it. It's for your own good.
> Love,
>
> Maisie.

This letter had its use, besides supplying Irene with amusement, for it provoked me to dispatch a bundle of MS. to the agent upon whose advice, she had heard, one could rely.

I suppose it's a form of self-consciousness, or as Maisie would put it, "conceit," that makes some of us avoid spectators. Until my marriage I shrank from the idea that anyone who knew me should read my thoughts; but having lived with Bill, who is so much more open and generous in his outlook, I seem to mind less and less.

Then the day before leaving the country this came:

> Dear Madam,
> I have read the MS. sent to me by your sister, and I find it quite good. It is too long, however, as we do not consider serials, but we would be glad if you would submit, before Thursday next, a

short story of 800 words.

Yours truly.

I hadn't a short story of any length and I hadn't the foggiest idea for one.

"I'll simply write and say so," I said to Irene, who came as usual to my room after breakfast to discuss the post.

"Good gracious, no," she cried. "You must have a try at least."

Then I realized that, of course, I must have a try and, what is more, a successful try.

Maisie's words also seemed like the truth—I had "rambled on too long."

So all that day I sat at my table, and after dinner exchanged the result for an article that Irene had been doing—in her airy fashion—on Rhodesia, which became less vague to me as I read.

And as she found my effort very much to her taste we afterwards went to bed rather hilariously.

Our gods chastened us soon enough for that. They sent Irene's article back to roost; and mine rendered their blow through the editor of the *Philanderer*, when several days later I sat in his office beside his desk.

"Yes; it's good enough in its way," he said. "But what our readers want is something more obvious than that!"

He had gray hair and a pince-nez and a keen clever face.

"Why does he prostitute his conception of things?" I wondered, saying aloud at the same time: "I'll do another then and let you have it tomorrow."

"Can you?" he asked.

"Of course," I answered, "if I choose."

What I should have said was: "Of course not, because I don't choose"—but to be baffled by the obvious pleased me little enough.

At home—the place where I used to house myself before my marriage to Bill—it seems impossible to work. The pandemonium of traffic rages night and day. Except today there is no privacy either, for now my old room has been commandeered.

"You can use mine if you don't expect me not to come in when I like; and you'll have to sleep on the inside, and not wriggle all the time!" Maisie said.

And as she spoke she arranged her head at the left-hand top corner and her feet at the right-hand lower corner of the bed. Until dawn and after that I tossed about open-eyed, disconnectedly piecing together the accursed short story.

"A man and a woman, and the other man or the other woman—that's the obvious," I thought; but what to make them do or say in the space of eight hundred words was as distant from me as sleep in the space left over by Maisie's adamant body.

When Purcell entered with the tea tray she awoke.

"You've kicked me all night in your sleep," she grumbled.... "I feel as though I'd been beaten black and blue!"

I looked at her—too wroth for speech.

"Well, don't let your eyes tumble out of your head," she growled, "and give me some tea for the love of glory.... I shall be ill if I have to share my bed again!"

Then the desperate inspiration came. The outcome of which was that the Babes—in whose opinion I have soared since presenting them with a brother-in-law—superintended a collection of food while I gathered together my pencil and writing pad and wits.

Joyously, before the dew had given itself to the sun, we spread our rugs under the biggest tree on the stretch of green overlooking the round pond.

I placed the babes before me. "It doesn't matter what you do" ... I said ... "if you don't talk to me before it is time to eat."

"May we go out of sight then?" asked Bey.

"No, you may not ... and you mayn't fall into the water either," I replied.

So Betty arranged herself on her stomach, propped up by her elbows, and began to read a book; while Bey, strutting about, crooned nonsense to a one-eyed Teddy bear.

I think we had chocolate and buns and hard-boiled eggs for lunch and I know that by teatime my tale was complete. Last evening the editor man rang up to say he liked it very much; but suggesting an alteration to the last line, and that destroyed the redeeming touch of sincerity, adding spice, I admit, but spice of the most blatant sort—spice for the *gourmand* rather than for the *gourmet*.

"You don't mind?" he said.

"Not in the slightest," I replied—and neither did I, for I hadn't been baffled by the obvious after all.

Just now Bill's letters have to be absorbed between events instead of being the one event of the four-and-twenty hours, but they are not less precious because of that.

They are my life. I have one for every day in the week. Today there is no post, but two came yesterday—one by the first delivery and one by the last. Here is the earlier one:—

My *bien-Aimée*,
For the first time this month a day without a letter from you. Because you were travelling, I suppose.

It is a perfect summer day and already I have done three hours flying, and later I am to lead a patrol!

I was out of bed this morning at 4 o'clock and in the air before it was properly light. It was quite an inoffensive patrol, for there were no Huns about—and it was a topping morning.

Breakfast was ready at 5.30, and after it I went to bed for two hours. Then at 10 a. m. I went out for a joy-ride. I flew up the line to Z—— and then tootled all around the salient and billets and bits of trench I had lived in last year.

On the way back I landed at another aerodrome and met half a dozen fellows who were at the home aerodrome with me.

You remember the second 'Hun'[1] whose argument with a haystack I described? He has had a further adventure.

While I was out on the aerodrome yesterday afternoon I heard Romney order my machine to be brought out. I hurried to ask if I was wanted for a patrol.

'No,' he said, 'I'm going to send up the haystack expert again.'

Fortunately my 'bus was not ready. Some alterations were being made to the cowling.

Another pilot had the misfortune to land at that moment and the 'Hun' was put into his machine. This time he got off the ground with a series of ungraceful hops, and once in the air did quite well.

Then he tried to land.

At the first essay he came in hundreds of feet too high and had the sense to open up the engine and fly round again.

The second time he came in much lower but still much too high. In spite of our shrieks and waving of caps and sticks he came down very fast right across the aerodrome, touched the ground about twenty yards from the further edge and then ran between a hangar and some cottages; fell six feet into a sunken road and stood on his nose!

---

1. "Hun" in this case means a beginner.

I don't forget I've been a 'Hun' myself, but. . . .
I've got a new stunt. Romney is enthusiastic about it.
It is called 'rolling.'
While the machine is going forward it is made to turn over sideways on to its back and to continue turning until it is normal again.
I told you the incident about B——, a great '*Hun-strafer*,' who got up against some Boche stunt pilots and had to 'stop the fight' to watch them stunting.
This was the principal trick they were doing.
I hadn't the vaguest idea of how it was done until some days ago when I was trying to improve on my 'Immelmann' turn. I hope if I ever meet a lot of Huns they'll stop the fight to watch me too.
Our hut looks lovely now—all draped in pale blue and with darker blue curtains and neat shelves and bookcases and pale blue bed-hangings.
But I want *you*, my wonderful lover. I long for you so much. Many times I do not sleep but think of you instead, and my thoughts are so thrilling. I love you, dearest woman.
All yours,
Bill.

I have been thinking that in all my experience I seldom have seen a woman and a man mated as Bill and I are mated.

At the best, in most cases, something has to be sacrificed for the sake of the something that is enjoyed.

There are those who are companionable mentally, but who draw one another by no charm. There are those who appeal emotionally and whose mind will be strangers until the end—and at the end more strange than now.

But when Bill calls me his "wonderful lover" I know it is because our minds, our senses, our spirits, make in communion the harmony that is complete.

Chapter 24

The short story was an incident merely, Irene's agent supplied the climax.

Feeling sick with the obvious I longed to take the nasty taste from my mouth and wondered how to do it. "I know," I thought suddenly, "I'll go to see the person 'upon whose advice one may rely'; and if he doesn't approve of what was sent to him. Bill and I can become tinkers, or two-step experts, or we might contrive a risky acrobatic turn on the ceiling of a music hall. Anyway we needn't scribble anymore."

The building was in one of those streets between the river and the Strand. As the lift-lady looked much too comfortable to be disturbed, indifferently I climbed the stair and, having knocked at a door, gave my name to a male being so ponderously minute that I think he must have stepped from his cradle to take this serious part in life.

Then, as one of the many benefits acquired by my amazing marriage is a less feverish desire for the haste that accomplishes nothing, complacently I stood by a window watching a vividly green creeper grow up the side of the brick foundation to a row of chimney pots.

It was a miracle of nature where all else was artifice except the sky.

After some time the war-baby reappeared to conduct me to another room where, immediately, I felt a most curious sensation of relief.

For here, whatever might ensue, was one who must detest the obvious as surely as Bill and I detest it.

When a big thing happens in our lives I think we are more normal than when some trivial excitement occurs.

During the weeks preceding my marriage, I was serene; and since then the serenity has grown, yet happenings have been colossal.

And, in that room, listening to words which revealed a justification of our work together, I felt that it was not news to me—and yet it was!

It was news of the most beautiful sort for vagabonds—promising freedom from the routine arranged by others; giving immunity from all purpose but our own.

There are those I know who uphold the slavery of system, and I myself agree that there are laws to be obeyed—but the machinery of life is for those who demand their problems cut and dried. It's neither for Bill nor for me nor for those who, like us, would explore.

Yet we must justify ourselves at least by evidence that we are willing to cope with the problem of every day.

We are too apt, I know, to sneer at the practical means of livelihood while still we eat and drink.

******

Calmly spoke the man "upon whose advice one may rely."

That very day, he said, proofs of articles accepted by the *Daily* —— had been returned from the censor: "to be passed by the writer's C.O." The same permission would be necessary for part of the material to form the book, for which there should be no difficulty in finding a publisher.

"And you know," he concluded, "with this paper crisis the sooner it is put in hand the better."

At first I thought I would telegraph to Bill, and then, realizing nothing could be gained in that way, I wrote enclosing the proof, to be sent back immediately with the necessary sanction.

Now I wait—impatient that a few more days must elapse.

I feel that if I could be certain Bill had shared my joy I would be content.

Those who love should know no barrier of space nor distance.

It is very stupid. He writes in the second letter:

My dearest One,"
Two perfectly lovely letters have come. They were sent last Saturday and Sunday from London.
Darling, how every detail of what you do and think thrills me. I love you.
I am sorry my first letter, addressed to town, was not in time, but you have it and more by now.
After writing to you yesterday I did a short patrol. The clouds were very low and apparently there was nothing doing—but later a call came through reporting a Hun machine 'spotting'

for the artillery near ——. I was sent up to look for it.

I got into the clouds at 2,500 feet and did not clear them under 6,000. Then I went due east by compass and when I thought I was far enough over I dived through.

I came out at 2,000 feet dead over the trenches, so up I went into the clouds again and found myself about two miles further on. I patrolled for ten minutes just under the clouds and saw no Hun and came home above the clouds.

I led my patrol of five not too badly last night, I think, but 'Archie' dealt rudely with us and I simply couldn't—and the others couldn't—keep the formation.

We went a good way east and got 'Archied' there. I spotted three Huns very low down, but each time I dived they got under small banks of cloud and I lost them. Altogether, yesterday, I did about five hours flying.

This morning I did a line patrol with Romney. There was a strong west wind blowing and we were constantly being blown over the lines. There were high banks of clouds at about 6,000 feet and we climbed to 16,000. The effect was very wonderful from above.

But there was nothing doing. No Huns—not even 'Archie.'

I didn't go into details about the rag because I thought I had implied all there was to say.

Anyhow there were seven of us and we got there at 5.45 p. m., and sat in a *café* and drank cocktails until dinner time, and then had dinner.

Voilà tout! Utterly romantic, quite foolish, and yet I avow without apology that I found it very amusing at the time.

It was when we arrived back—a very noisy and irresponsible tenderful that the Odd Man declared that he must come next time.

Whether to control or to join in the game was not quite clear.

Oh, more news! The 'air-hog' has just got an M.C. for general keenness and good work.

Our flight is 'standing by,' but I do not think we shall have another patrol.

This morning just before we got to the lines there was a big scrap in which our 'tripe-hounds'—as the facetious call the triplanes—got two Huns and our two-seaters got one, but two of ours are missing.

It appears that the Hun sent over about twenty machines in one raid. They haven't been seen in the sky today apart from that.

I have seen some fellows of —— Squadron who told me that FitzGarrick's mother has had a letter from him from Germany. I am wondering where you are at this moment Wherever you are, I am always thinking of you and loving you. Whatever I am doing I think of you all the time. "*Bien Aimée*, I adore you.

All yours,

Bill.

P. S.—The letters I had today were the one written in the train and the one of the day following. I loved both, but particularly about your journey. I recalled our journeys together.

Bill.

Isn't he perfect? I think I will go out into the park and think about him.

★★★★★★

In the park people were doing a church parade.

I sat under a parasol and watched them pass up and down in the sunshine. There were lots of women with new and very chic clothes, and there were soldiers with rows of ribbons. Those who had their "wings up" gave me a little pain in my heart, for I remember stitching the first pair on Bill's tunic. They had to be perfectly straight, you know, so it was more of a task than it might have been.

But I couldn't have allowed anyone else to do it, of course.

Then there were "The Creditors"—the maimed and blinded ones—some in bath-chairs; some on crutches; some holding each other by the arm for guidance.

They had young faces and I wondered if they must move like that until time should make their faces old.

I would have liked to speak to them—to comfort myself by hearing that their spirits dismissed restraint though their feet no more could carry them swiftly where they chose to go.

I hoped too that each had found his woman and that each woman had kept faith.

How marvellous, I thought, would be the spiritual revelation of such a union, if the man were great enough to accept the love and service, and the woman felt all joy in giving!

★★★★★★

Someone spoke my name.

Dragging my mind from its abstraction, I looked—and there was Harvey leaning on his two rubber-capped sticks.

I stared without speaking for a moment or two, and then feebly said, "Hullo!"

Chapter 25

It has been a warm and lovely evening. We dined in Piccadilly and afterwards came out into the gloaming to wander along under the deep sky.

Past the clubs overlooking the Green Park we went. Harvey unwarlike in his conventional dinner clothes, but warlike enough in his disablement, stumped along on his sticks at my side.

It seemed so familiar, so much a repetition of what had been, that I felt obliged to remind myself all was not as before; that now, released from the feverish bondage which had enchained me, I could walk calmly, guarded by the security of my true love.

At last, contemplating the brown earth of the empty row, we paused.

At dinner the talk had been superficial, as it is with two who have been intimate and between whom there is no more intimacy.

And during the walk we hadn't spoken; but now, abruptly, Harvey said:

"So you've solved the problem . . . your marriage is a success!"

For a while I had no reply. What is one to say to such a statement?

Whoever "solves the problem" and what is "success"?

Could I tell him, to whom ambition had seemed all important during the days when I would have given myself; given my body—and my mind, with its woman's capacity of which men have need though they may neither admit nor know it—that my marriage had taken me to an enchanted world?

I could tell him in a measure— and I did, in fairness to Bill . . . and myself.

Yet I had understood him so well.

His Destiny had given him his gods; those gods that mocked me to my utter desolation. Even war and his part in it had left them firmly rooted; and if, eager to escape, I had fled away at last, the fault was mine, not his.

My Destiny had led me to my garden—and the irony of it was that the gods fell as I turned to go. He was left alone outside without them—even without me! I had no wish—Oh, indeed, indeed I had no wish, for such a victory!

My hope now is that some other woman may come and guide him also into the place where truth is—

******

Bill's letter of this morning—Monday—still says nothing of the proofs and the stupendous news about the book. Counting the posts again I know that even Tuesday may not bring his reply.

But the sight of his writing is sufficient to dwarf everything else.

Cherie, another thrilling letter from you—the one written last Monday in the park when you stayed there all day with the babes.

Both I and my pen are speechless over it. I cannot say anything adequate. You are my life.

******

More news of the 'Air Hog!'

Last night he was seen to be hit—presumably by 'Archie.' His machine went down under control and crashed on the ground. This was about a mile behind the front line trenches.

Several hours later the Odd Man was able to find him in a casualty station. He had a compound fracture of the right leg and the left ankle was smashed up. He was quite conscious and could tell all about it.

His machine had been hit when he was flying low at about 4,500 feet. A gas attack and a big bombardment were on at the time. The shell hit the engine and burst on percussion. It blew out part of the engine, tore off the under carriage and made a big hole in the bottom of the fuselage.

The 'Air Hog' was hit in the legs by fragments of shell. He found himself sitting in an open framework with one leg dangling down useless.

With the other, the left, although the ankle was smashed, he managed to steer. Though the balance was all wrong, he forced his machine down in a steady glide, avoided some trees and chose a clear place to land.

He crashed on landing, of course, but crawled out of the hole in front and was found by the ambulance men a few minutes later. He was perfectly conscious and never lost consciousness the whole time.

It was a wonderful performance and a miracle too, to have a direct hit and still be alive. He may be badly crippled, but he is in no serious danger.

No more 'jolly old patrols' for him, however!

******

I interrupted the writing of this to play a set of tennis. It is frightfully hot and I am sitting now on my bed with a long drink on the table beside me—white wine, lemon squash, and soda.

I am not due out on patrol until this evening, but before that I am going up to test my machine. The original engine has been taken out to be overhauled after doing nearly sixty hours, and a new engine is being put in.

Tell Babe the Second that I promise to write to her soon. The golliwog she made still scouts for Huns.

******

I was glad about your decision not to see Harvey when in town. Yes, I think you could do no less than answer his letter.

Oh, my dearest woman, I love you. I send you all my most passionate vows.

Bill.

******

Reading those last words I wish that I had not dined with Harvey last night. I wouldn't care for Bill to dine with a woman who had kissed him before he knew me.

But at the moment it seemed to be making too much of it to refuse. The meeting of the morning was accidental too.

I hope the "Air Hog" has a woman somewhere who will give thanks for his escape; for I think that among all this waste the least wasteful exits are made by those who leave no one to weep. Then one dies instead of two.

Chapter 26

This has come.

Dearest,
Just a line to say I have submitted the proof to the C.O., but he has not returned it yet.
In case it is used it must not be signed. I am sorry.
I will write this evening at length.
All yours,

Bill.

Oh, I want his other letter quickly. I want to telephone to the man "upon whose advice one may rely" and tell him that everything can progress furiously.

Wait! Here is Purcell with a telegram. Now we can go ahead!

We can't go ahead!—The wire says "Permission refused!"

But this is impossible. There was nothing—*nothing*—in the proof to give "information" of any sort to the enemy. Why otherwise should permission be refused? This means that not only the articles but the book must be held over. And of what use will they be afterwards? Their whole value lies in the human appeal they would make to men and women at this very instant. How can I exist until tomorrow's letter comes?

******

It has come—the letter of explanation—but I am unconvinced. How could I be convinced with this:—

My dearest One,
I am sorry. The C.O. is afraid that the squadron would be too easily recognized, and I think the same.
I don't know what to do now. We can only wait until I come home on leave.

******

Yesterday I did two patrols—the early one at 4.30 a. m. and the last at 7.30. There was nothing doing on either.

Tonight we are having a special celebration dinner. Romney, who has been out here a long time, and has brought down many Huns, is going home tomorrow.

We expect he will get a squadron and his majority—in addition to his M.C., and *Croix de Guerre*.

He is an awfully dear fellow and absolutely the stoutest-hearted I have ever met. He is about 35 and married.

This morning I went up for a joy-ride and did an hour over the lines alone.

I hope you are not very depressed over the wash-out. I'm not—though I'm disappointed. We have *done* something in any case. And I love you and I know you love me. Dear, dear one.

               All yours,

                                    Bill.

How could he—what does he mean by writing to me like that after all my striving?

It was my "bit"—the only thing I could do for him while he did his share.

I was so glad because I thought he would be overjoyed.

It was utterly wrong for him to agree with the C.O. What does a "tousle-headed youth in pyjamas" know of our career? Couldn't Bill have argued with him and explained that anything identifying the squadron to any one, except the squadron itself, could be altered? But to leave it like that—just final!

And he doesn't seem to mind. I daren't write to him, I might say too much.

******

I did write yesterday after all, because I realised that I should be sorry afterwards to know that Bill didn't have a letter for each day.

I told him that I think he should have made some effort about this opportunity that will, perhaps, affect his and my whole future; but I don't think I expressed my amazement at his airy dismissal of it all. Now I hope I didn't, for it seems so trivial when one reads this:

Ma Bien Aimée,

Your letter of last Thursday saying you have managed to do another short story has just come. I am glad about that, for you must be disappointed about the other 'washout' after all your hard work.

※※※※※※

Things have livened up again considerably. After writing you yesterday I went out on an escort job over X——. I am leading patrols now all the time and am temporarily in command of my flight.

We flew very high to protect a two-seater taking photos.

After it had finished and gone I spotted two Hun scouts going south. We chased them to X——, and then about five miles further east, but could not come up with them.

After tea I went out a third time with one other fellow. At 17,000 feet over X—— three Hun scouts appeared suddenly above me. I was very surprised, for the sky was thick with our own scouts, but they were all further west.

For a few minutes we kept our positions. Then the Huns came nearer until at last I pulled down my gun and fired up at the nearest, who was about 200 feet above me. He did a sudden turn, when I had fired about 25 rounds, and dived steeply away.

The others twisted and turned, and I thought they were going to dive on me, but a patrol of our scouts came up and the Huns sheered off.

Towards the end of the patrol when I was losing height I saw four red Hun Scouts below me and dived on the nearest. (The other fellow with me I had lost. He had got mixed up in another formation.)

I fired twenty rounds at long range; and the whole four turned away!

This morning six of us—Kyle leading one and I the other formation—had to escort six machines that were going for photos again. It turned out awfully well. The photo people led at about 11,000 and we were above and at either side slightly to the rear.

The poor leaders got smothered in 'Archie' bursts the whole time and we sailed along above in comfort.

At last, when a long way over, a formation of Hun scouts and two-seaters appeared to the north-west of us. The Huns didn't see us and went for the two-seaters; and seemed surprised when we dived into the middle of them.

I picked out a fat two-seater and put fifty rounds into him. He sent out clouds of smoke and fumes and started diving away. I couldn't watch it because for the next ten minutes we were in a swirl of Huns and ourselves, all tearing round and round and firing guns.

When finally we got into some sort of formation again all of us were there intact.

I climbed up again with one other fellow following, to head off five Huns who were coming up from the south, and for twenty minutes we manoeuvred until finally the Huns went too far over the lines to follow.

We all got back and found that one fellow had got one Hun down for certain. All had had scraps at close quarters with results not seen.

I had rather a 'head' last night when I got down—after nearly three hours during the day at over 16,000 feet. However, I forgot all about it at dinner—our farewell to Romney—and today I am quite fit again.

******

I forgot to tell you that the Air Hog had to lose one leg below the knee. He is getting on quite well though up to now.

I don't think many people have so well won an M.C.

******

"Dearest, most precious one, I don't want you to work so hard as you have been doing—especially in town. You will begin to look tired again.

   Aimée, I love you.

              Bill.

But, Bill dear, what are we women to do just now if we don't work "too hard"? How can we sit in idleness and think of the risks you take? Indeed, in that case we should look more than tired. There would be nothing left when you came to find us.

Chapter 27

He "upon whose advice one may rely" thinks that the book will be of use afterwards, and that *Ad Astra* might, with advantage, preface it.

This will be good news to Bill and it is good news to me—but truly I admit my triviality.

What does a mere disappointment matter these days?

What does anything matter except that lovers should be re-united; and by lovers I think of them that love—mothers and children; husbands and wives; and those whose union is not recognised—all, all who love!

But yes, something matters more. It is that they who lose their lovers may not lose also Faith and Hope, and Charity.

Oh, there must be an afterwards. This can't be the End.

Bill says today—

Darling lover"

I cannot explain how anxious I am about your disappointment.

Your lovely letter which came this morning—written on Friday last, was so glowing with the thought of our success that it quite gave me a pain to think that by now you have my telegram and know we have come to a dead end—in that direction at any rate.

******

I think I got two Huns last night. It was on the last patrol again; it is becoming a regular thing to meet all the Huns just about sunset.

I led a formation of six and crossed the lines at 11,000 feet When I turned down south I saw five Hun scouts about two miles away east and manoeuvred to approach them with the sun behind me.

The sun is absolutely blinding at sunset when you're in the sky.

I got quite close to the nearest one and fired 30 rounds at him. He and the others dived east straight away, and in turning west I lost sight of them.

But one of my patrol watched for several minutes the Hun I had fired at and saw him falling and fluttering about right to the ground, quite out of control.

Twenty minutes later, when coming north again—all this was about six miles east of the lines—I saw a formation of red scouts. They were a long way below us, and I had also to go down indirectly to get the sun Behind me again.

At last I did this and then went all out for the nearest one. There were seven of them. I got quite close again and finished my drum, zoomed out and climbed west again.

While changing the empty drum for a full one I looked around and saw the Hun I had tackled slowly stall, stand upright, and then fall down sideways; sometimes he spun, sometimes dived. I must have got him too.

Having a full drum on the gun again I went back. I could see the various ones of my patrol diving on to the red scouts. I chose, as I thought, the nearest Hun and started firing. The gun stopped after one shot

But as I reached up to clear the stoppage I heard the horrible noise of a Hun's double gun just behind me.

I hadn't chosen the nearest Hun after all, but had passed one; and now he was on my tail.

I spun; the horrid noise stopped, so I stopped spinning.

Instantly the horrid noise started again.

I spun again. Once more the noise stopped and gently I eased my machine out of the spin and the dive.

But the Hun was still there.

When I heard the noise a third time I simply shut off the engine and *fell* down.

I had started scrapping at 12,000. I ventured to pull out level at 7,000.

Afterwards I learned that a scout of another squadron had dived on the Hun on my tail and had shot him down.

My machine wasn't hit anywhere. I didn't stay still long enough, I suppose.

Out of the seven red scouts another squadron got two and I got one—the others of my patrol didn't all get there in time to scrap, but they saw my first one fluttering.

Today is 'dud'; the first 'dud' day since I saw Dick nearly a fortnight ago.

Au revoir, my sweet woman.

I am all yours,

Bill.

Two Huns within a few minutes! Well, as he is there for that purpose I suppose the more he gets the sooner the purpose will cease; but I can't be persuaded that because some wives were born in Hun-land they wait less anxiously for each post—that the sight of a telegram has less power to stab their hearts!

I believe that, however it is spelt, anguish must mean the same thing. Yes, I think of the wives always. May their gods give *them* Faith and Hope and Charity.

Chapter 28

Irene has forwarded a letter from an old man I know. He says:

. . . I have searched my motor-map and Bradshaw for your whereabouts. What a Saxon nest for her for whom I invented an Egyptian classical name!

You see it pleases him to be facetious at my expense, but he does it in the form of flattery, and that is why I wonder he escaped marriage.

I like to think that he has been very true to someone, who was taken away. But I'm a sentimentalist nowadays, am I not?

Last night, in answer, I telephoned to say I had left my "Saxon nest" for a while; and tonight, at his flat, we dined together, for I refused his offer of "other guests." Other guests are all very well when you have had your say; but I wanted to bring our friendship up to date.

The dinner was perfect and the atmosphere so rare in its austere sincerity. Certainly the servant, who, at that table, hands one the most delicious food, is not quite so aged as my host, but his courtesy is equal.

To celebrate my marriage we drank champagne. I liked it.

Afterwards, over our coffee and cigar and cigarette, we discussed music, and my host's work on war-hospital committees, and Bill; and we gossiped too, without malice, about people known to both of us.

Then I asked him to come and refresh himself with a sight of our lovely Downs.

At his age he should sit in a garden, under God's own Heaven, instead of wallowing in the smoke and grime of cities—but he refused, pleading his hospital duties.

I imagine he feels the absolute necessity for activity. He knows rest must come soon enough maybe!

Bill said this morning:

Darling,
Another of those, fortunately, rare days when no letter has come from you. All the post brought was a letter from Dick. He says:

> What a sensation you made. . . . They are still talking about it in the battery. It was a fine exhibition.'

Darling, I *do* wish I could show you too, because you can't imagine how beautiful my machine looks stunting and flashing in the sun.

There was nothing doing all day yesterday, and after the early patrol this morning the clouds came down low again. But now it is clearer and I expect I shall be out tonight. In any case if there is no patrol I shall go out on the range.

The day after you should receive this you will be travelling to the country again. I would like to be there in your room when you get back to it.

Or, dearest one, to be near you. . . . I love you, my wife.

All yours,

Bill.

I can't bear it. . . . I can't bear it. . . . I want him to be there, in my room, waiting for me!

******

We have come to the "Saxon Nest" again; but neither Irene nor Nanny nor the family of one are here.

They are to suffer a month of duty visits; and so that this house may not become too wrapped up in its own reflections, I have brought the babes.

We have no maid.

One of the seven—or is it nine?—wonders of the world comes in the early morning to light the kitchen fire and clean everything to spotlessness. Afterwards she goes back to her cottage to cope with the necessities of four small children—which means cooking and cleaning, and cleaning and cooking, she grows her own vegetables too, and works in the fields and does all the washing and ironing for this household besides the flannels from the vicarage.

She never appears to hurry, nor to be tired, and her personal cleanliness is overwhelming. Her second husband is "at the war," and another child has a small grave in the churchyard here.

There's a life for you!

The babes are enraptured. Each has her room, which she keeps tidy; and we all make our own beds.

Then we cook too.

I don't know why we were expected to know that cornflour must be mixed in cold milk before being added to the hot milk.

We know now.

Then I would have you bear in mind that raw meat doesn't keep, although the butcher calls only twice a week.

The smell was horrible. The seventh or ninth wonder removed it and gave a short, crisp lecture on "partial cooking."

We grow wiser each day. Soon I shall be fitted to call myself a wife.

Yesterday afternoon, on the Downs, Betty helped me to boil a kettle, while Bey romped about without a stitch of clothing on except a shady panama hat. The sun loved her body and poured down his warmth upon her.

This is how we boiled our kettle. Before starting, into an empty syrup tin we poured a very small amount of paraffin oil and a small spoonful of salt. Then when we wanted our stove we uncovered and placed it in a hollow of stones piled a little higher than itself so that a draught could wander between it and the kettle. Into the paraffin we dropped a lighted fir cone. Two or three times the flame went out and we had to fish for the cone and relight it, but at length it blazed and the kettle boiled immediately. The salt, while keeping the paraffin from lighting so easily, prevents it burning away at once.

Our wisdom was not our own. We learned it at the vicarage while consuming an enormous tea the day before.

Betty said afterwards that probably they thought we had had no lunch, which wasn't exactly true—but nearly. The meat episode had taken place during the morning, you see.

✶✶✶✶✶✶

This letter of Bill's is too wonderful. It makes me ache with desire for him.

My dearest, dearest one,
The blank of yesterday was filled today by your two lovely letters of Saturday and Sunday.
Aimee, my dear wife, all your wonderings and questionings thrill me beyond words; certainly beyond written words. Were I close to you my first answer would be to kiss you till you

could not breathe.

But I can't put down on paper all that I would say. This I can say: that I am amazed all the time at the miracle of our marriage; amazed at finding myself capable of the richest love, for I have no reservations of which I am conscious; I am all yours and I want to deserve all you.

I am amazed and thrilled that so deeply tender and passionate a love should bring me such sanity and clearness in my mental attitude to you. I live only for you, my wife. I am utterly yours.

******

By now you will have written to me after hearing that the book and *Daily* —— articles can't go on.

In a short time now—the time we dare not speak of—we'll be able to put our heads together and make something, from the material, with which we shall have no difficulty.

******

Last night I started out on a line patrol, but the clouds were so thick that I got lost and came down 2,000 feet over the trenches.

I had only the 'Hun' with me—his first time over the lines. He was quite delighted because he saw a real Hun soldier in the trenches.

This morning we were up at 4.45, but the clouds were too low, so we went back to bed.

Later I went to the range, but when I started firing my gun didn't jam. On the contrary it wouldn't stop firing!

I scattered about 90 rounds over the country side and came back to strafe the gun-room.

This evening I am due out on an O.P.

******

I don't know if I told you about our contour chasing.

The squadron has gone quite mad over it. Nearly always on returning from patrol we come down low and chase around the roads and the camps about fifty feet off the ground. It is quite amusing and some funny things happen,

One fellow saw a band giving a concert one evening. He was about 300 feet high. Opening out his engine to produce its full noise he spiralled down directly over their heads.

For some moments nothing happened, and then he saw the conductor—a fat man—fling down his baton and throw up his

arms in despair. The bandmen could not hear themselves play!
"There was a big crowd of Tommies there, and as the machine zoomed up again they cheered and laughed and waved their caps, and the pilot laughed so much that he couldn't fly straight.

Doesn't sound fair, does it? However, the infantry still has a wonderfully good opinion of us.

I am going to the range now when I have posted this to you.
   All my most passionate love,
                  Bill.

Aren't all men babes?

I think it is well that in the midst of death they can laugh so easily at life!

Chapter 29

Betty and I are cooks!

I used to think those who could turn raw flour and other raw things into something one liked to eat must have a special gift. Now I no longer am surprised, except that any one should go on doing it day after day. We enjoyed ourselves because it was adventure; but I shouldn't care to be obliged to spend my time in a kitchen—even such a darling of a kitchen as this—whether I felt inclined or otherwise.

Our cakes are perfect, and the cornflour jelly stuff slips down like a dream. That's because it was flavoured with chocolate and had the beaten white of eggs stirred in at the last minute.

Prunes and rhubarb simply cook themselves while you fold your hands and sit on the kitchen table! I did so and re-read my letter from Bill.

My darling,

We are nearly sure that the enclosed cutting describes the scraps we had several days ago. Refer to my letter and see how nearly like it that is.

In some details it varies but not in much.

Then, again, the last paragraph obviously refers to the 'Air Hog'—except that he never lost consciousness.

I loved your letter of Monday, which I got at lunch today. I love your 'moods,' too. And you see how gravely I take them?

My dear, my dear, when we love we trust and understand, and we treasure all each other's quaintnesses. I love you always and am all yours.

******

'*Later.*

The flight got two Huns today. The new flight commander

Allison got one and Grahaeme, who is generally in my patrol, got the other.

It was on our return from escorting six two-seaters. Four Hun machines actually were over our side of the lines and Allison and Grahaeme climbed up while on the east of them and shot one each from underneath.

Grahaeme's was confirmed from the ground. It was seen to fall in the lines.

Today I got your first letter, written after knowing of the C.O.'s refusal.

I am just as sick about it as you are, dearest one. Don't, please, think I approve of the C.O. refusing; but all the same, I had to agree with what he said.

It is the rigid etiquette of the R.F.C. that, individually, squadrons and pilots should not be mentioned. (Ball is the solitary exception.) The C.O. said the squadron would be recognised. I couldn't deny that.

But, anyhow, right or wrong, having so much vital daily work to do, I simply cannot even argue with him over this now. When I get to England I must try to arrange something with you.

I am sorry, so sorry, my dearest, to think of all your work and your hopes standing by for such a flimsy reason. Please do not be too much disappointed. Wait a little.

Darling, you are so intensely precious to me. I love you and want you just frightfully.

All my love,

Bill.

Today I should loathe to cook. I have a "head." It's the one Bill had the other day and it has just travelled across. For that reason I welcome it—but I'm glad I don't have to cook!

There is enough food in the pantry to satisfy the appetites of Betty and Bey, and I shall live on tea and cigarettes for the next few hours.

That sounds like asking for trouble, doesn't it; but if you obey your instinct in these things you can't go wrong. Some "heads" wouldn't tolerate tea or cigarettes—and some will! Mine is the second sort.

Bill's letter is a tonic, though. I read—

Darling one,"

You are settled again in the country by now I suppose, and with The Babes. My longing to be with you grows more intense.

I love you with all my life, *bien-Aimée*.

✶✶✶✶✶✶

Yesterday morning one of our pilots was wounded. He had been here only three weeks and has done awfully well.

When he was wounded he was attacking a two-seater and was underneath it. The observer stood up and fired down on him and he was hit in the hip joint.

He came home and made a good landing, but is rather bad for he lost a lot of blood.

This morning Grahaeme went missing. He was out with Captain Allison and they got separated in the clouds. We may hear yet that he is down on this side, but there is a gale blowing from the west and we think he must be on the other side.

I did a line patrol last night and an O.P. this morning. But saw little. There were a few odd Huns about, but they stayed too far over east for us to dare to follow them in view of the gale from the west.

Later.

Grahaeme has just telephoned. He got mixed up in a big scrap and drifted a long way over the lines, lost his bearings, and landed finally at another aerodrome.

The mail is in, but there is no letter from you—only one from Joan. She says Dad spoke to you on the telephone last Wednesday.

I wish I could do that. My dearest, I long to hear your voice again.

✶✶✶✶✶✶

I have just developed a very bad failing as a pilot. I have started landing badly. The last dozen times I have returned to the aerodrome I have made simply awful exhibitions, and as these on several occasions followed a stunting show over the sheds they were quite humiliating.

This morning I broke my tail skid—tore it clean off. That makes the fifth I have smashed. I know why I land badly—afterwards. But I never know at the moment. It is a question only of tenths of a second. However, I will get it right again soon.

I did some shooting at the range yesterday. Going much nearer the ground, doing one quick short dive, and firing perhaps ten shots is, I find, much better than long dive firing all the time.

I did either eight or nine dives, and the early ones were long ones. Towards the end I did short dives and the result showed the difference. In the last four dives I scored one, two, one and three hits respectively. The last was quite good, for I had only five rounds left when I started the dive. But I got so near that I nearly touched the ground, then fired and zoomed.

When you are scrapping with a Hun the same thing happens. The Hun is moving as well as you, and frequently towards you, so that you touch almost before you fire.

In haste to catch the post. It goes in a minute.

        All yours,

                Bill.

Chapter 30

The old postman arrived today before I wakened properly.

Bey must have seen him come up the path for, half consciously, I heard her scamper down; then clad in her small *kimono* and bedroom slippers she tiptoes into my room determined not to rouse me, I suppose. Unable to resist temptation, however, she spent the next few minutes labouring to balance something on my nose. Knowing what was expected of me I slept soundly until this was achieved, and she had, with muffled giggles and gurgles, tiptoed carefully away. Then I opened my eyes and read:—

> My wonderful lover,
> '*Three* letters from you today—one written in town, the last from there; one in the train, and one from the country. Darling, I am frantically happy.
> Today the Odd Man received the June issue of his magazine, in which appears my article. I enclose it.
> On the whole, I think it is rather good; don't you?
> This morning I was called at 3.30 by the C.O. to go for a special stunt. For four days running a Hun, greatly daring, has come over the aerodrome just after daybreak.
> The C.O. proposed last night that we should leave the grounds the moment it was light if the clouds permitted, and try to catch him.
> We got off the ground at 4 a.m.—a few minutes before in fact. We climbed to 18,500 feet over the aerodrome and watched for signals from the ground.
> But no Hun came. Anyhow it was a lovely morning and, apart from the frozen fingers, I enjoyed the flip. We finished by patrolling the line for three-quarters of an hour and then came contour chasing home.

I was out again at 9.30 on another escort to two-seaters, who were taking photographs.

This afternoon I played tennis, and tonight I lead an O.P. at seven o'clock.

I expect to get another letter from you tomorrow. My dear one, I love your letters; they mean more to me than I dare say or think. I love you more every day, every minute.

    All yours,

                                          Bill.

P.S.—You are my *wife*, you know.

After reading this—feeling very glad about myself and Bill, I rose and went down into the stone-flagged kitchen, where the seventh or ninth wonder had left a bright fire burning. The kettle sang and the double saucepan waited for the porridge which I mixed so that it neither would be thick nor thin—then set it on the stove and came up to bathe and dress.

Bey already had bathed herself and was hurrying into her scanty clothing so that she might have time to play with the kittens in the sunshine of the garden before breakfast. Betty, who likes her sleep in solid chunks, called lazily for me to run her water when I'd let my own away.

And so about nine o'clock we sat down to breakfast in the nursery that, like every other room in the house, is as cheerful as it is simple and picturesque.

Later, after preparing the mid-day meal, I went for cream, which means a walk of four miles altogether. And these, as nearly as I can recall, were my thoughts:

"I hope the babes will be all right playing in the garden alone. . . . They ought to be. . . Betty is old enough now. . . . Bill's letter is so sweet. . . . I wish he were here. . . . Wouldn't it be too wonderful to have him I wonder what he is doing at this moment. . . . It's hardly worth while coming all this way for cream when it's so hot—but then it's so good for growing children. I wish our own milk people didn't make all theirs into butter. . . . Let me see, I mustn't forget to let Bill know that they had written from the *Daily* —— about his articles. . . . I'll say he might at least have taken the trouble to write to them, especially as I asked him to. . . . No, I won't say that. . . . I should be dreadfully sorry afterwards. I'll say I thought he had done so and that I didn't because I loathed having to refuse the chance. . . . Let me think—if I were to beat some of the cream very stiff, would it disguise the milk pudding enough to make The Babes not realize what they were eating? It's so good for them.... Oh, I mustn't forget to add some white of egg.... I remember the book said that....

"I feel certain Bill could have argued with the C.O. about those articles!... I should have done so.... I'm surprised he didn't bother even though he—what *shall* I do with the yolk of that egg.... It mustn't be wasted and I don't want it for anything.... I *know*.... I'll swallow it whole and let Betty and Bey watch me.... They'll love that. Bey will shriek with mirth.... Yes, I'll tell Bill that I didn't think much of the article he did for the Odd Man's magazine .., it wasn't a bit vivid.... Not on the same plane as his letters to me. I shall enjoy telling him.... He was rather bucked with it too.... Now if that chicken is to be hot for Sunday's dinner I can't *possibly* go to church.... How can I?.. And if I don't the babes won't—and we didn't go last Sunday.

"The village mothers don't go because they have the meal to cook. But they send their children. I'm sure Betty and Bey would not be sent—besides I'm not their mother! I quite forgot to ask the price of the chicken.... Goodness, I remember the woman on Salisbury Plain said they'd be worth their weight in gold. I hope this one isn't ... we haven't enough money in the house, nor in the bank either!... It'll be fearfully exciting cooking it. I hope Betty and Bey won't get too hot rushing about ... Bey's tummy *is* rather out of proportion to her size, ... but I suppose it's all right.... All small children have large tummies. It's where they keep their extra nourishment, I expect... I think I'll ask the grocer man if he ..."

You see what it is to be a housewife? I must pull myself together, mustn't I?

Chapter 31

My own wife,
We had a quaint patrol last night. All the flight did it. Allison led one patrol of three and I led the other. One fellow dropped out, however, and five of us crossed the lines.

We soon saw seven Hun Scouts leave their aerodrome and start climbing away from us.

Hoping to entice them to the lines, Allison turned west and re-crossed the trenches. We turned south, climbed hard for twenty minutes, and crossed again.

We were at 16,000 feet when we saw the Huns about 2,000 feet below us. There were, roughly, a dozen of them—all scouts and wonderfully painted. No two were alike, and hardly one machine was painted all the same colour. Green wings and red fuselage; pink and purple; yellow tails and white and black wings! They were hideous.

We had been in formation, but when we saw the Huns and Allison started twisting about to get into position, two of our pilots lost height and got underneath him.

I closed up to him, with Grahaeme close on me and the three of us tore round and round, like a circus—each on the other's tail.

Allison was looking for four of us and could see only two.

"Below us the Huns were going round and round also, but in the greatest confusion. It was screamingly funny. I don't think we were really happy—so few against a dozen and a dozen miles east of the lines—but the Huns were less happy.

First one and then the other would get out of control and start spinning, dive, and flatten out and climb up again. They had the wind up, all right!

Well we continued this round-about business for about five minutes, and I wondered when the leader was going to dive. I wondered also how we should get back such a distance to the lines if we lost height and got mixed up with the Huns.

At last Allison decided apparently that it was not good enough and he turned away west.

Ultimately we got into formation again. When we got home we had been out two hours and five minutes and had each only a few pints of petrol left.

It was really the better course not to have had a scrap under all the conditions, though perhaps we might have tried just one dive each and tootled home promptly afterwards.

✶✶✶✶✶✶

I didn't tell you about my fifteen minutes' battle the other day. I was out with an O.P. with one other fellow—the third had gone back with engine trouble—and when east of the trenches I saw a lot of English 'Archie' bursts to westward. A moment afterwards I spotted a machine making for the lines. We were at 15,000 feet and the other machine at 12,000.

I immediately dived a bit to head him off. He turned north and I turned north, too, to get in front of him. He turned south and the other fellow headed him off. Then he came east climbing. I climbed west, and he gave it up.

At last he put his nose down and came due east to pass under me. I dived straight for him, with my eye on the gun sights and the Hun at the other end of them and my finger on the trigger lever.... Then .... the Venetian blind effect appeared and I saw it was a tri- plane—one of our own machines!

Either it had been 'Archied' by mistake or there was a real Hun further west that I could not see.

Today I had your letter written in the garden on Friday.

I have just run out of paper of the size I usually use, but I can love you just as much on this as on any other—and I do.

All my love, my sweet wife,

Bill.

✶✶✶✶✶✶

We have had an event!

Just now—keeping a motherly eye on Bey while she cleaned her teeth—suddenly I heard Betty shriek from her room:

"Cows—cows! Oh, cows!"

Her voice carried all the shrill notes of excitement and I could hear her darting about.

"What is it? ... What do you mean?" I called back, and Bey demanded in her curiously deep and impatient tones:

"What is it on earf?"

"That's not the way to speak, darling," I dutifully began, while Betty came running, clothed in her undergarments, hair brush in hand.

"There's millions of cows in the garden," she panted.... "Crowds and crowds, and they're rushing furiously about, on the lawn—all going mad!"

Allowing for the exaggeration usual to females of Betty's age there remained a possibility of cows in the garden; so, as Bey ran out after her, I followed from the bathroom to the bedroom window—and there truly were the herd.

They seemed to be panic stricken—drifting sometimes; sometimes tearing in confusion, sometimes standing for a second and then leaping grotesquely.

The three of us watched, our heads all out of one casement, and our breath coming in jerks to match the antics of the cattle.

By and by the shadow of a human being detached itself from the meadow beyond.

It was weird and unreal in the gloaming, so that I scarcely could find my voice to call out and ask the meaning of what was happening. And when I did call, the head of the shadow tilted upward as though to discover us, but no answer came.

Away, beyond, the circle of the Downs looked black and rather terrible. One pure white animal, frantically leaping, seemed ghostly in the dusk. It crossed my mind how dreadful a stampede of untamed beasts must be;—the thud, thud of the hoofs of living things out of gear; the unreasonable infection of the panic; the horrible turmoil of the uncontrolled; the uncontrollable!

I pictured being down there, petrified, in their midst, while they trampled hideously about.

At last these real and harmless creatures gathered together in some sort of order and trotted out of the opening into their own country.

Then I realized that Bey ran a risk of pneumonia. Already she had been late, too, owing to the misdemeanour of Cotton-tail, who had hidden herself in the hedge.

So I bustled this babe into her "nighty" while she hopped about, ... sizzling with the after effects of the event. Soon she lay, looking too angelic, in her narrow white bed under the pale blue coverlet.

"Goodnight, sweet," I said, "sleep well."

She pulled down my head and kissed me fervently.

"G'night . . . G'night," she breathed, "an' ha'nt it been an ab-fo-lutely *wond*-o-ful tweat!"

I arranged the tall screen on which storks fly about to greet her in the morning; and leaving the casement wide open to the tender air I went from the room carrying my flickering candle carefully.

If a few cows in the wrong place at the wrong time provide one babe with an "absolutely wonderful treat," another babe with the pitch of excitement, and one grown-up woman with reflections on the uncanny, why, surely, life's a simple problem after all, I thought.

✶✶✶✶✶✶

I came to my room and drew the curtains across to hide the night. It was beautiful, but too sad for me. Bill's letter lay on the table—the one important thing in the muddle of books and papers and writing materials. I sat down and looked at it; then I took it from the envelope to read again. It was less likely than many to soothe a rebellious tendency.

> Dear, dear Aimée,
>
> We had the hell of a scrap last night. It was the sequel to the encounter of the previous evening which I described yesterday. Allison proposed that we should go out and look for the same crowd of Huns again. So six of us started, with Allison leading, and we crossed the lines and worked down south, well over on the Hun side, before two fellows had to go back with dud engine trouble.
>
> At last we came up to the Huns. I saw four about 2,000 feet below us, and then five further east and above us.
>
> I don't know whether Allison saw those above us or not. However it was, he dived vertically on the nearest Hun and I dived just behind him and went for the second.
>
> As I was going down on to mine I could see Allison close with his; then saw the Hun go down spinning, with engine full on, in a violent spiral. There was no room for doubt as to whether the Hun was hit.
>
> Most of this I saw semi-consciously, for I was sighting on to my Hun. I got very close and fired 30 or 40 rounds while he was flying level. Then when I almost collided with him, he dived. I

followed and finished the drum and zoomed out.

I turned west and climbed hard, but the other two fellows apparently kept the Huns busy, for none followed me. I proceeded with changing my drum and watched the Hun I had attacked still diving, not very steeply, but going directly west! I was then about 9,000 feet. We had all come down in the world a lot—and finally I saw the Hun crash in the ground among some patches of swamp.

Having changed my drum and climbed to 11,000 I turned east again and saw the scrap still going on.

I headed for them again and got in a burst of 25 rounds at another Albatross. He dived out of my sights and the same instant two Huns dived on me. They were almost directly above me, and I could only dive for all I was worth. They followed me to the lines, and by that time I had lost 7,000 feet.

★★★★★★

It was practically dark when I landed. I was the last one home. Allison had not arrived, and nothing has been heard of him since.

The other two of our four had started to follow us down, but had the high Huns on them immediately. They had had quite a struggle and had been shot about a bit. They had both seen Allison and me, however, close in with a Hun each, and both are certain the two were brought down.

I had one bullet through my right plane.

The colonel of the wing came over this morning to ask me all about it. We are sorry Allison did not get back. He was such an excellent patrol leader.

The post goes in a minute. I love you, sweetest one, and am all yours.

Bill.

I am no philosopher tonight.

Chapter 32

Midnight, Wednesday.

Darling,

I did not fly at all today. We were standing by most of the time, and in the evening I was to have led nine machines on the same quest as the previous evening, but about teatime a thunderstorm came on and the whole thing was washed out.

"Today makes exactly two months since I arrived at the squadron—56 days. Up to yesterday I have done 135 hours' flying—or 108 with the squadron here. There have been many changes since I came—five have gone missing, two wounded, two crashed, six gone sick, and two gone home at the end of their time—which makes seventeen that have left the squadron since I came.

Now I am ninth on the list in order of arrival—that is, eight of the seventeen who have been struck off were here before me, and the others have arrived after me.

It really is remarkable how, in every squadron, most of the people who are missing are new arrivals. All five from here arrived after me.

Tomorrow I get up at 5 a. m. to do a bombing escort, so I will finish this at midday (this is the second letter I have written you today) when the post has come in. Goodnight, dearest one.

Bill.

******

Today the papers are full of the new "advance."

Heaven above, what that means! What a fever of emotion—of physical and mental delirium. I hold my letter in my hand, but before I open it I say my prayer for the wives who have no letter from their lovers today.

I say my prayer for them—though to whom I pray I do not know.

Thursday, 2 p. m.

My dear, dear wife,

I was thrilled to ecstasy by your letter which came this morning—the one written on Sunday telling me of your love. I am amazed with the wonder and completeness of it all. *Bien-Aimée*, I worship you, in all your moods, just all the time.

★★★★★★

By the time you get this the news of another great battle will be several days old to you.

It started this morning—out of our area, but we started too. At 5.45 I was off the ground with seven machines to escort the bomb raid I mentioned last night.

When we got up past B—— we saw the battle burning. It was wonderful to be able to see it all like that; but, oh, it is so stupid and senseless. A patch of country about twenty miles long and twelve miles deep was just ablaze.

The 'push' had started at 3.45 a. m., and already at 6 a. m. the artillery barrage had moved forward several miles, leaving a smoking, churned, shell-pocked brown belt of destroyed country behind it.

To the west of, and right up to the original line of trenches, the whole of the fields and woods and roads were livid with the flashes of our guns—not just a dart of flame here and one there, but a dancing, pricking, shimmering mass of heat.

"Towards the eastern edge of the smoking belt was a constant band of white shrapnel bursts, like snowdrops overcrowded in a garden border, and before them and behind them and on both sides of them the continuous eruptions of red earth and dust where the increasing rain of high explosive shells was falling!

★★★★★★

I flew over this, 12,000 feet above it, and thanked some of my gods that I was no longer a landsman in combat.

★★★★★★

The squadron has done remarkably well at the start of the big push. Four Huns on two patrols. But one of our machines is missing—at least he is two hours overdue.

When the bombers were dropping their bombs and we were

looking on this morning three foolish Hun scouts dropped out of the clouds into the midst of us. One got on my tail—I was quite unconscious of it—and Grahaeme promptly filled him with over 80 rounds. He went down and was seen by two other pilots to crash. A second Hun was shot down before he saw us. The third flew level with me just for an instant, and then dived below me. I turned more quickly than he had done and dived vertically at him and fired 20 rounds. He continued to dive nd got out of decent range, so I climbed up to the formation again and we handed back the bombing machines safely across the lines.

We were all intact, too.

The wing commander came round about noon and was fearfully pleased with our start. While he was there the brigadier turned up, too, and was hearing all about it when six of a second patrol of seven returned with a claim of two Huns certain and perhaps others.

The squadron is rather pleased with itself!

Now this afternoon, it is appallingly warm, but there's no work for us until after tea. Then I may take a patrol about 6 p. m. and finish for the day.

Your picture of Babe the second is very sweet. I have one, particularly intimate, of you, which is so sweet!

I love you.

Bill.

Do listen to this!

I never knew anyone so adaptable as Bill. Equally he can appreciate the Odd Man's point of view and the inability of Grahaeme to express himself as the Odd Man would wish.

I think it is priceless to be able to put yourself in every one's place. He is teaching me that lesson among many others.

Friday, 2nd.

My dearest woman;

Another sweet letter from you written last Monday on the Downs.

As I felt when I first came out, so I feel now—how wonderful it is to have someone who matters so much to me; who gives me inspiration to live.

Aimée darling!

The weather turned 'dud' yesterday afternoon, so I had no further work to do. I was down for a patrol at 8 this morning too, but the clouds came over and I am still standing by.

I've mentioned Grahaeme several times, haven't I? He's my right hand man on patrol and is wonderfully reliable.

He's a Canadian and talks it violently and nasally—when he does talk, which is rare. Usually he is very quiet.

But when he is excited—say, when he comes back from a scrap—nothing holds him. His language, all unconsciously, is lurid. And as it generally happens that the Odd Man is waiting to know all about it, the result is thrilling.

'Anything doing?' says the Odd Man.

'Why, God Almighty, I should say there was!' shouts Grahaeme. He has still his helmet on, and as he can't hear well he thinks he has to shout. He goes on—'The sky's stiff with bloody Huns.'

The Odd Man does not continue for the moment, but just looks thoughtful. Someone else, less sensitive to blasphemy, goes on with the interrogation until the Odd Man, forgetting his feelings in the excitement of the story, chips in again.

'Did you get one down?'

'Hell, yes! There were three of them and I was diving on one when I heard someone pooping at me with his double gun. . "Hell!" I said. "There's another damned Hun on my tail." So I yanked up the old 'bus and got on the devil's tail instead and just pumped blue hell into him! . . . And away he went spinning to hell and gone!'

No comment from the Odd Man!

It isn't only on these occasions that Grahaeme's mode of expression is unusual.

At breakfast this morning the Odd Man was seated next to him and said:

'Out for more Huns today, Grahaeme?'

'God, yes!' said Grahaeme fervently and quite gravely.

Well, it's quite the right spirit anyway,' commented the Odd Man in the stifled silence.

******

The fellow missing yesterday was one of the second patrol. He was fairly experienced but not on scouts.

Someone in the squadron has heard from Hyatt. His memory is not normal yet, and he is still in hospital. The 'Air Hog' is in

London now and is getting on well.

I send you all my love, dear one.

Bill.

Saturday, 2.30.

Dear, dear woman;

It was such a tiny letter from you today, but so very sweet because you love me and I adore you.

A short note came from Dick too, saying he had received my letter by aerial post.

✶✶✶✶✶✶

I have just reckoned up my scraps and find I have got four certain, four probable, and one balloon (which is counted two Huns), total 10 (not out).

My note will be short as there is no very thrilling news. Though the strafe is tremendous and still goes on we are getting only one job a day.

I was out this morning at 5.30 a.m., but did not cross the lines. The clouds were down too low.

I went up the lines and saw all the progress that has been made. It is very decided.

All my love,

Bill.

P. S.—The last R.F.C. *communiqué* says:

> Lieut. G—— and Lieut. B—— (me), of —— squadron, engaged a hostile formation of five scouts and drove one down obviously out of control; and on the same patrol Lieut. B—— attacked seven H.A. and shot one down.

This morning I wakened and looked at my watch. It was nine o'clock. At twenty minutes past nine the taxi was coming to take mother to the station five miles away! She had been persuaded, much to her surprise, to come for a weekend, and in spite of her denial I knew she was pining to find herself back in town.

I leapt from bed and, without waiting to slip into my *kimono*, ran into Bey's room. She slept soundly.

As, usually, she rises soon after the birds, I thought the hands of my watch must have grown tired of going round and round, and had run races in the night; but, reaching the day nursery, I saw that the clock there said a minute past nine! I tore into the kitchen to find that the seventh or ninth wonder had been more wonderful than ever, for the kettle had reached boiling point at that very moment. Speedily I made tea, cut bread and butter and carried it all up to mother's room. She lay asleep.

"Your taxi comes in a quarter of an hour," I cried callously. "Get up. . . . Get up, or you'll have to stay here another day!"

That roused her. She opened her eyes wide.

"What!" she cried.

"It's five past nine," I said. "We've all overslept."

I was pouring the tea as I spoke; then I missed something.

"The letters!" I exclaimed. "I wonder where they are?"

Leaving mother staring blankly at the cup in her hand I raced down again, but could find no sign of letters either in the door or outside, where I had directed the old man to leave them if we didn't answer at any time.

Slowly I climbed the stairs.

Yesterday, Monday, there had been no letter from Bill; and when that happens, as a rule two are delivered on Tuesday.

I didn't like the morning any more.

But there was mother to be seen to, so I went back to her room.

"What does Bill say?" she asked—still sleepily.

"I don't know. . . . There's no letter," I replied.

And then I heard the gate click and, glancing out of the window, saw old Mrs. Witchell hobbling up the path with her hands full of envelopes. I shall love her evermore.

★★★★★★

There were seven for me—three of them from Bill.

While mother dressed, vaguely I read the other four—making comments all the while.

"But what has Bill got to say?" she insisted.

"I don't know," I said again, but added this time, "I like to keep his letters until I'm alone in my room."

At this she said nothing but looked disappointed, and I knew she was curious to hear the latest news.

"I'll open the last one," I conceded, breaking the flap apart as I spoke.

It was short—one tiny page torn from a note-book. It said:

Saturday,
4.20 a.m.

Just got this; all unexpected! But I still love you.

Darling, it intensifies my delight a thousand times to have *you* this time to tell the news.

All yours, bar and all.

Bill.

I stared at it. A pink slip fell from the envelope on to my knee. It was separated into little oblong squares like a telegraph form—each word having a box of its own. My eyes gazed, then I understood.

"Oh, Mummy," I cried, "Bill has got a bar to his M.C!"

******

Soon afterwards the taxi appeared. Bey had wakened and came along the passage in her small blue *kimono*, squashing the black cat in her arms.

"What's all happening?" she asked. . . . "Why's Mumsie up?"

"We've slept late, darling . . . and the taxi's waiting . . . and Bill's got a bar to his M.C.," I cried.

"Good ol' Bill," she murmured. . . . "Lie still, puff-puff! . . . Mumsie don' go back to nasty ol' town. . . . Stay wif us here!"

******

We got mother off at last

Bey went to the gate, and Betty, who ran out of her room at the last minute, hung with me from the window.

"Don't forget to change," I called. . . . "And it's the *other* side of the platform!"

"And don't forget to get out at the end," giggled Betty hilariously.

"G'bye, Mumsie. . . . An' don't forget an' leave you' specackles in ve twain," we heard Bey shout.

Then the engine of the taxi gathered speed and over the hedge we caught glimpses of the top of mother's head, and a waving handkerchief.

"I hope she won't take the wrong train," I said.

"She's sure to," dismissed Betty casually as she lifted the lid from the teapot and looked for tea.

By which you see that we treat mother as though she were not one of the cleverest, most practical women in the kingdom.

But she's so very absent-minded in little ways, and as someone said: "She never takes the right turning if she can find the wrong one!"

After this I went downstairs and made more tea, which I brought to my own *sanctum*.

"You can look after yourselves, this morning," I called to the babes in passing; "I'm going to read Bill's letters in peace."

Then I closed my door.

Chapter 33

Before he went Bill said one day:

"When I go to France again what shall I bring you—a little silver rose, or what?"

"Why a little silver rose?" I asked.

"Well, I thought you might like another M.C. And for the second one they give you a bar to the medal. And you wear a little silver rose. It is worn just there!"

He pointed as he spoke, to the centre of the inch of ribbon on his tunic, then he added meditatively:

"But I don't think we want a silver rose—it would hide the pretty purple stripe! What else would you like instead?"

I smiled at him.

"I'd like *you*. Just bring me back yourself," I said.

And now that he has his "little silver rose" I don't know what to think. I suppose war is too abhorrent to women for them to be able, unreservedly, to appreciate the rewards.

In a prayer lasting all day and every day I give thanks for the glad philosophy which makes my Bill a happy warrior; for the understanding that makes him a kindly one.

That he should be an able warrior doesn't enter into my prayer; yet one pays homage to vitality, and determination.

As for "the little silver rose." Why, how can heroism be sorted out and docketed like that?

The deed for which he won the right to wear it probably was less heroic than some unapparent victory of which he, himself alone, was aware.

But when all is said we shall be human.

I loved my mother's pleasure. We shall love to see the face of Bill's mother when she admires it

The "pretty purple stripe" will be hidden after all, but I daresay we shall enjoy the "little silver rose" just as well.

Here is his next letter:

Darling Aimée,

No letter at all today from you!

After writing yesterday I went over and dropped a note for Dick with the news: then, led a patrol and got another Hun!

It was the nicest, most gentlemanly, scrap I have had.

First of all, when coming up from east of —— I spotted a Hun two-seater coming from the lines about 2,000 feet below us. We were at 15,000.

I didn't tackle it well, but the trouble was that none of the others saw it in time. I was afraid to go straight on to it, fearing the observer's gun, and tried to get underneath it.

The Hun fired a signal light as usual, and opened all out and walked away from me. Had the others seen it we could have headed it off.

Bearing in mind the signal light, I turned south again, climbing, and came back to the place about four minutes later.

There, sure enough, were five Hun scouts a thousand feet below us, coming south.

I let four pass and dived on the last one.

Another fellow—Kelly—dived on a second Hun and Scott on a third.

My Hun saw me coming and put his nose down. He caught up with the others by doing this, and then I saw that the leader had turned and was trying to get above me.

I gave up the Hun I had picked out originally and turned on the leader, who was nearly level with me. He swung right across close in front of me, trying to avoid me, and I fired 40 rounds into him. He turned quickly, then went over on his back and fell down all sideways.

I zoomed up hard and found myself level with another, fired at him until he dived off my sights and then turned and found a third an easy mark.

I didn't get very close and my drum ran empty just as he dived away. I probably hit them both, but they were under control.

Kelly and Scott saw no apparent result to their shooting. The Huns just dived away.

As I climbed west to change my drum three more Huns appeared a long way east and well above us, so I decided we had had enough and headed for the lines and home.

This success created more enthusiasm than any previous one, coming on the announcement of the afternoon.

Kelly and another pilot saw my Hun going down.

Why it was such a nice scrap was that we always remained level with or above the Huns. Not one of them ever got his sights on me to fire, and I'd a Hun to go at every time I looked for one.

******

This morning was dud, so I took a tender and went off to see Dick. I got back at 3.30.

It was awfully nice to see him.

He was with his gun in the battery position, but everything was quiet. I had lunch with him.

His dugout and gun-emplacement are wonderful—equal for cosiness and cleanliness to a gun turret on a battleship. He says it is becoming quite a show place.

******

No more news and no more bars just now. I am longing for tomorrow to come for your next letter.

I love you, sweetest woman.

All yours,

Bill.

It seems strange that I don't know Bill's brother when they are such rare friends. I wonder if he resents the thought of me? I haven't written to him, but if I do I shall say that if anyone stays at war for two years without a leave they must expect things to happen.

I daresay he is indifferent merely.

Chapter 34

Aunt Fanny used to say:
"You'll be sorry for it someday—you mark my words!"
That frightened me very much. I used to brood about it, and "Someday" became mixed up with Hell and the Day of Judgment and Revelations. We lived in Scotland, you see.
This, in a mild form, is one of the "Some days."
I know exactly how Bill felt after writing to tell me of the silver rose. He ached for speech from me, although it couldn't be a reply to his news.
Then next day brought no letter, and the day after that one telling mostly of how little I cared for his article in the Odd Man's magazine.
I know well, too, the chill that comes in the very moment of enthusiasm.
My criticism would have kept until a day when I could kiss him directly afterwards.
He says—

Ma Bien Aimée,
Your letter of the 7th came today. Though I was not displeased with the article myself I felt somehow you wouldn't like it. I still like it, however.
There was no work yesterday, and all night it poured with rain and thundered so hard that we couldn't hear the war.
Up to the present it is very overcast, so I may be able to go to S—— to buy the little silver rose to wear on my ribbon.
The squadron is getting a name, but even we didn't know until last night what a name.
A new pilot arrived and was recognized as a fellow-cadet by R——, who told him he was damned lucky to come to us.

'Oh, yes, I know,' the new man said. . . . 'They told me so at S——. They said it was *the* squadron in France.'

We were frightfully bucked to hear that for what anyone says there is being said throughout the corps in these parts.

The best of it is that we know it's true. Since the day before the last push we've got down ten Boches certain.

I've been saving up a story to tell you; the wonderful adventure of our crashing 'hun!'

Three mornings ago I took out Faulkner and the 'hun.'

It should have been an offensive patrol of six machines, but the clouds were too low, so I started on a mild and inoffensive line patrol. After half-an-hour of dodging the clouds I gave it up, gave the signal for 'washout' and tootled off north alone to have a look at the strafe.

When I got back and landed Faulkner was back, but the 'hun' was still out. About ten minutes later he came in. As he flew over the sheds he was waving frantically. He made a very rocky landing.

His machine was an amazing sight. It was shot and torn to ribbons. We counted fifty-eight holes in it, at least half of them showed that the shots were within a fraction of being vital hits. It was a miracle that the fuselage had not broken in two.

The 'hun' was very excited and it took a long time to understand his story.

When I had signalled 'washout' he had turned down the line, seen a balloon away over and decided to strafe it.

He crossed at about five thousand, and when near the balloon saw two enemy two-seaters. He changed his mind and attacked them. One he hit and crashed. Then from above came four red scouts and from below 'Archie.' For ten minutes, while he struggled to get back to the lines, losing height fast all the way, the Huns dived at him and fired at him.

He felt his elevator go slack suddenly, and looking round saw that the control on one side had been shot away. The whole machine seemed to go sloppy and groggy. A shot hit one cylinder and his engine began to miss.

Finally as they neared the lines, when a Hun dived at him, he stalled and turned and the Hun overshot him. He fired then and raked the Hun up and down the fuselage, and he went down almost promptly and crashed. They were now only about

200 feet off the ground.

At last our 'hun' crossed the trenches, being fired at by the Boches and cheered by our Tommies as he crawled over.

He came home flying low all the way. His machine was a 'write-off.' There was hardly a part of it untouched.

As his temporary flight commander I strafed him violently for playing the fool, and told him his luck was more than he deserved But to myself I acknowledged that it was awfully plucky to struggle on as he did. It was his fifth trip over the line and his first scrap—though he had seen one other.

He will not attempt to repeat the performance. When his excitement wore off he had a big reaction, and he realizes now what inexperience may do. We have great hopes for him as he gets his balance.

Well, that's all the news—except that you may not have heard that I love you.

   All yours, every moment.

                    Bill.

For one thing I am thankful, and it is that Bill is able to remain cold in moments of greatest turmoil. I have this comfort, that though he will shirk nothing through fear, he will allow reason to be his guide.

Chapter 35

At last he has had the sort of letter—the only sort of letter—a man should receive from his wife. He answers—

Oh, my dear, when you write as you do today, when you tell me of your longings and your thoughts, I can hardly bear to stay here.
For I want you too, my wonderful lover; and just to want you so intensely and to know you want me is exquisite happiness.
You make all my life so complete.
I am sitting in my hut now clad in a shirt and shorts—my Suvla ones. I have been having a cold bath after a very hot game of tennis, and feel beautifully cool.
Before lunch I led an offensive patrol. There was not much excitement; one Hun two-seater got in our way and only just managed to escape. I dived on him but could not get very near, and though I fired 50 rounds he continued to dive, straight down——we were looking into the streets of ——, and at 8,000 feet I gave it up, as that was too low to be safe so far over the lines.
I spent half-an-hour alone after the patrol trying to persuade another two-seater further north to come over our side of the lines and be shot down, but like all these German people he was very unreasonable and seemed to prefer that I should do it over the Rhine. I didn't follow him quite so far, however.
I dined last night with —— squadron at their farewell dinner. They are moving to another aerodrome.
I got lots of congratulations, and it was rather quaint to be talking 'shop' on equal terms with men whom in England we heard of as among the best fighting scout experts.
After dinner I risked what is now my wife's money to the ex-

tent of 10 *francs* at roulette. At any rate I borrowed 10 *francs* to start playing, as I had none in my pockets: and promptly paid that back and finished 12 *francs* up.

My luck is always in!

Last night—earlier—I did a line patrol on which nothing occurred.

During the patrol, while I was at 12,000 feet, I spotted Dick's battery by a gun flash.

When I was there the previous day the major had challenged me to find it from the air because he said they had been in the same place for weeks and the Boche hadn't spotted them yet.

Of course I had the advantage of having been there on the ground. When I looked for it I simply followed with my eyes the route I had taken—and just at the moment my eye stopped at the exact spot there was a flash from the gun itself!

Afterwards I went down low over the position, 'chucked' a few stunts and waved to Dick.

******

Mother's letter is quaint. But they worry a great deal too much. You will do them a lot of good when you go.

Just going to tea now. I send you all my love.

Bill.

P.S.—Today, by the way, your letters were of the 6th and the 8th. One of the 7th came yesterday and one of the 5th two days earlier. The 6th has been hung up somewhere.

I'm feeling awfully pleased with things today because you got my news this morning—Tuesday.

******

I have no time to think.

On Monday the babes go again to school, and it is staggering to discover that nearly every garment worn by either needs buttons or hooks or dams.

As well as that they must be fed three times every day.

A woman with children to care for might just as well resign herself to the fact that to them must be devoted every single moment of her waking time.

Someone has to do it. Plainly I see that.

Every second spent at this table means neglect of a necessary trifle.

I shall miss them when they go, yet I shall breathe once more—and I won't cook at all!

But even now I refuse to scurry over Bill's letters; so, having seen the babes begin their porridge—Bey eats hers willingly because a Mr. Quimper lives at the bottom of the bowl and waits for her to say good-morning—I carried my tray up here to my *sanctum*. He begins—

> Aimée, dearest one. Your words were so wonderful again when I read them today in your letter of Saturday.
> Just as dreadfully as you I am longing also. But we have not too long to wait.
> Things are very quiet again and I am getting only one job a day.
> I was to have done at O.P. at 6 this morning, but when I got up at 5 a.m. it was so cloudy that I changed it to a line patrol and took only two others.
> It was difficult to see, and we came back after 40 minutes.
> Since then I have slept most of the day, as it is too hot to do anything else.
> I don't think I've any news and very little to talk about.
> All my love, sweetest lover.
>
> Bill.

Foolish one, it is your handwriting, and your words of love, I cherish. What is "news" to me? I can read the morning paper for that, can't I?

Chapter 36

The church bells ring—but I sit here wrapped in an overall. Betty is covering the kitchen table with "ingredients." We are to make a cake for school.

But I must read first what my Bill says and then all the while we stir flour and eggs and chocolate flavouring and things I can be thinking of his words.

My own wife;
There was no letter from you today. The post is very stupid. I love so much to talk to you and hear you talk to me *every* day. This morning I did a line patrol, as it was too misty again for an O.P. There was also a westerly gale blowing and at 17,000 feet we could hardly move—in fact, we lost ground and were blown over the lines unless we put our noses down and did 100 miles an hour against it. We saw nothing all the time.
I went to the range yesterday, and won 10 *francs* from the brigade machine-gun officer.
I told you, I think, that he has a competition in which we pay him one *franc* for every drum we fire at the target unless we score five *per cent*, or more—in which case he pays one *franc* per cent. I fired 130 rounds and got 13 hits in seven dives—or 10 *per cent*.
The weather is intensely hot again, and I shall sleep this afternoon.
There may be an O.P. to lead this evening, but no orders are through yet.
The new flight commander is due here tomorrow, so I shall relinquish command of the flight again then. He is a good man. He was here when I first came, and went home sick about a month ago.

The O.C. is still in England and is due back next week. He knows nothing of our success since he went. He will be fearfully excited when he comes back.

Last night I lay awake for a long time just thinking and longing.

My dear one! All yours.
Bill.

Oh, I wish we—whatever it is that makes us, and it is not our bodies—could go out consciously and meet in the night time. I, too, lie awake—thinking of him. Why can we not know it at the time? What is this barrier and why can't we triumph over it?

Chapter 37

Most precious One.

I've been waiting so impatiently for your letter acknowledging my news.

It came today, and I am more thrilled than when I heard about the bar. It is lovely, isn't it, to have our sympathies so intensely, so vitally mutual? I live only for you, dearest lover, and when you are happy I am thrilled to ecstasy.

It turned out as I expected.

Your mother heard the news before leaving. My people have not written about it yet.

★★★★★★

This morning I led an O.P. It was quite an amusing one, for right at the start one impudent Hun sailed over our heads while we were climbing—*on our side* of the lines.

We were at about 9,000 and he was at 14,000 or 15,000 feet. He just ignored us, and though I climbed all out I couldn't reach him. Ultimately we lost him.

When we crossed at 14,000 I chased two Huns off the lines and then turned south-east. Two more Huns appeared below—one a bit east and the other further south.

I made a feint of going for the south one while closing up gradually on the other; then turned suddenly and dived on him.

He dived too, and I never got nearer than 100 yards. We dived—the Hun and the whole of our patrol—from 16,000 to 9,000 feet, and I fired 45 rounds and another fellow fired 30 rounds. The Hun went on diving, however, and ultimately went out of sight.

When I turned and climbed I looked down, as I thought into the streets of ——. But after ten minutes hard flying against the slight wind I looked down again and I was still over the streets of ——.

We had been over the other side of another town miles further east.

I saw two more Huns a long way over, but they simply would not come and give us a chance at them.

The weather is still intensely hot. Yesterday afternoon I played tennis in pyjamas, and after perspiring beautifully had a cold bath in my hut. This afternoon I have only just energy enough left to lie down and sleep until teatime.

Do you know that I love you? Darling Aimée, I want you and soon. . . .

        All yours,

                      Bill.

Oh, I wonder how soon he means when he says "soon"?

I want to know and I'm frightened to know. I want to be able to count the days, and yet I think I shall be worn to a shadow if I do—and what joy would a shadow be to Bill?

We want each other to kiss and love, and we want to see each other.

It's very difficult to explain why spiritual union is not enough, any more than mere bodily union would be enough. I suppose it's because—on this earth anyway—we are human; and because there must be something beyond—above!

When Bill comes back to me I think I will weep. Tears come to my eyes even at the thought.

Chapter 38

We are in the train at last.

At 6.30 this morning the seventh or ninth wonder dragged me from sleep. Hers was the ruthless knocking of one who has to rise right out of her dreams and take hold of a scrubbing brush.

A moment later Bey ran into my room.

"I don't know which'll be the nicest of all the journey, darling," she sighed with flushed cheeks.

I clung to my pillow.

"Nicest?" I cried—then I realised that at seven and a half you appreciate trains and railway stations even if you have to start in the dead of night with the promise of a broiling day.

She sits now at the opposite end of the compartment,—which our gods have given us all to ourselves,—and looks a picture of cool enjoyment. I suppose you may when your skirts finish just below your waist and your socks just above your ankles.

She is nursing her "baby" and explaining in an undertone that we are moving and not the fields and trees and sky.

Betty is devouring a sequel to *Daddy-long-legs*.

And at last I may read Bill's letter.

Every moment has led up to this one. The thrill of breaking the envelope never grows less. It is the summit of my day. He says—

> Dear, dear woman,
> I got the finished copy of your big photograph this morning.
> I don't know why you are always on the verge of being apologetic about it, and I don't quite know why other people are not satisfied with it. I love it.
> But after all it is only a photograph, and whatever it is that is lacking in this one is lacking more or less in every photograph.

I'm sure my last one, with which I'm quite satisfied, conveys nothing more to anybody than a flat reproduction of the shape of my features.

I love your photograph. I love it, just because it helps me to visualize you physically; and when I can do that it is much easier to picture your more abstract attributes—your sweetness, your comprehension—Oh, you dear pagan!

******

I am sitting under an open marquee, on a huge double deck-chair made by the Odd Man, listening to ragtime on the phonograph. It is burning hot and I am wearing just a shirt, cotton breeches and socks and slippers.

I haven't flipped yet today; I expect a patrol at 7.30 this evening when all the Huns will be up.

The Odd Man's big deck-chair is quite wonderful. It will seat ten. It is made of rough timber and cocoanut matting.

******

Talking of ragtime! Did you ever see my ragtime words written to the ragtime music composed by Martin under the influence of Heidseick? I wish he were here!

But that is not my greatest wish in the world!

I got a quaint combined letter from home today about the bar. Mother is pleased. She hardly dare say how much—but she pleads with me not to try to get any more decorations!

She said exactly the same thing over the first award.

******

Last evening after dinner, before a large audience, the Odd Man and I had a topping discussion on the war, the peace, Germany's future position and our attitude to her, the Russian revolution, and then later, conscientious objections, industrial unrest and Socialism and Christianity.

If it had been an argument, or a debate, I would have claimed a complete decision on all points. But it wasn't. It was a discussion, and was therefore so much more satisfactory.

It was really good. I wish I could reproduce it, but I can't.

Do you remember that when you said you'd like to meet the Odd Man I wondered and doubted whether you would, because apart from his good-nature and sincerity and quick repartee he had little to appeal to you—having the stereotyped 'country gentleman' attitude of his type toward political and sociological things? However, I do think he tries to get outside these traditional prejudices—and it must be difficult.

******

Your letter of Wednesday last arrived today also and made me all happy all over—all over again!

Bien Aimée, it is so wonderful to possess you, to have such a dear, dear wife. It is becoming almost too much now that I can count the days until I see you.

Darlingest, I want you unspeakably.

All, all yours,

Bill.

******

Now we are in the second train and soon we shall reach our station. Having decided upon the one way to fill in the hour's wait we commandeered a corner table in a refreshment room, which would have been intolerable on a cold or rainy day, but today was preferable to the suffocating blaze of sunshine outside. Betty ate four bath buns. Bey discovered cracknel biscuits and rejoiced. With them she drank lemonade and needed it, I'm sure! But Betty sighed for tea. So did I, and we had a large pot full.

******

Their delight at the thought of meeting everyone, from the "Head" downward, makes me realize gladly how the methods at this school must contrast with the rigid, stupid discipline of the place to which I used, loathingly, to return each term.

"We've loved being with you, darling," Betty has just announced.

"Yes, we have," seconded the smaller babe.

Betty proceeded:

"But of course if you've *got* to do lessons you might just as well fire away—otherwise you'd find yourself in the same class as infants like Bey!"

This couldn't pass, of course. The protest came at once. "I'm not an infant—I'm seven and a half!" Bey shouted.

Betty looked all her condescension as she glanced downward from her height.

"Well, what's that?" she queried. "Wait until you're *my* age and you'll see!"

What Bey had to wait for wasn't explained, but I hope—though long after she has passed Betty's milestone—a husband as splendid as Bill!

Chapter 39

The babes are safely at school.

I shouldn't care to have been one of the staff when the whole concern moved from the coast to the country, but I should imagine that now they feel relieved. Blessed babes! How I love them and yet—

******

Stoics perhaps, but not ordinary mortals, could preserve calm of mind in the throes of raids by air, and bombardment by sea, while responsible for fifty children belonging to nearly as many sets of parents.

For forty-eight hours I haven't heard Bill speak—or *seen* him speak, I should say, perhaps.

A while longer on this journey and half-an-hour in Barnes' old crock of a taxi that feeds nowadays on a mixed diet and resents it rowdily, then the seventh or ninth wonder will appear carrying a bundle of letters—two at least from France. It is so lovely to have a husband—not any old husband—but my husband!

******

There are three!

Two were written on one day, and each is very short. The first says—

Dearest one,

A line in case I don't catch the post with a longer letter to-night.

Am just off to —— to get my hair cut and shall be back, I hope, in time to write.

Out on patrol this morning I was hit on the forehead by 'Archie.' My goggles, which I had pushed back, were smashed, but saved my head.

    I love you.   Bill.

Well, "that's *that*," as Bill would say! I am obliged to sit here and read that my whole world has been hit on the head by a piece of shell; that he was saved by the merest chance!

I can just manage to remind myself that all life is "chance"—and so keep calm. What else can I do?

The second letter was written during the afternoon,

Dearest,
I have just got back to find your letter of the 14th waiting for me. We had a nice lunch at —— and bought lots of things— pyjamas and underlinen and pictures and toilet creams.
Just in time for the post. I still love you.

Bill.

The third one, posted next day, contains the news I have waited for and longed to hear.

My Wife,
I knew you'd be disappointed at the scrappiness of my letters yesterday, but I hadn't time to write more.
Things are still very quiet—partly because the weather is so unsettled. It is raining and thundering again now.
After lunch I went to the range and fired a drum and then went for lunch with —— squadron.
Holt was there too, and when we came away we got up to 2,000 together and at my signal we 'rolled' at the same moment. This we did four times, keeping quite near each other all the time. Then we spun and did Immelmanns and finally dived together at the sheds.
When we got over our own aerodrome we did the same performance equally successfully. ✶✶✶✶✶✶
The time gets nearer for my leave.
Two fellows went yesterday and I am one of the next two.
We shall leave, if present arrangements continue, a few days after their return.
Where do you wish to meet me?
At Folkestone or in London? I rather think the latter.
I got your letter of Saturday when I got back.
I loved to read of you making the blue *crêpe-de-chine* things because they are for me.

All, all yours,
Bill.

P.S.—I'd nearly forgotten the news. Grahaeme has been awarded the M.C. As I told you before, he is my right hand man. He always flies close behind me, and I always know he will be there.

I had a little bit of M.C. ribbon all made up ready, and when the wire came through last evening I was able to fish it out of my pocket promptly, and pin it on to his tunic.

✶✶✶✶✶✶

Do you love me?
    I worship you.

Bill.

Chapter 40

Old Witchell came this morning to pick fruit to send to Irene. When I heard the bell I hung out of my bedroom window.

"Hullo!" I called.

He looked up—his round face beaming.

"Good-marnin'!" he called. "I was just a-wondrin' if you was a-comin' t'help me gather them chirries!"

I laughed at him. He makes you laugh.

"I'm not dressed," I answered, leaning on the ledge to indicate that I didn't intend to dress either.

"Well you are the lazy one this marnin'!" he exclaimed.

"Oh, no, I'm not," I contradicted. "I've been very busy—I've been writing my letter to my husband."

With a doubtful expression he scratched his head.

"Well, I do be wondrin' what you have t' say t'one another ivry day," he cried, and added, "How do he be?— Gettin' on nicely?"

"Splendidly, thanks. And how are Jack and Jim?"

"Fine, thank 'ee. Jack he be back we' his ship be now. He were a bit quiet like. Not the same lad his mother tould him."

"What did he say to that?"

"He didn't say nothin'. But I reckon he do have seen things t' make a lad quiet. And when do 'ee be expectin' 'eer husband home—have 'ee any idea?"

I drew a deep breath. It had to be said sometime—the thing I dared not say even to myself.

I looked across at the sky where it meets the ridge of the Downs.

"Oh, make it true," I prayed, and aloud I answered:

"A fortnight today he hopes to be in England!"

And when the words had passed my lips I breathed again.

My fear left me.

He will come, I know.

******

Old Witchell's voice brought me to myself.

"Be-ant 'ee lonely ail be 'eerself in this big house?"

Truly I believe that if I had explained to him that I am not alone—that Bill is with me all the while—he would have understood.

But I couldn't call it out of my bedroom window, so I just said: "No—I'm hardly ever lonely!"

"'Taint reet for no one," he replied, seriously. Then he brightened up.

"I tell 'ee what—'ee come along this afternoon an' have a cup a tea wi' me and the Missus. She'll be reet glad!" he said.

******

Bill's letter was lying on the table. I took it up to read again:—

Darlingest;

"Because there were two editions of the mail yesterday I got no letter today. *Car même*, I can read your other one again. We are all just setting out by tender for a Canadian camp, where a big baseball game is taking place. Grahaeme of M.C. and blasphemy fame is in charge of the outing.

This morning I led the early patrol. It was a perfect morning and we went a long way over at 16,000, but saw nothing.

I have been trying to make everybody in the flight roll, and two of them do it now. So when the patrol was nearly over I gave a signal and rolled—Grahaeme promptly did the same and Holt also;—and we came back over the lines in a big 'V,' throwing ourselves all over the sky. Once I turned over on my back and flew like that for half a minute.

******

After breakfast I went to do the climbing test and stunting I told you of, before the H.Q. Staff. It was quite unexciting. I just did everything I could think of and then came home.

The Odd Man left today for England. He said he would try to look you up. I hope he does.

Do you know how I love you? I cannot calculate it. My lovely lover.

Bill.

Chapter 41

Someone has written an article *On Leave*. It is the outburst of a soldier who goes back to a pleasant calm country and hears his own people "*talk* war."

They ask him questions and he answers vaguely, for he knows that if he were to speak his bitterness as bitterly as he feels it they, though kind and forbearing, without comprehending in the least would think him a little mad.

He sneers.

"What do they know of this Hell of war?"

How *can* they know? With the most vivid imagination how can they know?

But, on the other hand, what does he know of the Hell of those who stay at home?

What of all the fathers who, willingly, would give their lives for their sons; and the mothers whose soldier boys are their babies; and the wives who wait and fear and ache for them.

There are two sides to this, soldier!

Who is to say which suffers more—and who is to know?

✶✶✶✶✶✶

My lover says today—

Aimée, dear one,

The letter I received from you this morning—written on your railway journey—was just lovely.

By now I suppose you are back again. I hope your mother will have returned with you.

Have you noticed—of course you have—that my letters get much briefer lately? I find much less to write about than formerly. The new impressions seem to be pretty well exhausted—and besides that we do so little lately that there's not a lot of news for you.

But I'm waiting to hear something of your short stories. What about them?

In the latest official *communiqué* appears the following:

> Hostile Aircraft.—In the evening Lieut. B—— (your husband) while on offensive patrol drove down a German machine out of control. He then attacked a second, which was driven down and crashed. Lieut. G—— of the same squadron drove down a hostile scout out of control.'

Bloodthirsty!

But I love you, dear lover.

    All, all yours.

Bill.

Chapter 42

I don't know how other wives feel when their husbands are due for leave.

Nothing so wonderful ever has happened to me before.

Our marriage was an adventure—and I love adventure! It promised a lot of things—companionship, interest, someone on whom to concentrate affection, and from whom affection would be given.

It promised much, but not this ecstasy that is so calm, so radiant.

It envelops me. I am possessed by a miracle of—what it is?

I think it must be *love!*

★★★★★★

Bill becomes less articulate as the time of our meeting draws closer. And in my letters to him I am more garrulous, I notice. I tell him silly details—about my new frock and hat, and the shoes which *Monsieur*, who makes for queens and kings, won't promise to deliver until the very last moment, although they were ordered a month ago and he charges the earth! His expression suggests, "Take it or leave it." So, of course, you just take it, and leave it at that.

If they don't fit, goodness knows what I'll do, for my others are in rags.

Then I tell him about the new *crêpe-de-chine* things, and the new "*boudoir*" caps, and the absurd little jacket to go with them—to wear when we sit up in bed with our heads close together drinking our morning tea.

It isn't the slightest use of any one complaining that these details are superfluous in war time. They are more necessary than ever they were to the man *who has lived war* for months.

He says—

My Dear, Dear Wife,

I got your letter of Thursday the 19th today. I love it. I liked the bits about your clothes and things.

You want to know how I am. Awfully fit except for a touch of that Suvla indigestion during the last week.

And now! What are your plans for when I get to England? Where will you meet me and where shall we stay?

Faulkner left today on his leave, and if the other fellows return to time I may leave here on the 3rd or 4th and get to London the following day. That is a week next Wednesday or Thursday or Friday. Of course when I know definitely I will wire you.

I got the enclosed letter today from Dick. I hope to see him again before I come on leave.

Darling lover, I want you more than I dare realise. Do you love me? All my love.

Bill."

Chapter 43

How *am* I to exist until he comes? On Sunday, as we sat round the tea table in her tiny parlour crammed with coloured glass ornaments—"presents from somewhere"—and crinkled paper and enlargements of photographs, Mrs. Witchell said: "I don't hold wi' flyin'. . . . The Lord He di'n' give us no wings. . . . 'Tain't proper. . . . 'Tis callin' forth His mispleasure 'tis!"

"The Lord didn't give us fins—and yet Jack sails on the seal" I reminded her maliciously, because the little arrow of foreboding cut through my heart and, as she had sent it, humanly I wanted her to share the pain.

I went on chewing at the large chunk of homemade cake and watched her expression grow puzzled, then uneasy; but soon it became placid again.

"'Tis diff'rent . . . 'Tain't the same," she said—and that was enough.

As she seemed to know so much of what the Lord thinks, I wanted to ask her if He approved of war; of the big shells from the big guns with which Jack and Jim are obliged to massacre their kind; of all this perversion of reason; of the useless, silly waste of it all.

But instead I went on eating cake.

Old Witchell, in his pale blue shirt sleeves, best satin spotted tie, and best black trousers and waistcoat, sat on my other side. Jerry and Gwendolen-Ivy, solidly munching, stared, goggle-eyed, at whoever spoke. Mary's baby lay on the horsehair sofa, with Mary—so motherly glad—on the edge to keep it from rolling off. And every time Witchell turned his beaming scarlet face toward her the baby yelled.

"Yew fill his lil' belly too full— that what I says!" he cried at last in exasperation.

"That I don't," denied Mary, with a toss of her head. "'Tis a princess could be no better looked to than my babe.... 'Tis yew wi' your great voice a'-shoutin' at the lamb like what you did that day!"

Into her arms she gathered the small bundle.

"There now," she crooned. "His Dad be a'-comin' soon he be.... Never 'ee take no heed then... His Dad what never see his lil' face—he be a'-comin' soon—soon!"

And as I heard the poetry of her voice I knew herself was with the sailor who since three weeks before their babe was born hasn't seen his wife.

Jack's best friend is Mary's man. The two work together on the big ship somewhere on the wide sea—when you pass your days encircled by the ridge of the Downs, all beyond also seems beyond measurement, you know—and as Jack is one of those who live in other's joy you can imagine how the father is allowed to pivot every conversation round one subject—Mary and the babe—the babe and Mary!

******

Oh, I wish I could lose consciousness until he comes—or wish he could be kept in a glass-case until the day. He says—

My dear one,
I'm out on the advanced landing ground again. It is rather a dud day and so far we have had nothing to do. This morning I was up at three o'clock as I had to lead at O.P. as soon as it was light, but the clouds were too low, so I went to bed again at 5 a.m.

I had no success yesterday. When I got to where Dick had been I found that they had moved away. I had tea with the C.R.E. and whole bundles of brigadiers and red tabs again, and I got home at 9 a.m. There was a lovely letter from you waiting for me.

I am just going to fly back to the aerodrome for the mail. It is Friday now and by next Wednesday—just imagine! I can't. Can you hear me shouting for my machine, and can you see the mechanics running out?

Later.
The Aerodrome.

I landed here ten minutes ago and found the most lovely letter of all—the one written on Monday telling me delicious things. Dear, dear Aimée, my ecstasy is almost too much.

All, all yours,　　　　　　　　　　　　　　　　　　　　Bill.

Chapter 44

Today I came home.
Suddenly I couldn't bear the solitude. Although it is Sunday and I had arranged to come here on Monday or Tuesday I just couldn't wait. The noise and racket are welcome. The restlessness catches my mood. Mother understands. She wasn't a bit surprised to see me.

I can't sleep. I don't want to. I want to talk about Bill.

Mother listened until her eyes, which are most alert at midnight, began to close, and now I am reading his last letter again. He says—

You darling,"
You thrill me too much. A lovelier letter than yesterday's came for me today and made me faint with delight. My dear, dear woman, I love you—your mind and your body—beyond all expression.

The letter from you was written on the 26th in bed and on the day when you got no letter from me.

And now, the news. I've got a flight; and in about three weeks I expect to be gazetted captain and flight-commander.

It isn't 'B' Flight; that is my only regret. I so much wanted 'B' Flight, and all the fellows in it and the personnel wanted me to have it too.

You see since Romney left the squadron I have been running 'B' Flight with the exception of a few days.

More news. Kyrle has been awarded an M.C.

The wire came last night. We are all glad. He is, as I have often told you, a wonderful pilot and a topping patrol leader, with lots of strafe and lots of caution.

Still more news. The wing adjutant rang up this afternoon to say that my leave will start on Wednesday or Thursday; more probably Wednesday.

If I fly over I ought to be in London the same evening; if not, about mid-day the following day.

I must catch the post with this, as it may be the last letter you can receive before I arrive. But I will go on writing until I leave here, of course.

Do you love me? 'Yes, Bill.'

Bill.

Chapter 45

We had had lunch and were drinking coffee.
Purcell entered with a telegram, which she handed to me.
I tore it open and read:

Leave commenced sooner than expected. Arriving Victoria 2 p.m. today. Meet me Savoy Hotel.

I looked at mother and Maisie, who were staring. Then I looked at the clock. The small hand said "two" and the large hand almost covered it. I sprang from my chair.

"Mother!" I cried. "Bill's train will be in the station *now!* . . . Oh, what shall I do?"

✶✶✶✶✶✶

Mother and Maisie and Purcell helped me into a frock. The new hat had come and proved to be one of those perfect affairs that adapt themselves to an emergency; the shoes we had wrenched from *Monsieur* earlier in the day; and when the long chain of turquoise matrix had been clasped, and the last whisper of powder had been whisked on, to what Maisie calls "the flaps" of my nose, I kissed them all and flew down to the waiting taxi.

✶✶✶✶✶✶

At the Savoy, dozens of soldier men—lots of them with Flying Corps caps—drifted in and out. I sat in a corner from where I best could see, and my heart did all sorts of silly things.

Though most men may not be as wonderful as Bill, their uniforms are not unlike.

✶✶✶✶✶✶

The twisting doorway turned again. I saw him.
There was no mistaking when he came at length.
Straight to the desk he went—for we had arranged that I should

take a room, though not so soon.

I saw him speak, and after a pause, during which the official consulted a book, I saw him receive an answer, then slowly turn away; and I knew that, immediately, he would telephone to ask my whereabouts.

I knew, too, that he would go to me at once.

Then I stopped being another person. I knew that it was necessary to move.

Next moment I had touched his arm. "Bill!" I said. He turned to look at me. He seemed to look and look—and then he spoke.

"Aimée!" he whispered.

And I knew the word meant "Beloved."

Chapter 46

Today Bill goes to France again. A moment ago we stood outside the aerodrome, and all about us the fields shone in an amazing splendour. Beyond these fields was the sea.

Overhead, like black or silver streaks against the blue heaven, aeroplanes darted about. Engines buzzed and droned; shots followed one another in *staccato* succession; a machine rose vertically from the target, to whirl and dive again.

I felt Bill's excitement—his eagerness once more to handle the mechanism, to return to the work into which he throws every ounce of his capacity; to the men in whose skill he delights with almost an artistic appreciation.

His eyes followed a little speck on the horizon.

"Oh, you would love it. . . . How I just long to take you, too," he cried.

Quickly my gaze came back to his face, for he had voiced my most ardent wish.

"That would be wonderful," I said. Then so that he should know I didn't grieve and how glad I felt in the sunshine, I added: "But I'm happy. . . I'm perfectly content that you should go." And as his clasp tightened on my hand I smiled, for my joyousness surely must mean all would be well—that he and I were parting only for a little while!

But I wanted an assurance from his lips, and my eyes looked into his to *see* the truth for fear he should utter words merely for my peace of heart.

"You are coming back? . . . You *know* you're coming back?" I questioned.

Seriously he turned to me and spoke with absolute conviction. "I'm certain—quite certain," he said.

After that no cloud remained.

******

For an hour we had motored through lanes and villages—and now the man at the wheel is taking me on alone.

It's funny how glad I feel.

Chapter 47

In the train there were two very small boys.

They wore pink and white striped blouses and minute pink linen trousers, fastening on the shoulders with straps.

They had corn-coloured mops of hair, blue eyes, and impossibly perfect complexions. The mother, a woman who looked as though she had no thought to spare for herself, wiped her face with a handkerchief.

"They've been travelling for hours," she said. "They are just about fed up!"

Then, while the younger one clambered on to my knee to tug at the chain round my neck, she went on to explain that they were going North to a grandmother to escape the bombs which had fallen several times about their part of the world.

"That one—his nerves is awful! . . . But don't let him worry you like that," she pleaded, bending forward to try to lift him away.

Puckering up his face he clung to the chain; and at this the other one, realising that he missed an excitement, stretched across until I had to clutch him also to prevent a fall.

The mother sighed. Her expression suggested that the gods were using their last straw.

"Why not leave them to me and go to sleep?" I said; and then after that, while they turned me into a game quite ruthlessly, I reflected on grandmothers and mothers and how they come to pass.

It was when we changed, however, that I longed for Bill to see us.

"My porter will bring your luggage," . . . I assured the mother. . . . "Don't bother about it at all."

But when I saw that no words would persuade her to leave it, I said I would be responsible for the live stock, and to this she agreed, but on the platform they seemed to become shorter and fatter, until they looked like round fluffy balls.

One on either hand they toddled placidly until one of them without warning yelled:

"Mummy!...Mummy!...Where Mummy?"

Fearfully I looked back, to see his mummy in the throes of suitcases and a perambulator, so, stooping down, I gathered this infant into one arm, without daring to leave hold of his brother.

"Mummy's coming soon,"... I whispered.... "Be a good boy and I'll give you lots of nice things."

Whether or no he heard didn't matter, for he rediscovered the chain about my neck, and with little grunts and babbles of delight began to tug at it for all he was worth.

A very immaculate elderly man stepped aside from the door of the compartment and frigidly helped us in.

Then after staring with disapproval and perplexity for some moments he made up his mind to speak.

"Your husband at the war, my dear?" he asked.

Panicked at the thought of the damage they might do themselves, I clung to the struggling infants, clutching both in one bundle on my knee.

"Yes!... He's an airman," I gasped.

Over his eyeglass he drew his brows together.

"Dear me.... Dear me!" he muttered—and I knew he was pitying Bill.

******

This "Hydro" is a terrible place. At dinner I felt uncharitable and my own distaste annoyed me, for I would like to feel well disposed toward all people.

I left before the meal was half way over and came to this corner of the lounge to write to Bill.

To look at some of the people here is to dread age; but I know that in the course of things we must grow old someday; and when that happens to me I want to be like the woman who has tucked herself into the corner opposite.

She is wearing a frock that hangs in folds and draperies, and her white hair is piled up on her head with a jewelled comb.

She puffs away at a cigarette in a long slim holder; and glances humorously at me.

She loves and respects her age, and she means everyone else to love and respect it too.

Tomorrow Joan should come. I am longing for her; but even more I long for my first letter from Bill.

Now I will go to bed and morning will not seem so remote.

Chapter 48

It has come—my letter!

Darling,
Gazetted today! Am just leaving on one of the newest type of scout machine.
All my love.

Bill.

I might have been certain he would find a moment to write and send me all his love!

Again I feel as I felt after our last parting—that I am not alone. Even in this strange place Bill's thoughts are with me.

Wasn't I cross last night?

It was disgusting of me.

Indeed it is a pity that I, who have so much, should fail to understand that all men and women are the result of circumstance and that to criticize is to prove my limitation.

I wonder if Bill's waking thought was of me?

But of course it was, for I am with him all the while.

Now I will get up and go to meet Joan.

It was a splendid idea for us to spend her holiday together. I expect we shall talk of Bill most of the time.

******

Joan is very content to sit on the veranda, or to walk without an aim, listening to the tales Bill has told me, and to the account of his leave, for she saw him only during the three or four days at home.

She is most thrilled to hear of the evening in town with Romney and Faulkner and Grahaeme and the others. She wishes she had been with us and I wish it too, though I was selfish and wanted Bill all to myself.

Next time he comes on leave we must persuade her to go to town with us and give her a riotous time.

Anyway she must be with us in Paris afterwards. She has too many of Bill's possibilities to be allowed to waste herself in one groove.

I have told her also of the five perfect days on the golf course by the sea; and of Bill's pleasure in my "style," though I played so atrociously, and of his lecture on concentration because I became absorbed in an account of our opponent's hospital work instead of thinking of my next shot.

She laughed much about the little man who, in spite of the fact that bombs fall regularly in the street where he has his office, has tempted providence by supplying himself with socks enough to last for many years—because wool is going to be so scarce and expensive after the war.

******

Each day brings nearer the first letter from France. Tomorrow it should come. The days seem unreal and so do the people here—except Joan, who is of the same flesh and blood as Bill.

Last night there was a dance. The music got into my veins and I longed for my lover to come. He didn't though—and so I enticed Joan into the corridor and bullied her into learning a foxtrot and a one-step and a hesitation waltz. Tonight someone concocted a concert in aid of the military hospital. The whole thing seemed to be like a caricature. Very fat men and very thin women—or very thin men and very fat women—all crusted and rusted into grooves, sat and listened while performers from among them did their turns.

The few young ones seemed all pose and meaningless sagacity. Uncomfortably I wondered what ailed my point of view, and was relieved to find that Joan wanted to leave the place.

"Let's go to bed," she whispered, and as we passed the alcove I saw the woman whose growing old has been accomplished with grace.

She lay among her cushions, knitting leisurely—her long cigarette holder gripped between her teeth.

Both the holder and the teeth probably were expensive, but it is not her bank balance that gives her distinction, for all the others look full of cheque-books.

Just a tiny glint of irony tinged the tolerant amusement of her glance.

She is very wise, I think.

I want Bill.

I feel all incomplete.

Chapter 49

The letter has come at last.

It seems ages since I heard from my love, but really it is four days only.

Now something should arrive from him each morning and the days will be worthy of the sunshine once more.

Darling,

I got back to the squadron half-an-hour ago—too late for the post. I find lots of things have been happening—but I must tell you first of my crossing.

It wasn't at all nice really. I'd never seen —— a scout before, nor the type of engine used in it, but when they asked me if I could fly one I said 'yes' promptly.

I think it would have been all right if everything had been normal, but the petrol and air adjustment was frightfully difficult to work. A fitter spent half-an-hour trying to get the engine started and to keep it going and to show me how to do it, and then I spent twenty minutes trying to taxi out across the aerodrome.

Finally I got desperate and the next time the engine started—about the eighth—I opened all out and went right off.

After you had left me I watched the taxi disappearing down the lane and wondered what were your thoughts.

I met a fellow I knew and talked with him for an hour, and then about 11.30 I was told there would be a —— scout for me, so I went down to the mess and wrote a note to you before I left.

Getting away was an awful business. I had to pack my haversack in no space at all, and as I had to wear a big life-belt—in case I landed in the water—I was horribly cramped and felt sure I'd never be able to fly a strange machine like that.

When I did get off I hardly knew it. I was barely breathing for wondering if the engine would stop for the ninth time when I crawled over the sheds. The engine wasn't going all out but just enough to lift me from the ground.

However, it improved after I got clear of the aerodrome, and I climbed up to 1,000 feet before it gave me any trouble.

Then it started dropping its revolutions, and when I tried to readjust it, stopped altogether.

I got it started again when I had fallen to 1,500 feet, and without further trouble climbed to 7,000 feet and headed out to sea.

Then it gave out again and I had to turn back.

I felt horribly wild with it now, so when, after losing 2,000 feet, I got it again, I headed straight across for the French coast, which I could see.

I can't describe to you the tenseness with which I watched my engine for the next twenty minutes. Every two or three minutes it started to fail, slightly, and I had to work cautiously at the hand pump to keep up pressure in the petrol tank, and very gingerly to alter the air and petrol adjustment.

I don't think I was nervous about coming down. I thought of that eventuality quite calmly and decided how I would glide down as near as possible to one of the dozens of naval vessels which I could see below me.

But the result of watching my engine closely was that I never saw the coast again and found myself well into France looking for my destination over absolutely unknown country.

Either by luck or instinct I went straight to it—and then I did feel nervous really. I daren't throttle down the engine for fear of it stopping altogether, so I left the adjustment quite alone, shut off the petrol at the supply and glided down to 1,000 feet over the aerodrome; then opened the petrol again and the engine came on all right.

For the last little bit I used the thumb switch—making the engine buzz just now and again to give me sufficient speed to touch the ground in the required spot.

I put her down without breaking anything and felt extremely pleased.

When I landed I found a side-car driver of the squadron waiting about and asked if he had come for me. He said he had come for an officer who was flying over. That's me all right,' I said, and went down to the town for lunch.

After feeding I bought extra stars and had them sewn on my tunic and then came here.

I could not conceal from myself the eagerness I felt to get back. The side-car driver told me a few of the things that had happened since I was away—of the number of Huns down and the scraps with big formations, and of one of my flight missing—Donaldson, a comparatively new pilot here.

When I arrived I found that the side-car wasn't for me at all. Another pilot had had to fly an old machine that was being returned and the side-car was sent ahead to bring him back. When he arrived and found I had taken his side-car he blasphemed for half-an-hour and wired for another.

I had quite a nice reception. The C.O. and the 'Odd Man' were playing tennis, and my flight was just starting an patrol. I offered to go, but the C.O. said it wasn't necessary.

Holt has done very well with the flight. He has got two Huns and two other fellows one each.

I started writing to you last night, but I was too tired and sleepy to continue. I slept until 7.30 this morning and was wakened then for patrol and the advanced landing ground. However, it was raining a little and was very overcast; and the work is washed out for the day.

This gave me an early chance to tackle the C.O. I have planted the MS. right on him and sat on his bed until he had read every word of the letters, and—I think—a lot more.

He said he saw no reason why it shouldn't go through all right and suggested a few minor alterations. And he liked it too!

So *now* you can go ahead. Tonight I will post it with the C.O.'s written permission.

Just at this moment Holt, sitting on his bed, is deep in it and chuckling over your bits of humour.

Well, I think that's all the news I can think of.

I haven't said anything about my leave. But it isn't necessary, is it? It was just perfect.

And I love you.

Bill.

Many times I have read this letter. When I read it I like to recall his answer to my question, "You're coming back? . . . You *know* you're coming back?"

"I'm certain, quite certain," he said, didn't he, and you remember I was looking into his eyes at the time!

★★★★★★

I also am unable to speak of our time together—except when I tell Joan of superficial details. I wonder if those who believe in Heaven could imagine anything more enthralling, more complete!

Chapter 50

The "little Saxon nest" is like a dream. The clear days of work and easy thought; the woods when, under the vivid green of the trees, bluebells grew so lavishly that they covered the dead brown leaves that in turn covered the damp earth—all these are distant, a lovely part of memory.

The ridge of the Downs against the sky will stay always before my eyes—so long I looked at it and prayed for my lover to come.

Irene and Nanny and the family of one are real; and someday I hope they will allow me to go back to them; but now I will go to Bill's people, who are my people—to stay with them till he comes again. To be with his sister is so sweet; to be with his mother will be sweeter still, for she gave him to me, and he is my life. Every day I thank her in my heart.

Today's letter, though it is short, is very precious.

My dear one,"
By this time—2 p. m. Thursday—I think you will have received my wire about the C.O.'s approval of the book. Will you be glad?
I didn't wire you about my arrival because I hoped to let you know even the same day that the C.O. had given his approval, but I got here too late to tackle him.
I told you, didn't I, that Holt, who represents quite an intelligent reading public, was fearfully thrilled with the MS.
He read every word of it and loved your bits.
I am hoping to get a letter from you tomorrow, Friday, telling me of your journey and of your arrangement to go home with Joan.
The weather is wild and the clouds are low again, so I may go to the 'pool' this afternoon.

The record of *Cheep* came and is quite good.
Will you send me my flying log-book? I left it by mistake in my hand-bag and I don't want to lose count of my hours.
It is a short letter today, for I have no news.
All, all yours,
Bill.
P.S.— In reading over the MS. with the C.O. I remembered how and why I had come to start one letter to you 'For whom I live.'
It was after I had had a letter from you in which you were troubled about Greta and also at a time when I had been having quite a lot of rather desperate scraps. I had wondered to myself why I had the luck to get through as I did, and it seemed to me I was just living for you as I wished.

Voilà tout! I love you.

Bill.

Chapter 51

This afternoon we went into the enormous drawing-room which no one uses, and Joan played a nocturne of Chopin. It makes your heart weep.

I lounged in a deep chair with a picture before me of the evening, just about a fortnight ago, when she played to us at home.

Bill's mother and dad were there—both content to have their boy again even for those few days, and glad to have me because I am his.

Near mother he sat, on the other side of the fireplace, twisting his pipe from one corner of his mouth to another, and whenever I looked up I found his eyes seeking mine.

Afterwards, when we were alone, he said:

"Aimée dear, did you *feel* me loving you?"

"Yes," I answered, for I think I am conscious of his slightest thought.

I wonder why I am so confident that he will come back to me? Every day I see the Roll of Honour and am forced to realize that there is no reason why I should be spared a grief that others have to bear just now.

And Bill's work is most constantly full of risk. Yet I am so perfectly at ease.

I think it is that I have faith in my own instinct and even more faith in his instinct; and he said:

"I'm certain—quite certain!" didn't he?

Today's letter is rather disappointing, for he has had nothing from me since he left, and I wrote at once of course. But he knows that. I needn't fear that he would doubt that.

Dearest one,

There was no letter from you today, but there is sure to be one tomorrow.

This morning I led the first patrol. It felt quite strange for the first twenty minutes. I couldn't feel the machine properly and couldn't tell where I was. However, it worked out all right and I kept a very good formation behind me.

We saw no Huns but got quite a lot of 'Archie.' At the end I landed at the advanced aerodrome with another fellow and stood by until 9 a.m., when we returned for breakfast; since I have slept until lunch.

Yesterday five of us took a tender to ———. We sat in a big French *café* for an hour and drank '*aperitifs*,' and had a very good meal afterwards, with the wine you liked at the Savoy.

It was quite a decorous party, though I completely lost my voice through singing 'rags' in the tender on the home journey.

There is another M.C. in the squadron too—Kelly. We are quite pleased, because though his judgment is not always good he is absolutely without fear and does his job thoroughly.

When I get your first letter I will have more to write about. I am longing to hear your reply to my wire.

All my love.

Bill.

P.S.—Don't worry about my flying log-book. I find I brought it after all.

I smile at that last sentence. It brings another picture to my mind—of our bedroom overlooking the sea, close to the golf links where we spent those glorious days away from the rush of town and all the people we knew, and seemed to bump into at every corner.

It was midnight, and Bill lay in a cosy chair with his feet on the bed, chewing his pipe and leisurely blue-pencilling the type-written copy of our book.

I stood about in my *kimono*,—having emptied all my belongings onto the floor,—wondering how I could cram all his golfing clothes into my suit cases.

As the problem seemed beyond me, I went and sat beside his feet on the bed and, taking his pipe from his mouth, lighted a French cigarette from the glow under the ash.

Bill lifted his eyes from the book and smiled.

"I'm thirsty!" I said, smiling back.

"What would you like?" he asked—eager always to please me.

"Tea," I announced—looking at his watch and thinking how unreasonable was my wish, for it was not the sort of hotel that keeps its staff going in relays.

Yet for all that Bill went down and came back with tea, and for half-an-hour we drank it and discussed the four corners of the earth.

But while he was away I spied his precious flying log-book sticking out from the muddle on the floor.

Taking it up I kissed it and slipped it into the pocket of the haversack hanging on the post of the bed.

"That, at least, he must have if he leaves me and everything else behind," I said to myself.

And now he writes:

> Don't worry about my flying log-book. . . . I find I brought it with me after all.

That is why I smile.

Chapter 52

At last we begin to talk properly. It seems rather one-sided until each answers the other.

Sometimes I am surprised that letters reach their destination at all these days, but at other times I'm all impatience because of the loss of time between writing and being read.

I read today—

My darling,
Ten minutes ago I was waiting on the aerodrome for the post to come in. It brought your first two letters.
Then I got into my machine and flew to the advanced landing ground. Now I am sitting under a haystack where I have just read your letters. They make me very happy—the one written in the train especially.
Last night I did a patrol and met nine Huns, but had no luck.
The first idea was to send out the whole squadron, but afterwards it was proposed that one strong patrol should go out, and that a few others should go out on their own and keep the patrol in sight.
Then, if a large formation of Huns was met they would be kept busy by our formation, while the odd roving ones, flying high above, might pick off a Hun or two.
Kyrle, Kelly, Hastings and I volunteered as the odd men and B Flight did the formation.
It was nearly a success, but just failed. After roaming about nearly three-quarters of an hour at 15,000 feet, the formation turned away up north just as nine Huns appeared from the east. Kyrle and Hastings went with the formation and Kelly and I were the only two who saw the Huns.
We manoeuvred against them for twenty-five minutes, and

were within long range of them most of the time.

But I couldn't get near enough to fire, and was afraid to waste ammunition so far over.

Several times five of the Huns came directly underneath me, but two others were just above and I daren't go down, and at last, after we had worked a good way north we had to come away.

This morning I came to the advanced landing ground, but returned as it was perfectly dud. It cleared up a bit at lunch, so I have come out again, but there is nothing doing at all.

I shall go back for tea and to post this to my wife.

    And I send her all my love.

Bill.

Oh, how I wish I could be with him! It seems such a waste for him to sit under a haystack alone.

Chapter 53

Yesterday morning, at the Hydro, we had breakfast in our room. No letter had come from Bill, but cheerfully I told myself it would arrive by the afternoon post and would be more precious for the delay.

About half-past nine Joan dressed herself and was mending a tear in her "nighty" when the maid knocked at the door and said one of us was wanted at the telephone.

"Was it 'Mrs.' or 'Miss' they asked for?" Joan enquired.

"Never mind which it was," . . . I interrupted. . . . "I can't go down like this, so you'll have to go anyway!"

Then I added so that she would hasten:

"Perhaps it's Dick—on leave!"

That sent her speeding away, and when she had gone I leant on my elbow and scribbled lazily at the beginning of the new diary for the second volume of our book.

Very soon she returned.

"They've been taken off—whoever it was," . . . she grumbled. . . . "Isn't it silly?"

"They'll get on again," I said, not caring much, for I knew that if it were Dick he would persist.

Joan fidgeted about for a moment or two, then said:

"I think I'll go down to the lounge and write letters, and be handy if the 'phone rings."

"All right," I answered, adding: "If it's not too hot we might go for that walk you spoke of. . . I'll be down in half-an-hour."

As soon as the door closed I got out of bed, and after looking for some clean clothes began to brush my hair.

About five minutes later the handle turned.

"Who's that? . . . Is it Joan?" I asked.

The answer was indistinct.

"Wait a moment," I called, and, slipping on my *kimono*, unlocked the door.

She stood there. Her face was quite grey. I moved aside to allow her to come in, but I couldn't take my eyes from her eyes.

"What is it? ... Oh, Joan, what is it?" I managed to say at length.

Then, as she seemed unable to speak, I caught hold of her hands.

"Joan—tell me what it is!" I cried.

"I can't.... I can't," she began, and her voice was all broken up.

"It's not Bill?" I whispered—but of course I knew.

******

We packed our clothes. We would have liked to leave the silly things and run away at once, but of course we just had to go on being perfectly sane.

Joan was wonderful. She went and settled the account and gave our address for letters and asked the porter to send for the luggage.

Our one idea was to get to mother as soon as possible. We kept on hoping that dad had been with her when the wire came from the War Office; and sometimes I said that I knew Bill was all right—that he couldn't be otherwise because he had promised to come back.

After the first change of trains we travelled with a coarse fat woman in sweltering black clothes. With her were two small fat boys, also warmly wrapped in woollen garments.

As soon as we started one of them asked for a drink of water.

"I 'aven't no water, love," the woman said. "'You've 'ad it all, you know quite well."

"I want a drink of water," he moaned, and kept on moaning in spite of her repeated assurances.

Very soon both were scarlet in the face, and the sweat was pouring from them.

The woman sat on the edge of her seat, as fat people often do; and in turn mopped her own and the child's forehead with a dirty handkerchief.

All at once Joan opened her bag and brought out some biscuits.

"Here you are," she said, persuasively. "That'll do instead of a drink, won't it?"

For a moment there was silence, while the other child, who had been sitting quietly watching nothing, grabbed his share and both stuffed their mouths as full as possible.

Then the thirsty one began again, for after his dry biscuits naturally he wanted his drink more urgently.

"You'll be 'ome soon. . . . Tain't many minutes now, love," the woman recommenced, trying her utmost to console him—and then she turned to us to explain that they had come from Blackpool and had been on the way since early morning.

Soon after this a fight broke out. The one who wanted the water did it all, while the other one made placid efforts to shield himself.

After a few unheeded remarks the woman picked the troublesome one up by his middle and plumped him on to the seat.

Defiantly he stared at her and slid off. Again she picked him up, and off he slid once more—staring stolidly at her all the time.

I don't know what made us laugh—his expression or his persistence; but all at once we started to giggle, and soon the tears were pouring down my face.

I wanted to shriek with laughter and I wanted to howl with crying—but I managed to tell myself that if I started to lose control I might not be able to regain it.

Joan must have felt the same, for she stopped also.

By this time the child was howling lustily, for he had to be smacked very hard.

"I can't let 'im 'it the other one," the woman explained—panting now and purple. . . . 'Ee would kill 'im. . . . 'Ee would pull 'is eyes out, 'ee would."

★★★★★★

The last word was said as we stood by the van on the station here waiting for our luggage.

"Hi!" we heard, and the call came so explosively that we turned without thought The fat woman hung out of the compartment—her hat was awry and her face seemed as though it would burst through its skin—but she was looking beyond us to the porter.

"Hi!" she repeated. "'Oo's tin box d'you think that there is . . . that one on the platform? . . . You put it back where you took it from, you fat-head, or you'll 'ear about it, you will!"

The porter smiled, and calmly proceeded with his work.

"All right, mother," he said, "keep your 'air on. . . . Don't get 'ot or you might be sorry for it hafterwards!"

The woman's voice rose to a shriek.

"I'll keep my 'air on, you'll see, an' all! . . . In with that there tin box or they'll be trouble about. . . . Fat lot it 'ud matter to you if I gets 'ome without me belongings. . . . 'Urry with you, or by—"

"'Ush, mother, 'ush. . . . See there it goes. . . . Now be calm!" Saying this goodnaturedly, he heaved the tin box into the van again, adding:

"I wouldn't be *your* 'usband—not for somethink!"

Before the answer could be heard the whistle sounded and the train began to move. The woman had her last word, however.

We saw her at it, though we couldn't hear.

******

Mother was there when we opened the door.

Her face was smiling.

I couldn't bear that. She held me to her.

"I'm so glad you've come, at last," she said.

"We're all hoping for the best.... We're just hoping all the time."

Then she turned to Joan, and I went into the kitchen because it was the nearest place. Dad came and kissed me and went out again.

Bill, dear, I knew you'd be sorry if I cried. I knew you'd think it utterly foolish.

Besides, you are coming back. You promised to come back. You *must* come back.

******

We had tea.

Mother told us how she was alone when the telegram came and how she couldn't read it.

"I just kept the girl waiting there," she said. "I couldn't get it read."

The people next door sent for dad, and he hurried home at once on his bicycle—the bicycle you used when we were on Salisbury Plain, you know! It took you to the aerodrome in the morning and brought you home at lunch time; and then took you away again and brought you back in the evening—except when you crashed in that field and had to stay at the farm all night. But always it brought you back. I want to go on my knees beside it and kiss the pedals and the seat and the handlebars where you held them!

After a while dad had telephoned to us. Joan had said to him:

"I don't know how I shall tell Aimée.... I can't tell Aimée!"

Wasn't it like her to think of someone else and not of herself?

******

We read the telegram, and it seemed to give us hope.

After all, many airmen have gone missing and afterwards have been reported prisoners of war.

Isn't it strange how much a matter of comparison everything is?

Yesterday, before ten o'clock, to know that you were a captive in a strange country where we couldn't reach you; enduring hardships of which we could know nothing; to contemplate the days without your letters, would have seemed unendurable; and today the news would bring relief beyond all words.

About eleven o'clock we said goodnight and went to bed. The others looked so weary. Their faces seemed to have become old and colourless—almost without life.

I felt very wide-awake.

I slipped downstairs and found the St. Moritz albums and brought them up to look at all the snapshots of you and at your Cresta Run colours.

Joan was in bed with me—in the bed where we slept together just two weeks ago; and when we lay down she put her arm round me. Somehow she seemed so small and helpless that it made me cry. The tears trickled on to the pillow until it was wet.

I kept on remembering little things you had said and all your ways.

I love everything about you. You know how utterly I love you, dear!

Soon I felt I couldn't breathe and had to sit up.

And though you told me not to grieve if anything happened to you, I just couldn't stop crying.

Joan was crying too, then— quietly and helplessly like me.

She sat up and put her face against mine.

"Never mind," she whispered. "He's coming back. . . . There's no need to worry. . . . He's coming back!"

"I know," I sobbed, "I know he's coming back. . . . He was certain of coming back—but I want him now—at this moment! . . . It's so lonely not to know where he is!"

After that we put on the light again and looked all through the albums once more and talked about the things you have done and how joyous you are and how lucky always.

But of course you would be lucky in any event. It's us who . But we don't think of that. . . . We know we shall see you again.

Chapter 54

Dad has written a lot of letters—among them one to Cox's to ask them to let us know if they should have a cheque, made out by you, from Germany.

And I have written a note to the "Odd Man" telling him how anxiously we hope to hear that you are a prisoner and even wounded. Darling, is it too selfish of me to want you in little pieces rather than not at all?

I want you with any sort of wound except one that will take your reason from you.

I will be your limbs—your eyes. I will be everything to you.

You said, didn't you, that you would find compensation always, and I know I could make you happy. We could live in Paris just the same, and we have our work together. Our love would be just wonderful. It *is* wonderful. You are my life. You are living for me, I know.

******

Darling, although I can't send the letters, I feel I must write to you every day.

I want to tell you that I can't imagine life without you. I can't believe you aren't alive. You seemed always to be just about twice as much alive as any of us.

Today lots of letters have come—several of them from the squadron.

The C.O. and the "Odd Man" write so finally—as though they are certain you were killed. They say lovely things about you and your work, and speak as though only a knockout blow could have sent you spinning down.

But Holt gives details.

He explains how you went out early on Sunday morning with several others, and how, when you were going up to meet some Hun scouts, which appeared unexpectedly after you had dived on to some others, the anti-aircraft shells burst in thick clouds, breaking up the formation. Suddenly you were seen to spin. For three thousand feet you were seen to spin—and then the others had to look out for themselves.

About an hour later Holt, at the advanced aerodrome, had a message from our anti-aircraft people that one of our machines had gone down out of control behind the German lines. They reported a wing missing, but those who were with you vow the machine was intact and think you must have had a direct hit.

He finishes, however, by saying that there is no reason to believe that if you were stunned you couldn't have regained consciousness in time to flatten out before hitting the ground.

All speak of your wonderful control over your machine and of the loss you are to the squadron.

That, knowing you, I can understand—but why do they have so little faith? Why is it left for us, here, to believe in you? I think death matters so little to them that, having gone from among them, you might as well be dead.

To me, too, death matters little—except if you are dead; and if you are I will come also.

As soon as possible I will learn to fly, and one morning early I will go up into the blue heaven and then let go! I will spin down and down, and down!

Oh, if I could go up at once. If I could move—quickly—quickly! . . . If I could go battling against the wind and gun fire and enemy machines. . . . If I could move—move all the while, I could grip this pain and laugh at it—and come to you very soon.

But here—Bill here in this house! Never to be alone—never to walk alone! To know, above all, your faith in me—that I should comfort mother and face her and all the world with perfect calm! It is too much. You couldn't realize how much you expected of me—you who had to go ahead always with your brain and your body!

Don't you know what you asked when you left me this to do? I think I can't go on.

Chapter 55

Darling—This morning I think you have broken some ribs.
Do you mind?
I think it because I dreamt about an umbrella with broken ribs.
It must be a code dream.
"Umbrella" is Morse or something for you.
I know you won't mind being an umbrella or any old thing just to please me.
Anyway you can have my ribs.
I have some extra ones, haven't I?
Or was it that you gave me some in the beginning?
Have them back, darling. . . . Have them back at once! Really it seems immaterial which of us has them, because, as you know, we are one.
Yesterday I pictured myself wheeling you in a bath-chair along a country lane, and then sitting down on the step by the wayside while we write a book.
How d'you like that? You can't possibly complain.
It would mean, of course, that you had come back with only one leg. Well, we can learn to walk beautifully with three, can't we?
You used only to have two legs before you married me, so you've gained one really. And even if you had none at all you would still have two!

******

Do you know what I have been thinking ever since we heard the news, and what I believe in most firmly except in those despondent moods which we all have because the tension is so great?
I believe that if you had been killed mother or I would have had some message from you—some sort of spiritual communion.
What it would be or how it would happen I don't know, but any-

way it would be tangible to us whose thoughts never left you—never leave you—except in sleep.

This has nothing to do with any religious conviction, for, as you know, I have none except an idea that this can't be all we were created for.

I am convinced that you, who would be so eager to comfort us and to relieve our pain, would come to us in some way; and I feel that in some form you would stay with me and be my companion all the time.

Darling, everything about you is my companion. I have no slightest wish apart from you. When you found me all the vague and ceaseless longing for "something, we know not what" left me—for you had come.

Dear, were two minds ever more in tune, or two spirits ever happier in the release—each to each? To be with you made the perfect night, the perfect morning—because all of you sought me, and all of me was yours.

How then could you leave me without a sign? You couldn't leave me so much alone.

Chapter 56

Darling—Desirée has just gone. Yesterday she came to tell me she knows you are alive. She repeated what she had exclaimed after our marriage when she was feeling rather sore about it.

Do you remember—I told you?

She said:

"Before I saw him I hoped he would fall out of his aeroplane and break his neck.... And now I've seen him I know that if he did fall out his neck wouldn't break!"

That, you know, was to announce her vexation, because, after having heard all her confidences and given her all mine since we wore frocks above our knees, I had dared to marry without telling her beforehand.

I understood, for I should have felt the same.

She repeated, too, what she had said when we all met in the Savoy lounge about three weeks ago—that she was convinced you would come through.

Her unreasonable confidence is life to me just now.

******

As she had travelled so far mother asked her to stay a night. She slept with me, and we talked for hours. She tried to persuade me to go back with her, but I told her I couldn't rest away from your people and that I couldn't leave them to wait for news of you.

Joan has decided to continue with her work. So you see mother and I are alone most of the day.

This morning, very early, I lay thinking, and it dawned upon me that on this earth one *must* have some refuge which is not material. Life is too much master of the situation otherwise.

Here are we—or here am I anyway—unable to get away from the crude fact that I *must* have you back at any cost.

It is impossible—not that I should have you, oh no, not that—but the blank refusal to accept any alternative.

If I could believe in the survival of individuality after death; if I could be convinced that the spirit lives and is conscious of those who still must stay here; then I would be content to wait without your bodily companionship. I would know that by being true to you in word and thought and deed, I could keep you with me until my own spirit should leave this cage.

I could find strength to be kind to the others; to do my utmost to help mother and Joan and those who have depended on you for pleasure and interest. If I could believe this I could become—not outwardly resigned because I must show no surrender—but radiant, so that in seeing me all people could renew their hope. I could live most truly, as we are told to live, helping all with my double strength—yours, dear, and my own.

As it is, under this solid exterior, I am rebellious full of self-pity and irritability. I am useless to the others. I am useless to myself.

The "Odd Man," in his letters, says: "God give you strength."

Bill dear—who is God?

He doesn't tell me that.

Chapter 57

Darling—I want to live out of doors just now—all day and all night. I want to go to sleep under the sky and to wake under it. I want to see no houses and to have no walls about me. And I want the wind to blow and blow.

All the while I want to have a vision of you that is eluding me just now. All day I am with you. My last thought at night is yours. In the morning I wake and turn to you.

But I think under the open sky my spirit would find your spirit in the darkness—and that is what I want.

Perhaps you, also, are between four walls. Are you? Oh, send and tell us that you are! Send and tell us you are in a bed—a little hurt but not too much for your comfort, dear. And if you are in pain may I not come to you?

******

Last night I was impossible—utterly selfish and impossible.

Joan had been playing softly on the piano, and you know her haunting touch. It was evening, and the sadness of the gloaming took hold of me.

Suddenly I cried, imperatively: "I want to go out."

Joan stopped playing.

"All right," she said; "I'll come with you in a minute."

"But I don't want you to come with me. . . . I want to go alone," I answered.

"Oh, no! . . . You can't go alone," she exclaimed.

"Why can't I go alone?" I persisted "I love being alone. . . . I hate always to be with other people!"

Poor Joan. You know how sensitive she is? I knew why she didn't want me to go alone, and it enraged me to think she should be afraid to leave me. Yet I realised my brutality and tried to soften it by adding,

"Take no notice of me tonight. . . . I'm bad-tempered!"

"You couldn't be bad-tempered, Aimée," she said most gently. "You're just tired, that's all."

Bill, I could have screamed. I was afraid of myself.

Just then mother came in.

"Aimée wants to go for a walk alone," Joan said to her helplessly.

"No, I don't," I muttered. . . . "I did want to, but I don't now."

"Oh, no, you mustn't go alone," mother began.

"I tell you I don't want to go alone," I interrupted; then, from sheer inability to leave it there I began to argue.

"How can I work," I said, "if I never can be alone to think? . . . You can't think when others are with you all the time."

"Oh, but you don't want to work just now—not with your brain. . . . We can't work with our brains just now," mother broke in. . . . "We can only just keep on—just keep on hoping from day to day."

Bill, dear, I could have taken up all the things in the room and smashed them into tiny pieces—and the windows and the walls and the whole silly house!

"Joan will go with you. . . . She won't speak a word. . . . You'll be just the same as if you were alone!" mother continued—and then, mercifully, I saw her face.

I don't think that ever in my life I have seen any one look so weary. I could have howled with crying over her. I didn't know what to do or say. I was ashamed.

I think we all sat under our juniper trees last night, dear one.

Chapter 58

Today I said to mother:

"You know, dear, how convinced I am that Bill will come back to us because he said he would.... But I have been wondering what your religion would mean to you if you had to let someone go whom you love."

It was, perhaps, rather a cruel thing to ask, but I felt that if her belief meant anything she might be pleased to tell me and to let me share in her comfort.

She seemed willing to talk quite calmly.

She said she knows that those who are taken are alive in spirit always and conscious of us who are left.

"Then why do you grieve at the possibility of losing any one?" I asked—adding: "If I had that belief I should be content.... Nothing could hurt me if I believed."

For a little while she was silent. Then she said:

"I grieve—I would grieve—just because I'm human, and I want to feel that those I love are on the earth.... I want to be able to put my arms round my children.... I'm a mother and I can't help being human, that's all."

Then I told her of the letter I had had from the "Odd Man's" wife.

"Whatever happens," she wrote, "it is no loss.... We have them always."

"What does she mean by 'no loss'?" I asked, worrying the problem to shreds because it all means words and nothing more to me; and I think that those who have come to some conclusion should be able to make it plain.

"I'm sure I don't know," mother said. "It is a loss, as we all know, if our dears don't come back.... I tell you it's because we're human it's a loss."

"Oh," I cried, for I wanted to solve the riddle and it wouldn't come right. "I don't believe in anything—and nothing you or anyone says makes me believe."

"Don't say that.... You don't mean it.... You can't mean that," mother whispered in a voice of pain.

"But I do mean it.... Can't you see that I'd give anything if I could believe—but I don't," I reiterated, stung and goaded by this stone wall of words, written and said!

Mother didn't speak for some time, and when she did it was to say:

"We must pray.... We must pray hard and we will get what we pray for.... I believe that if I pray my boy will come back to me."

"Mother," I asked, quite desperately, "have all those who prayed and who believe had their dear ones back from this dreadful war? ... Think of your own friends alone! ... Have they not prayed?"

Again she was silent and then bravely she spoke.

"It's true," she said. "But whatever you say you can't take away my belief."

Ashamed of myself once more, I went and put my arms round her, kissing her.

"Darling," I whispered, "I don't want to take away your belief, but I just ache for you to give me some of it."

"It waits for all of us to see how we can stand the test," she answered tenderly. "But just pray, dear, and it will be easier.... Just pray '*Thy will be done.*' ... That's what I'm saying all the time."

Chapter 59

We wait for the post on tenterhooks. It's no use objecting, Bill. We do. And telegrams are nightmares. When dad is away at work I open them because mother can't. That one from the War Office was too much of a shock.

Yesterday afternoon another came.

Mother had opened the door and she called to me. I rushed downstairs and took the envelope from her hand, tearing it apart. They must be read speedily, you know. We should find them unbearable otherwise.

This one said:

Home on leave. Arrive tonight.—Dick.'

Will you forgive me, dear? The tears blinded my eyes. You were so anxious for Dick and me to meet, and now it happens like this!

To mother, who had not seen her boy for two long years, it seemed like a miracle—a direct answer to one of her prayers.

******

He has come. I can't take my eyes from his face.

It isn't like yours in feature, really, but there is a look—a mannerism. And the voice is yours!

When he smokes his pipe—twisting it from one corner of his mouth to another and biting the stem, it is you!

He means just everything to us all just now. He is so perfectly optimistic. He says he simply can't be downhearted because he knows you'll come through all right. He whistles and sings rag-time, and brings a gust of life to this house.

After his bath, when mother and dad were tucked away in bed, he came into Joan's room and brought some French cigarettes.

Then we showed him the C.O.'s letter, which we hadn't dared to show to mother and dad because it seemed so final, and after all he knows no more than that you were seen to go down out of control. Dick read it slowly. At least it took him some time, because the smoke got into his eyes.

Then he said:

"What a doleful blighter!"

"Yes, isn't he?" I agreed.

✶✶✶✶✶✶

Darling, Joan is playing rag-time for Dick's benefit.

I can't bear it. I think of the way you caught me to you when the music started and how, with our bodies close together, we danced and danced.

Bill, I can't picture the earth without you.

To have had you and to lose you,—it simply must not be!

I am utterly selfish. I want to come to you at once if you have gone.

What is this place without you? You didn't mean just this or that part of life.

My lover, my friend—everything! Always you said:

"Are you happy, dear?" or "Are you tired?" or "Do you wish for anything?"—and sweetest of all—"Do you love me, my wife?"

Yes, I love you, and I'm tired and I want to come to you, wherever you may be!

Chapter 60

Darling—For three days I haven't written to you—and during those days I have faced the possibility that you may not come back.

It seemed to me that to have the full lesson of the trial we are enduring we must not shrink from any view of it. My thoughts have been muddled up with my emotion and it is difficult to separate the two.

Emotionally I feel I can't do without you. I *must* know your amazing need of me. My perfect artist—what should I do with my need which is your need?

Yet all else would I sacrifice for the delight of your clear brain—for the chaste, the unutterable satisfaction of your mental companionship.

There again we seemed to give and take with absolute equality.

Tonight I make no feverish abandoned complaint. It's the waste that appals me. I can't get beyond that. Indeed I can't get beyond that.

******

Today Dick took me, in a slow train, by the station you used when you went to the grammar school.

He showed me the old stone house where you lived then, and the path across the fields, where you ran every morning while the train grunted impatiently.

He showed me, too, the old seat where you spent hours with a notebook taking the numbers of the engines as they passed.

We hung out of the window together, and as the train moved Dick said:

"D'you notice those steps? . . . Well, I can see him tearing up them always at the last moment—but never too late!"

I was wondering how they could allow anyone else to use the steps after you, when he added quietly:

"He was my ideal then—and has been ever since. . . . All through these three years of war, if ever I've been in a tight corner I've said to myself: 'Bill's been in tighter ones and come through.' And that has brought me out all right; every time."

You see, dear, we all need you. You simply can't be spared.

★★★★★★

When we reached the town we went to book seats for a "*revue*." The others were to join us later and in the meantime we went to a little *café*—all corners and alcoves.

We tucked ourselves away, and ever coffee and French cigarettes Dick talked of his time in Paris with you and of your days down the Seine on the skiff. And I told him of our marriage—for I know you wanted him to hear. He loved it all, and laughed so much at the bits which seemed most characteristic of you.

About six o'clock we met the family and arrived at the "*revue*" just after the curtain had risen.

The lights in the auditorium were low, and from then onwards, in that crowded smoky-place, I saw you vividly. Never since the news came have I seen you so vividly. I heard what you would say as each one appeared on the stage, and I heard your laugh.

Your stick, the one made from the broken propeller, with the band of the fragment of aileron control, was in my hand. It goes everywhere with me.

Suddenly—while in front of a black cloth a number of girls were doing a rag-time dance—I saw *you* against the blue morning sky. . High up against the blue you were! . . . I saw the "Archie-bursts" around you. . . . I saw your machine stagger and begin to spin. I saw it spinning—down—down .

And when it reached the ground, my heart stopped—to tear madly on again, for you stood up, and after saying "damn" quietly, just once, you fumbled in your pocket and brought out your pipe and tobacco pouch.

Dear, the pain of the blue morning sky overwhelmed me, but you—you are coming back!

Chapter 61

Today is Sunday.

It is two weeks now since you went down.

This morning I made my usual pilgrimage to the bicycle shed to say my prayer.

I ask the old bicycle to bring you back again, you know.

This happens very early.

As soon as I wake, before I dress, I slip downstairs and out through the back door and along the little passage leading to the garden—and then I come in and make the morning tea, for, by doing so, I keep everyone else in bed until the letters have arrived.

Today it was later. I wakened with a start. The hands of the clock pointed almost to the time when they say you went spinning down. Springing from bed I ran to the kitchen and out to the garden, and as I went the sun came from behind a cloud. Most gloriously it came—enveloping me in a wondrous light. Suddenly the tightness left my heart.

"He is coming back.... He is certain to come back!" it sang. And I waited there, drinking in the promise thirstily until my brain and my spirit were revived.

Later we went to chapel.

It was mother's wish, of course. "If he's able to think at all, he'll picture us there this morning." And that stopped my hesitation.

We looked so cheery and festive that all miserable inquiry was squashed. People are kind, I know, but many seem to think it improper of us not to have red eyes.

I sat next to Dick, and showed him those three children who amused you so much. He bawled forth the hymns like you do, and then I opened the book at a place which said a lot about delight and blowing trumpets and joy coming after sorrow. It was lovely, and when we went out the day was lovely too.

★★★★★★

Tonight mother told us all to go to bed.

When the house was quiet, Dick came into our room: and Joan and he and I have been sitting with you in the candle-light. We felt you so much with us and were so merry—in whispers.

Dick brought out a lot of French cigarettes that had fallen into his bath and had been dried on the cylinder.

We talked of you and Paris and St. Moritz—and of the fun we shall have together afterwards.

All at once mother appeared. She was very cross.

We felt guilty and extremely young—but I was pleased to find that such a trivial thing had power to move her. We all seem more alive today. You must have been ill, and now you are out of pain!

★★★★★★

Dear, we must wait. We know we must wait, and as mother repeats:

"We must go on hoping—just hoping all the time!"

For you said when I asked if you were coming back: "I'm certain—quite certain."

And I was looking into your eyes at the time.

You are living for me, I know.

Chapter 62

And so, after all, this *is* the end!

You who were certain of coming back, and I who was certain of it, too, have had to own ourselves completely baffled. On that Sunday morning your life went out "into the ether," and you left me here.

From higher than the highest hill you came spinning down.

Your body, that belonged to me, must have made a big hole in the ground.

And I, who could have rendered living beautiful for you, even if you had been crippled, or disfigured, or blinded, may not touch nor hear nor see you anymore. My useless tears are falling.

I can't believe that Life—the abundant share of it which was yours—could finish utterly; or that the individuality which made you mine could go back into nothingness again.

Yet, if that is not so, why did you—whose first thought was for me always—not come and make it known?

If anything that was you still exists, why don't you come now?

Why don't you come and take me too: or promise that I shall mate with you again?

Last night, in the darkness, I lay and realized what it means to be alone. And I thought:

"When he lay beside me before I spoke he knew my mood. I had no vaguest wish he didn't grant; no problem he didn't solve; no pain he could not soothe. . . . My pleasure was his pleasure; my sorrow he took from me. . . . And now when the greatest of all sorrow has come through him, he doesn't speak.

"That *cannot* be his wish.

"What does it mean?"

******

Well, dear, that's over!

And now I'm going to pretend.

I'm going to pretend from this moment that you are alive and with me all the time.

I'm going to pretend that you never leave me night or day; that we are as much together as we were when I could see and touch and hear you.

If there should be spells when this is not satisfactory entirely we will laugh them away—or if laughing doesn't act we will discuss them seriously as our habit is.

I've been thinking of how many women must be feeling alone just now, and I wondering how they tackle the situation.

Some, I suppose, have a definite religion to see them through. They will bow their heads and say to their God:

"*Thy will, not mine, be done!*"

Others must be rebellious, and are spending their vitality in a fury of pain which time will wear down to resignation.

Others, who married because marriage happened to come their way, will find consolation from expressions of sympathy and from the dramatic possibilities of mourning.

Those who, like me, have had to renounce what made them whole—the someone before whose coming they were consciously incomplete, and at whose coming they became as, consciously, complete,—will face the inevitable according to their ability, until the time comes, when they too go out into the "nothingness" or to the "everything" that must come eventually.

At first they may believe—as I believed—that nothing would do except to follow at once—at once: that they must force Death to pause in his greedy harvesting and gather them too—but a small voice may whisper to them also:

"Death knows his own business. . . . If you tamper with your Destiny you may miss him whom you seek. . . . It is all too incomprehensible for you to interfere!"

Chapter 63

Good-morning, Bill!

You see I say "Good-morning" just as though you hadn't been with me all the night!

You have been, of course; but I shall chatter like this on paper because I can't go about speaking out loud in any other way—and you know how I love to hear my own voice?

Such a lot of things happened yesterday, and you were with me through them all.

I found myself smiling at your remarks—especially in chapel—but we'll talk of that in a minute, for first I must explain why I don't speak of how the family are taking the final news of you. I don't speak of it simply because they don't know—because they haven't received it.

The Odd Man wrote to me—and I simply can't speak of it so soon! Before the post came I had put the kettle on the gas, and had been out to the bicycle shed to say my prayer for your return.

Then, while the kettle boiled, I read the letter; and afterwards hid it away in my *kimono* sleeve—and there you are!

Mother goes on "hoping—just hoping all the time," and if you think I ought to have told her you will understand that these few days before the official word comes can't make much difference to her—and that I must have them to myself to bury my dead. By "my dead" I don't mean you, dear. You are living for me and with me all the while I know. I mean the idea of the tangible "you"; for it takes a little while to lay upon the altar of whatever power there is the something which seemed so essential to our staying here at all—the body, the touch, the kisses, the human presence! It takes a little while to force our lips to say:

"Thy will, not mine, be done." Especially when we don't know whose will we mean.

That's why I guard my secret; why I listen unmoved when they speak of you as a prisoner of war; when Joan comes home with another story of someone whose husband or son has written after many weeks; or when mother says: "We'll send him such lovely parcels, see if we don't"; or, "If we could just see his name on a cheque, that would do for us, wouldn't it?"

And if, when I may have failed to answer and she repeats "Wouldn't it, Aimée?" I say "Yes, mother!" it is because I must; knowing all the while that no signature of yours will be seen by us anymore.

That's why I come up here to my attic to be alone with myself—and you.

✶✶✶✶✶✶

On going downstairs at lunch time yesterday I found Mr. Blair in the dining-room.

As a previous minister of the chapel he had travelled to make his speech at the formal welcome to the new man, and had come first to hear the latest news of you, whom he chooses to call "one of his boys."

When Joan and dad and "the kid"—who, by the way, goes on, in the back garden, playing at air-battles as though you had not fought your last; and at artillery duels as though Dick were not risking his life in one at this moment—had gathered at the table, and mother had served the food from her place at the end, we ate and laughed a lot about nothing, and then I went into the kitchen to see to the coffee.

While it was going through the process of being made I, having done no work except to cover up one bed and "brew" the morning tea, "washed up"; and as usual, quite valiantly you did your bit—which was to stand about filling your pipe, urging me to hurry and come and have a cigarette instead of wasting time poking about in a pan of greasy water.

Didn't I always agree most heartily when you vowed you never would wish me to do any housework of any sort whatever—except to make coffee, that being an aesthetic pleasure to us both. At last, having carried in the tray and handed round the cups, I slipped away to go up to the bedroom where I lay appreciating, with you, the humour and quaintly expressed truth of *A Knight on Wheels*, by Ian Hay.

You remember Dick wanted us to read it! And I knew, when you said "It's so very sane," that you meant the way the writer views life over the top of preconceived ideas.

Presently Joan appeared.

"Dad's gone and mother's asleep and Mr. Blair wants you to come and give him a few hints about publishers.... He has some writing he wants to see in print," she announced.

Lazily turning over, I answered into the pillow: "Tell him I don't know a thing about publishers. I've met only one and I don't know anything about him except that he lives with his mother."

At this Joan seated herself on the edge of the bed. She's much too wise to try to coerce any one.

"I'd rather stay here myself, too," she said, knowing quite well that she would be obliged to go and talk if I didn't.

I knew it too and yet I said:

"Go down and give him the address of the man upon whose advice one can rely.... And then come back here as quickly as you can."

Just as I finished speaking, darling, you interfered.

"That's not fair," you whispered. "Besides, old Blair is quite good fun—not a bit a preachy sort.... And he thinks no end of me"—you added, with one of your occasional touches of self-appreciation.

After that you can imagine it didn't take me long to hop out of bed. I slipped into my dress and powdered my nose and tidied my hair and was down in two minutes.

Mother lay dozing on the sofa. Mr. Blair sat by the grate smoking a cigar and, when Joan and I had fitted ourselves into the big armchair, in low voices we discussed books and manuscripts and the placing of work; and then the talk worked round to you.

"Everything was as easy as could be to him," said Mr. Blair. "Without a bit of trouble he just carried away all the prizes at school—but he never cared.... *We* got excited, he didn't!"

"Yes," agreed Joan, "he always seemed a bit aloof from it all, in spite of being so jolly and all that."

As they said this, darling, a wave of remembrance of your complete giving of all of yourself came over me. Nothing you kept back—nothing you held aloof. Just all of you was mine and all I took.

Now, as I sit here, I recall, too, something that occurred in our bedroom overlooking the golf links by the sea.

I had spoken some half-formed wonder that you should go on caring for me as you did. It was just the whimsical statement of a woman who can't let well enough alone; for truly I knew that with our conception of life and of each other, our union would grow with the years. Eagerly you came to me.

"Dear, you are mine always," you whispered, making me meet your eyes—and then your voice became more calm.

You held my hands:

"I should have said," . . . you continued quietly and with grave confidence, . . . "that *I* am *yours* always—all, *all* yours."

******

Well, to get back to yesterday, Bill, old boy!

At three o'clock mother invited and resented criticism upon the angle of her hat; then went with Mr. Blair to chapel to hear the first sermon of the day.

"Hurra!" cried Joan in the tone of voice that reminds me of you when, every now and then, you decided to get a hundred seconds out of a minute, "we've three hours and a half all to ourselves. . . . What shall we do?"

"Three hours and a half?" I queried. "How's that?" She snatched up a leaflet from the table.

"See here;—Service, by Mr. What's his name three thirty until five. . . . Tea in the schoolroom five until six thirty—nine-pence. . . . Fancy they can eat for an hour and a half for ninepence, and in war time, too!" she rattled on fatuously. Her mood was infectious, and feeling gloriously irresponsible we rammed our hats on our heads and let off steam by a quick tramp over the fields: then, coming home again, we shed our outdoor clothes and lounged about in *kimonos*, making tea and collecting from tins in the larder all the nice things to eat.

We were too late for the second service, of course, and the ministers, who were to address us, already filled the place where the choir usually sits, under the pulpit facing the congregation.

With them was the mayor who, after a few jokes and a few sensible remarks about the practical side of religion, apologized for handing the chair over to a deputy—because he had to attend several other meetings in the town.

When he had trotted away and when the vestry door had closed upon him, the deputy introduced another "brother," who stood up and, rather unexpectedly, began to pray.

I couldn't decide whether to kneel or not, so, as there was nothing to kneel upon and I was wearing the costume you like so much, I just leant my forehead against the edge of the pew in front and talked to you.

The brother's voice was oddly pitched, and he played about with some of his words and once you exclaimed: "Oh, fids!" which made me giggle, and at that the woman in front sat up and nearly knocked my hat off.

You see, we had a tolerably exciting time.

Then, darling, the girl with the *contralto* voice went on to the platform and sang. To the accompaniment of the organ she put her heart and soul and all her lovely tenderness into her song.

We were close together, dear heart—and when she finished with "Ships that pass in the night," I held you very firmly, for we didn't just "speak each other in passing," did we?

We became one, and you are with me evermore.

A thought has just whispered to me that when I die you will be waiting, as you did at the marriage office; and you'll come forward, as you did then—so eagerly and tenderly—and you will take my hands and say "Aimée."

Oh, I wish Death would hurry and come this way! One extra couldn't make much difference to him when he is taking such crowds and crowds. And if he must have an exact number, couldn't you persuade him to spare someone who wishes to stay here, and to take me instead?

Couldn't you go to him and say: "Look here, old man, I've left my wife across there. I don't want her to think I've forgotten about her. Perhaps you wouldn't mind just putting back your old skiff a moment—and if there's anything we can do for you, don't mind asking!"

If he's a decent sort at all, Bill, that should be enough; but if he seems inclined to stand on his hind—I mean, on his dignity—just say "Sir" instead of "old man," and perhaps "ferry boat" or "launch" instead of "old skiff."

There's no sense in getting his back up and taking any risks.

I'm not grousing, Bill. It's only a suggestion, and if it doesn't meet with your approval, I'm ready to admit that you were right most times. If you decide that there are things to be done here for a while, I'll stand to all right, you know.

✶✶✶✶✶✶

But all this time I'm trying to tell you that the meeting at least gave me an insight into the "other person's" point of view, for I heard enough to convince me that while I could find a God more easily up here in my attic with you, or out in the country where the sun shines and the wind blows, some can get beyond what seems to me a muddle of words that hinder thought rather than develop it. When a minister said, with an earnest wish to spread his conviction:

"God is in Heaven," I wanted to ask, just to begin with:

"Is God like Bill?" For really when you come to sift it out the only God any of us can understand is our Most Beloved, and the only Heaven any of us desire is to be with our Most Beloved without fear of parting or of love becoming less.

Can any of us, with our human comprehension, get beyond that?

Chapter 64

Last evening when Joan and I returned from a long tramp over the high fields against a stiff wind, mother, who had been baking bread and now stood at the kitchen table, said:
"Dad's in the dining-room."
"Alone," said Joan, briskly.
"No," he's not alone. . . . He's with—"
"Oh, I know! With old Methuselah what's his-name!"
"Now, Joan," censured mother, "don't you be so quick. You're too brisk by far nowadays. You don't know who dad's with, so let me speak!"
"Sorry, mother," said Joan, giving her a jaunty kiss. "Go ahead! Who is it?"
"You're so quick, you never let me open my mouth," continued mother, quite aggrieved and unable to proceed.
Joan smiled at her and going to the sink began to pull a lettuce to pieces without waiting to take off her hat.
"There you go, and you'll spoil that skirt, too," chided mother seeing her unrepentant.
"All right, I'll cover it up," said Joan agreeably, unhooking an apron from the peg, and adding, as she did so, "I'm sure I don't care who's in the dining-room. . . . I'm hungry. I want some food."
At this, perversely, after a little pause, mother said:
"It's the man who was in Paris for a fortnight—the one Bill showed round."
Suddenly Joan stopped splashing the lettuce leaves, and began to laugh.
"Oh, Aimee," she cried, "it's that man who went from here! . . . The one dad gave Bill's address to. You remember I told you. Bill wrote home: What on earth have you sent out this time? He doesn't smoke

or drink; he doesn't like music or theatres—and he's never spoken to a woman in his life!"

And I wrote back on a postcard: "Don't bother about the man. He's no special pal of ours."

And, of course, Bill left it lying about, and the man may have read it, for one day he handed it to him saying, "This is yours, I think!"

✶✶✶✶✶✶

But here again, Bill, I had an insight into the other person's point of view, for when, after supper, we went into the dining-room to please mother, the man, with a break in his voice, spoke of his time in Paris as the happiest of his life.

You were so good to him, he said.

Being unadventurous he mentioned with awe your airy disregard of most things—especially your own safety.

"He had so many narrow escapes," he finished, wishing to comfort us in our anxiety: "He'll come out of this all right, you'll see. He's such a lucky chap."

"Well, that's what we believe," said mother. 'We're hoping for the best . . . We're just going on hoping all the time."

Then it was, dear, that I wanted to say quite calmly: "He's lucky still. . . . He's dead." But the words didn't come; and realizing that I had done, as usual, less than my share of housework that day I rose and went into the kitchen to wash the supper dishes.

✶✶✶✶✶✶

I've been to the dentist.

If you've got to stay on this planet you can do it more pleasantly without a hole in your tooth, can't you?

After gagging my mouth and putting that grinding thing right into the roots of my head, he said, working away at the wheel:

"Now, just raise your left hand if I hurt you!"

I thought:

"My son, it would take more than this to make me sing out nowadays. . . . I'm fireproof, more or less."

But I daresay if he had been too familiar with a pet nerve it would have been just as hateful as it used to be.

Life's rather amusing—taking it all round.

Chapter 65

Beyond doubt the greatest difficulty is mother.

Mothers, it seems, have no interests of their own. They see life through their children, and what happens when, as now, their children go away and come again no more.

What can we do for them?

I, Bill dear, feel very helpless. I'm so impatient, too. Always I have wanted other people's way to be my way—and not mine theirs.

Small restrictions irritate me to impatience—and yet one must be above impatience, of course.

Because of this irritation in myself I find it perilous to talk below the surface of things to mothers. My tone, and the fact that they are unaccustomed to argument, make discussion seem like a personal attack. And yet I know of no way to friendship except discussion, and without friendship how can one be of use?

I wish I had your big calm way. Perhaps if I pretend enough that you are expressing yourself through me I may conquer my futility.

******

Yesterday we went into the park. "That," said mother, nodding toward a circle of grass, "used to be a cricket ground.... Many a time we spent an afternoon here, before the war, watching them play.... We had county matches and all, you know," she finished, so that I shouldn't imagine it to have been merely a provincial playing field.

When we had admired the circle of cultivated grass, and walked on again in the sunshine she continued:

"You should have seen them—how lovely they looked in their white clothes against the green all round!"

Overjoyed by the picture she visualized—of the players with their alert bodies springing upward to catch a ball; or running and bending with the grace that balanced muscular development gives—I smiled, and was smiling still when she cried in a voice full of rebellion:

"It's a shame—it's a dreadful shame to think of so many of them killed and gone!"

I traced a pattern on the ground with your stick. Bill, dear; and I answered, musingly, unguardedly:

"I don't know.... Is it a shame?"

Incredulously she turned to me.

"Not a shame.... And them so young and full of health?"

Having started I went on:

"Death has to come sometime.... It must be lovely to die when you're most full of life," I said.

"But do you think *they* would have chosen to die? ... They who could have lived many a happy year!" she persisted, hardly crediting my words, I think.

I answered:

"No one chooses to die—or very few of us; but who is to say that the years would have brought happiness to them? ... It isn't certain, is it?"

Mother seated herself on the bench beside which we had stood.

"Then you don't think this war is a terrible thing?" she asked.

Quickly I answered her, able to agree at last.

"I think war is a senseless and horrible mistake—and I think if there is a God he must weep for our stupidity.... But it's us who are to be pitied, isn't it—not those who are dead," I said.

Mothers are so very sweet—and so pathetic. I wish we could help them!

Chapter 66

Bill dear, last night I felt wonderfully happy. Joan was asleep. I had been reading, and afterwards, in the darkness, had no wish for sleep.

You were with me. I was content. How can I explain it?

Not many days and nights ago I cringed from the very suggestion that you might not come to me again as I had known you hitherto.

That you could be with me after I no longer could touch your body or hear your voice seemed too incredible to bring even the vaguest sense of comfort.

I felt too forlorn—too alone.

Now, without reason, beyond all argument even of my own making, I know that you are mine, that you are *me*, more completely than when I lay in your arms breathing your very breath.

On looking back it seems that upon our most holy moments there fell a shadow—a shadow cast by the knowledge of human chance and change; of partings and vague fears.

We two faced living with so much to make us courageous and buoyant—but I, for one, was afraid.

I was afraid of Sorrow.

I would have gone a long way round to escape meeting Sorrow face to face.

And now that he has taken me by both hands and has forced me to stand and meet his gaze, I find I am looking into your eyes; that it is you who hold my hands; you who whisper that you will go with me to the end of this earthly journey helping me to fulfil the tasks that destiny has pre-arranged; that it is you who will gather me into your being when the last task is done.

You are God now, for your human body has released your spirit that is one with the great spirit of Love.

Oh, I realize acutely the limitation of words. I see why symbols, worn out and ill-conceived, are voiced by those who would give spiritual guidance to others who grope with Reason for a light in their blindness!

There are no words. The revelation is beyond speech. Neither music nor sunshine, nor the wind on a mountain, could convey the joy of it.

That is a pity—for just now so many beat their unseeing eyes as I beat mine a short while ago, and I would like to share my faith.

But what do you whisper?

"Let all, when they must, meet sorrow face to face.... Let them stand as you stood, blinded by tears—and when the tears are passed they shall see, and have no more fear.... In the meantime let your love, your happy love, reveal that we who are dead are living with you all, all the while.... Just carry on.... We'll see you through."

Thank you, Bill.

There is no death but forgetfulness; everything that has loved and has loved to the end will meet again
　　　　　　　　　　　　　Mazzini

Letters to His Wife

R. E. Vernède

R. E. Vernède

Contents

Introduction 209
Letters 219

Introduction

My first idea in printing my husband's letters was to have them, in a complete and more convenient form, for private circulation among those few intimate friends and relations to whom I had sent copies of each letter as it arrived. During the last few weeks, however, I have been asked by so many people to have his letters published, that I have at last decided to let them appear as they now do. But I do this very hesitatingly. To those who knew my husband, and who know his writings, no apology is needed. To others I feel I should like to give some explanation. The letters were written under very great difficulties. How great, I think, few people can realise without having known the man.

He was French by descent, his branch of the Vernède family being Huguenots, who left southern France in 1685 at the Revocation of the Edict of Nantes, and emigrated to Holland and then to England. His horror of cold and damp I always thought was due to his southern French blood; it was such a real and physical thing. He could stand any amount of heat, but the cold, especially damp cold, seemed positively to numb him. It still seems almost incredible to me how he survived those two awful winters in the trenches. And it must be remembered that he was over forty, doing 2nd lieutenant's work with boys mostly about half his age.

The spelling of the letters also made me rather doubtful. It was a trick of his always to misspell certain words in writing or mispronounce them in talking. They are all of them family words, generally with a story attached. At first I thought of spelling the words properly, but in many cases this seemed to make the sentences so much more pompous that I have kept them as they were originally written, and can only hope they will not strike anyone as either affected or irritating.

Before he went out to France I made him promise that he would tell me everything just as he thought of it and not try to make things out better than they were. He kept that promise, and I think it was a help to him to feel that he could say things just as they occurred to him, though once or twice he was doubtful as to whether he was worrying me by telling me too much. But I repeatedly assured him that my imagination was quite vivid enough to invent the things if he did not tell them to me. And I think he was convinced of it.

A short sketch of his life up to 1914 may be of interest to some people.

Robert Ernest Vernède was born in London, June 4, 1875. He went to St Paul's School, won the Milton prize in 1893, for an original English poem, and a classical exhibition at St John's College, Oxford, in the following year. He took Greats in 1898.

On leaving Oxford he lived at home in London and took up writing as a profession. He began by writing articles and short stories. His first novel, *The Pursuit of Mr Faviel*, was published in 1905. It was very successful, and has since been republished by Nelson's in their 7d. edition, and, under the title of *The Flight of Faviel*, in America. It was followed by *Meriel of the Moors*, (1906); *The Judgment of Illingborough* (1908), and *The June Lady* (1911). A book about two boys, called *The Quietness of Dick*, written some time earlier, appeared in America in the same year. He also wrote for some years for *Black and White*, and later for the *Bystander*. But his two books of travel, *An Ignorant in India* and *The Fair Dominion*, both published in 1911, and some short stories for *Harper's Magazine* and *Blackwood's Magazine*, were, I think, what he most enjoyed writing, and poetry he always loved to write.

His first war poem, *England to the Sea*, appeared in the *Times* of August 7, 1914. He wrote several more in the next few weeks, and after that he wrote occasionally when he had a little quiet time. After being wounded, and while down in Sheppey, November, 1916, he finished *Before the Assault*, which he had had in his mind for some time and which he mentioned in his letter of March 1, 1916. It was published in the *Observer* of December 17, 1916. Two other poems mentioned in his letters were *The Sergeant*, published in the *Daily Chronicle,* August 31, 1916, and *A Petition*, published in the *Times* of May 5, 1917, a month after his death. These he wrote in the trenches in the summer of 1916 and sent home to me in a manuscript book before he went into action on the Somme. When his kit came back from France after his death, I found two more poems that he had written or finished since he went out in December, 1916, *At Delville* and *A Listening Post*; they are included in the collection of his poems recently published, (as at time of first publication), by Messrs. Heinemann.

His poems brought him appreciation from all parts of the world, and since his death I have had many other kind letters which show his influence was far greater than we knew. I should like especially to mention a letter I have had from Canon H. D. Rawnsley. He wrote saying he had never met my husband, but that he had read his poems with very great pleasure, and had expected great things from him if he had been spared. He also sent a sonnet which appears on another page.

In 1902 we were married, and came to live in Hertfordshire in the depth of the country. He loved the country life and became an enthusiastic gardener. He was also a keen lawn tennis player, and took a great deal of trouble in making a good tennis lawn, besides planning and making the whole garden out of a piece of waste land which was covered with nettles and scrap iron when we took the house, He hated English winters, and we always tried to go away in the winter, instead of in the summer when our garden was at its best. One winter we travelled in Holland, Denmark, Sweden, and Finland. And another winter we spent a month in Switzerland. He enjoyed the sunny cold—or at all events the *sun* part of it,—but decided that on the whole he liked warm climates better. Another winter we spent in Pau, where we played much tennis.

But the winter that he enjoyed most was when we went to India and spent three months with his brother, who was a Collector in Bengal. He revelled in the climate and was much interested in the people. On our return he wrote some articles in *Blackwood's Magazine*, and later published the book already mentioned, *An Ignorant in India*. He was much gratified by the appreciation of this book by Anglo-Indians. Only about two years ago his brother's wife in India met the adjutant of one of the Indian regiments, who, on hearing her name, asked if she was any relation of R. E. Vernède. He went on to say that *An Ignorant in India* was 'a Classic in the Mess,' and they made every newcomer read it.

He went to Canada for a three months' trip in the autumn of 1910, and after his return he wrote *The Fair Dominion*. I was unable to go. This was the only time we were separated during the whole of our married life until the war began, except for a fortnight's walking tour he took in Portugal in May, 1914, about which some articles appeared in the *Bystander*.

When war was declared my husband was four years over age, but after reading *The Call*, which he wrote a few days after war began, I knew he felt that he must go.

He tried to enlist several times, but was refused because of his age; at last, on September 4, he enlisted in the Universities and Public Schools Brigade of the Royal Fusiliers. Even there he was nearly refused because of his age. He was determined to join, but he would not mis-state his age. He gave his age as 39, but they wrote it down as 35 and accepted him.

The brigade—4000—assembled in Hyde Park on September 18. They marched to Victoria Station and went down to Epsom by train.

They were billeted all over the town, and he was lucky enough to get a very pleasant billet, where I was able to join him at the end of November. I was there until the middle of March, 1914, when the men went out of billets into huts in Woodcote Park.

Before enlisting he had been advised by many friends to take a commission, but as he knew nothing of soldiering he would not hear of it. However, after some months of training he had become convinced that he would be more useful as an officer, and applied for a commission. His greatest friend, F. G. Salter—the 'Frdk.' mentioned so often in the letters—had enlisted at the same time. They were at Epsom together, took their commissions in the Rifle Brigade at the same time, and went out to France together. They had been at school together from the age of nine, and were up at Oxford at the same time. It was a bitter disappointment to my husband that he and Frdk. were not attached to the same battalion when they got to France, but when, a few weeks later, the latter was seriously wounded and returned to England unfit for active service my husband felt it a real relief, as he wrote to me, that his life was safe.

He had already had one disappointment on getting his commission. A close friend of Epsom days, J. H. Vaughan, who had applied for a commission at the same time and for the same regiment, had not been gazetted to the Rifle Brigade, but to the Royal Inniskilling Fusiliers.

Robert was gazetted to the 5th battalion The Rifle Brigade on May 14, 1915 (the 13th anniversary of our wedding day). He went down to the Isle of Sheppey a few days later, and was again lucky in getting a pleasant place where he could be billeted, and where I joined him. We were there until November 18, 1915, when he went out to

France.

The letters tell the rest of his military career up to April 9, 1917, and the following letter completes it. It is from Captain Spurling:

Dear Mrs Vernède,
You will before this have had the official notification that your husband died of wounds on the morning of the 9th between the First Aid Station and Dressing Station. It is with the greatest regret that I have to report his death, as we all admired him immensely, and although senior to me both in age and term of service, never for a second made me feel it.

He was in charge of his platoon on our advance and went forward with a Yorkshire officer, who was in charge of the coy. on his right, with his sgt. and cpl. and a couple of his men, and as far as I can gather, came right on top of an enemy machine gun and was very seriously wounded. His men got him back to the Aid Station, but he did not survive the journey on from there.

I did not see him personally after he was hit, but his corporal, who looked after him, said his last words to him were: "Send my love to my wife."

Please accept my sincerest sympathy with you both from myself and his brother officers in your irreparable loss.

Always ready to help and most thoughtful for others, he will indeed be a great loss to us. In my opinion he should have had command of a company long ago, but joined us just after promotions had been made.

His grave is in the French cemetery of Lechelle, and yesterday we put up a new cross, and put stones round the grave and planted out a large bowl of daffodil bulbs which we had flowering in the mess when we were here together some days ago.

Robert was decidedly French in appearance—very dark, with an oval face and the most beautiful smile I have ever seen. His voice was low and soft and peculiarly pleasant; it was in its way a counterpart of the ease which characterised all his physical actions, and I think reflected his mental outlook too. Every child and every animal loved him.

The youthfulness of his appearance was quite extraordinary, and we had many amusing episodes from it. I remember once while on a short walking tour between the Rhine and the Moselle, we arrived at a small village one day and stopped at the inn for lunch. Our host came and sat with us, smoking a long pipe and chatting as we ate. He spoke German, and kept on addressing my husband, who did not know the language well. I explained, saying, '*Mein Mann spricht nicht viel Deutsch.*'

He looked quickly at us both and said in amazement, '*Ihr Herr Gemahl?*'

I said 'yes.'

He looked again and said with true German curiosity, 'Ah, younger than you are.' I said firmly, No, he was older. But his interest was not to be quenched, and he tried to guess the age, beginning at least ten years too young; when he reached the correct age, he was so utterly amazed that he apparently believed it to be true. I think he felt we should never have invented anything so incredible.

While we were in Sheppey one of the subalterns having just found out my husband's age, pointed at him in the mess and said to the rest of the room, 'Guess how old this man is.' Most of them guessed 28 or 29. One man, probably feeling himself very clever, said daringly, '35.' The subaltern's joy at being able to say 40 was great. I mention these incidents as they explain his jokes about his age, and what he meant when he said that he must be 'ageing visibly' because they guessed him as being 32.

He was very quiet and reserved with people he did not know well, though a great talker with people who interested him. His second captain in the batt. in writing to me said:

'We so often in C Coy. were given, usually most unexpectedly, some extraordinarily sound and what must have been well-thought-out ideas with reference to tactical or disciplinary or other army matters.'

'Usually most unexpectedly' exactly describes him. He would sometimes sit, smoking quietly, for nearly half an hour while other people talked, and then suddenly say something which showed that nothing had escaped him. A friend, writing of him, said:

> Two things endure with me. One is that many as his high qualities have been—his writing, his physical grace, his tender heart, his good taste, his good humour, and so forth—what was so distinctive was the congruity of the whole. Everything fitted in so beautifully that it was a delight to be with him in any mood or any surroundings.
>
> The other thing is that silent as he appeared to many, he had

the true gift of conversation as so few have. He would tackle a subject, and keeping the other person with him in a manner so different from the mere sayer of bright things and in a manner so much more tender than the Socratic one, he would stick to it until one had reached down to the essence of the problem and felt on surer ground than one had ever done before.

I will end this short introduction by quoting the note which appeared after his death in the *Pauline*, the magazine of his old school, and which was contributed by his old friend, Mr. G. K. Chesterton:

> The death of Robert Ernest Vernède, who fell fighting as a lieutenant of the Rifle Brigade in the great advance on the Western Front, while so heavy a loss for those of us who loved him, may well be felt by the many more who admired him as something like a gain; an addition or completion to that new and shining company of poets whose patriotism turned them into soldiers, and gave them a life and death more worthy of a legend; those poets who have become poems. He had indeed other strings to his lyre, or labours for his pen; his books of travel and criticism had already revealed his appetite for adventure both material and mental; his novels had embodied romances other than his own.
>
> Tragedy itself cannot eclipse the gaiety of that farce in the grand style, *The Pursuit of My Faviel*, the reading of which was like a holiday, not to say a honeymoon. It was perhaps the one work of our generation which was genuinely full of the April foolery of *The Wrong Box*. But his poetry will necessarily be the note that vibrates longest in the memory, especially for those most affected by his end. In the first days of the war we read that address of *England to the Sea,* lines of which really had what a good critic has called, in another good poet, 'the gesture of magnificence:'
>
> *Say, them, who hast watched through ages that are lengthless,*
> *Whom have I feared, and when did I forget?*

This alertness, even in a literary sense, was typical of his conduct throughout; he was in this also early in the field—as he was in the battlefield. He went to the war of his own will, when past military age; he went to it a second time when he had been wounded and might easily have been excused. On the second venture he was killed.

I write of such things in words altogether weak and unworthy; but it is at least natural to me to be writing them in the *Pauline*, for, though I am proud to think our friendship was never broken, it is as a *Pauline* that I still picture him most vividly. Many personal accidents accentuate the feeling; not least the fact that he always remained, even in face and figure, almost startlingly young. There went with this the paradox of a considerable maturity of mind, even in boyhood; a maturity so tranquil and, as it were, so solitary as to be the very opposite of priggishness. He had a curious intellectual independence; I remember him maintaining, in our little debating club, that Shakespeare was overrated; not in the least impudently or with any foreshadowing of a Shavian pose, but rather like a conscientious student with a piece of Greek of which he could not make sense.

He was too good a man of letters not to have learnt better afterwards; but the thing had a touch of intangible isolation that surprised the gregarious mind of boyhood. He had in everything, even in his very appearance, something that can only be called distinction; something that might be called, in the finer sense, race. This was perhaps the only thing about him, except his name and his critical temper, that suggested something French. I remember his passing a polished and almost Meredithian epigram to me in class: it was, I regret to say, an unfriendly reflection on the French master, and even on the French nation in his person; but I remember thinking, even at the time, that it was rather a French thing to do. There was a certain noble contradiction in his life and death that there was also in his very bearing and bodily habit.

No man could look more lazy and no man was more active, even physically active. He would move as swiftly as a leopard from something like sleep to something too unexpected to be called gymnastics. It was so that he passed from the English country life he loved so much, with its gardening and dreaming, to an ambush and a German gun. In the lines called *Before the Assault*, perhaps the finest of his poems, he showed how clear a vision he carried with him of the meaning of all this agony and the mystery of his own death. No printed controversy or political eloquence could put more logically, let alone more poetically, the higher pacifism which is now resolute to dry up at the fountainhead the bitter waters of the dynastic wars, than the four lines that run:

Then to our children there shall be no handing

Of fates so vain, of passions so abhorr'd
But Peace . . . the Peace which passeth understanding . . .
Not in our time . . . but in their time, O Lord.

The last phrase, which has the force of an epigram, has also the dignity of an epitaph; and its truth will remain.'

C. H. Vernède.

The Paper Mill,
Standon, Herts.
August, 1917.

In Memoriam
Robert Ernest Vernède
Rifle Brigade
Died of wounds in France April 9, 1917.

'Unversed in war,' but not unskilled of pen,
You who heard England calling to the sea,
Who knew the things that keep us great and free,
Who felt Right's cause with Honour amongst men,
Mercy and Truth, had given the heart of ten
To those who fought though death alone was fee,
You who bade all the fallen at rest to be
Seeing the end they fell for was in ken—
Peace and the power to live as no man's slave,
Secure from tyranny of the War-Lord's hell;
Sleep! for the dream you dreamed shall yet be true;
You gave your best to her whose best to you
Was given; your prayer is answered, from your grave
Sounds out 'I died for England, All is well.'

                                  H. D. Rawnsley.

Letters

Folkestone, November 18, 1915.
Somewhere at Folkestone, in the dark, the train having stopped for about an hour and a half. It is now 5.30 p.m. H.[1] and I have eaten a tea of tongue sandwiches and brandy and water. F.[2] and A.[3] are asleep. It is much warmer and drizzling. 8 o'clock just starting for pier!

Somewhere, Friday, November 19.
This is written at 10.30 a.m. in a small *café* where the subaltern draft is drinking coffee and writing after an extremely prolonged crossing. We got across by 10 p.m. Hideous wind blowing crowded boat and lingered on the quay till 1.15 a.m. when we got a train as far as this, which is a base camp among the sand dunes, which we reached about 2.30 (today), finally getting to bed on the ground in tents with some dished-out army blankets at 4.30. It really was very amusing, though, and more 'characteristic' than anything I have struck. Jolly cold and freezing all round. We aren't a bit settled for writing, but I think we are here for a few days anyway, and have, in fact, arranged to mess together at a restaurant at five *fr.* a day. These youths are very pleasant, and if F. and I can get in the same Bn. (with H. and A. perhaps) it will be very well.

Address doubtful, and will probably change before you reply to this.

Saturday, November 20.
(Written on hotel paper headed Grande Place a Etaples, Pas de

---

1 2nd Lieut. R. E. T. Huddart, The Rifle Brigade, killed in action, 30th June, 1916.
2 2nd Lieut. F. G. Salter, The Rifle Brigade. See introduction.
3 2nd Lieut. G. H. G. Anderson, M.C., The Rifle Brigade. (See page 101).

Calais, but erased.)

Still at base camp, not knowing when we move on. We mess together, the nine of us, in the railway buffet, not at all bad, and share two tents, jolly cauld. It freezes at night and thaws slightly by day, but in my valise last night I was pretty warm and F. never slept better. We are near the sea, among the sand dunes and pines, very nice winter country because it's not wet or muddy. This *café* pen makes me write like F. I hope you will be able to read it.

This morning we marched out a couple of miles and threw a bomb or two and marched back again: lecture this afternoon.

This altogether is rather a halfway house sort of place and one feels rather strayed on the passage; and not knowing at what moment one will move on is rather annoying, but it's not without humour. I told you, didn't I, that we had the pleasure of carrying our own valises several times for some distance. We left them under cover eventually at the station on a seat, but when they were brought up by the transport they had been dragged through pools of water. I should have liked to give the transport fifty days C.B.

Till we get to the trenches I can't give you a proper address—and it's no good trying to settle down to write a proper letter because I can't in this slack sort of hustle.

Sunday, November 21.

We haven't been posted yet. Last night was bitly cold; we shaved in our one tin between 5 and 8 a.m. Roll call at 10, after which F., H., A., and I went for a walk to a place called Flecie, where we lunched in the Inn by a nice hot stove, and were swindled into paying four *frcs.* for it by a stout old Frenchwoman without shame. Never in her life, I should say, had she had two *frcs.* before for such a *déjeuner*, and these things are not calculated to make a lasting *entente*.

The village where we lunched was filled with a Canadian ammunition column run by a major from Montreal with whom we chatted. He and his officers were billeted at the *chateau* belonging to Count somebody and seemed very pleased with themselves—nice men.

Still very fit and go about in my fur all day. F. wears nothing and looks like an icicle. Apparently there is no chance of arranging our Bn., so if F. and I get together it will be pure luck. We would like H. and A. as well.

This is written in part of a hut where the men are singing, one small end being reserved for officers, of whom there are now hundreds here—why, nobody knows. The tent is a grisly squash, and I have not washed yet, to speak of. I made tea there about an hour ago in my canteen, which seems to go well. Several Epsomites here.

Monday, November 22.

We have just returned from a lecture on sand-bags, not bad, by a major who this morning took us in battalion drill of pre-Zulu days and then told off most of the officers on parade (all the Rifle Brigade except F.) for not appearing in Sam Brownes. *How to win the War?* We are a rum folk.

The routine at this place seems to remain the same—parade in the morning, lecture in the afternoon. Most of the officers, we were told, were to be posted today, but only a few to the front, which leaves things as vague as ever. Meanwhile we are not given rations and have to feed ourselves at the rate of about nine *francs* a day. However, I was warm last night, in spite of a fairly hard frost, which looks well for the future. We all hope we shall get away from here, as it is pigging it without any necessity. I mean to get a bath tonight if it's possible. The worst of the place is the nowhere to sit and general overcrowding. It's either this (Y.M.C.A. Hut) or a *café*, which latter costs money. Frdk. is reading Henry James on a stiff chair in a very bad light. I am going to find a bath.

November 23.

It's begun to be misty moisty (5.30 p.m.) and we have just heard that —— and —— are posted to another Bn. and go off at 3.30 a.m. tomorrow morning, and the rest of us are likely to go at much the same time elsewhere. That, however, may be the usual rumour, and I will keep this till the last mo. and then write on envelope or somewhere probable address, and you must write quick to me.

I am much afraid that F. and I won't get together, but you never know.

24. Am appointed and go off tonight. Of course F. and H. are in the 2nd. Never mind.

November 24.

We had such a night officers being shouted for and going off at all hours; rain at intervals coming into the tent; F. and H. departing at 2.30 a.m., ourselves at 5.30, as far as the railway siding, when it was discovered gradually that the train would not be in till 8 o'clock. So we went off and routed till we roused a *café* there to give us breakfast. Since then we have travelled through various places for about six hours, finally being turned out here to change trains at 4 p.m. We have therefore had lunch and shaved in the kitchen of the Café Vasseur—quite a friendly Inn, where I write. We don't in the least know whether we shall arrive at the Bn. and the trenches tonight or not.

Just off to train—must finish later.

9 p.m. Have arrived been posted to C Coy. and had dinner. But first of all I've got what you will think good news, I expect, which is that the Bn. is out of the trenches altogether for a month, taking a rest, so that for that period you need not worry yourself one little bit. Personally, I think I shall find resting in the army out here rather a nuisance.

There are about seven officers to the Coy., and we are billetted together in a farmhouse, moderately dirty, in a village which I have not seen yet as we only walked in in the dark; but there is much mud.

25. We changed our billets this morning and are now in a village four miles away from the other—four in a room in a picturesque enough farmhouse, with its pond and farmyard in the middle, the house and outbuildings built round it in a quadrangle. The men are in the out buildings, in straw, not at all uncomfortable, I should say. We sleep on the floor in empty rooms. I would rather have gone into the trenches, as here, again, one has the outsider's feeling, the others having all done it except oneself.

Still November 25.

There is nothing doing today, and one of us is 'in billets' while the rest are out, and that happens to be me, so I may as well chat, though I don't think there is much to tell here. Apparently the time here is going to be very much the same as at Minster, and except that I have to censor my platoon (No I2's) letters, I don't expect to find it very amusing. Making a whole circle of entirely new acquaintances at this time does not add to the amenities of war, and not having got with F. still annoys. I expect I shall grouse for some little time but you must not mind that.

I haven't seen the village yet, but they say there is not a shop in it even to buy matches at. Luckily I got a rather poor pipe lighter in Etaples, with which practice will no doubt make perfect. The mess food in the middle of these excellent French housewives is cooked apparently by army cooks—and resembles it. (Grouse.)

I might possibly get time, but doubt it, to finish off some poems.

26. Very cheery today—nice and bright. People not bad. Send me some socks and a good towel when you can.

November 28, 1915.

The time passes in a manner neither pleasant nor unpleasant, but simply of no particular interest to me, I suppose because one has no personal control of things, which never did suit me. It is freezing pretty hard, and I should think there would be skating if such things were to be done. Instead we spend our days (except Sunday, today, when there is nothing doing) as follows:—

6.30 a.m. Rise. (Horrible.)
7.30. Breakfast. (Porridge and bacon and eggs dryly cooked.)
8.30-9.30. Squad drill with the sergeant-major.
10-10.45. Parade with our platoons for musketry practice.
11-12. Sergeant-major again.
12.30. Lunch.

After lunch we are supposed to supervise our platoons at some form of exercise, such as cross country running, football, etc.

Football, if you please, is compulsory for the officers, so yesterday you might have seen me playing sokker for the first time in my life at the age of 40 with men who really play it quite well, and me not even knowing the rules. It's very absurd: however, being fairly nimble I don't think I made so considerable a fool of myself as I might have done, and anyhow, the day before I found I could easily outrun most, if not all, of my platoon, with the possible exception of the platoon sergeant—a nice man and a great athlete. Most of the elderly men (of over 34!) simply give up and have to be coerced.

I suppose I am imagined to be about 28, and I think I shall not reveal the truth this time, as I don't fancy elderly subalterns are much appreciated.

I imagine this bn. represents typical Regular Army, as far as you can get it now, and is, so far, more interesting than what one has seen, but I do think the whole thing is too undemocratic, and distinctions of rank demoralise human relations. I do hope Frdk. is not too much revolted by it and hasn't been forced to play sokker. I expect, however, that he is in the trenches, and I wish this bn. had been.

This is all very stodgy, but that's what I become, you know, when I've got up too early in the morning and my soul isn't my own, so to speak.

November 30.

The tiresome thing is that if you sit near the fire here you can't see to write; and if you sit away from it, you are frozen. Not that there is any news. I'm very much afraid that I shan't get any verses done. If I had the proper concentration, I might, but there are seven people strewed about the room at most times, one lamp (without a shade) and N.C.O.'s popping in at intervals.

The men are all very grousy about their rest, and certainly I have not run about more since joining the army—all the morning from 8.30 and a football match or run in the afternoon. I joined the riding school party this afternoon and gallopped about quite happily barebacked. Half of them can't ride at all.

I think for a youth this would all be great fun—though you mustn't think I'm having at all a bad time.

December 1.

I have just got my first letters from you. I can't answer them properly tonight. Everything is going on all right. These people are very pleasant and I dare say I shall even find some real friends.

December 3.

The deerskin waistcoat from L.[4] has arrived and is fearfully nice. I put it on and then ran two miles, without stopping, with my platoon with that and the other one on—so got very hot.

4. Miss Lily Player, a cousin.

I have written to L.

I have just re-read your letters in my valise after a hot bath following the run. That sounds luxurious, doesn't it?

Don't bother to send papers. We get them regularly in the mess only a day late, and none too much time to read them.

I hear another bn. has also come out of the trenches for a rest, so Frdk. is out of it too. We are pretty sure to be here for another fortnight at least.

I am just beginning to know my platoon. Have two very good sergeants. One of them beat me by a little in the two mile run today, but I had too many clothes on, and two miles is too short anyhow.

Yesterday we took the coy. for a route march to a town seven miles off, where they could buy cigarettes and things it's a great grievance that they can't get anything here. A lovely day. On the way back one of the other subalterns and I stopped at another village where we had to attend a lecture on gas attacks, so lunched there before the lecture—excellent lunch of five courses (at 2.30 p.m., after hours) served in about five minutes of our arrival. The French are good at that sort of thing. Then the lecture, which I retailed to my platoon this morning.

Very muggy and rainy today.

1. Gave gas lecture.
2. Listened to musketry lecture.
3. Lecture on treatment of frost-bite.
4. Two miles run with platoon.

All very practical, I think, but rather too much of it.

What shall I give to my platoon at Christmas? I think they have rather a thin time of extras and accommodation; though well-fed otherwise. Officers ought to fare like the men, I do believe, in spite of the arguments against it. Here they hardly can wash, for instance; or do anything in comfort.

This is our billet—

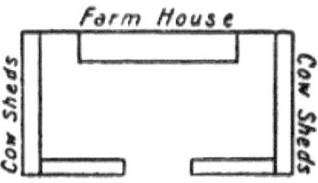

We are in the farmhouse—men all round in barns and cowhouses—the centre a lively, noisy manury farmyard with a pond in it and every variety of turkey, goose, duck, hen, pig, cow, horse, and dog gobbling round. It is quite picturesque. The farmer very fat. I find myself quite fluent with my French, except occasionally.

December 5.

I don't seem able to get at the poems. Today being Sunday, I thought I would, but have been hoicked out for revolver practice, making lists of drafts of men, and watching a football match, which C Coy., which is the best in the Bn., won easily. I haven't yet had much to do with my platoon, owing to these other parades, but shall try to chat with the men, whom I'm only beginning to know by name.

I enclose Frdk's letter, from which you will see that he seems contented with his lot, which I'm glad of.

This is only a scrap late at night. Another route-march tomorrow, and, I believe, an inspection by French the next day.

December 9.

It has been disgustingly wet today and we spent it mostly in a barn much worse than ours, giving short lectures to the men on all sorts of things. I didn't give any, being in charge, but put on platoon sergeants, who start with great zeal and suddenly stop at the end of two minutes, having exhausted all their eloquence. I think practice in smoke helmets is what the men hate most; the things make you feel choked and sick for some minutes from the chemicals inside, and they would probably all much prefer to be gassed some weeks hence to wearing them now.

I sleep most comfortably in my valise. Would it interest you to know that it's rather the thing when one comes in at the end of the day to change into gum boots, which, with woolly soles inside, are most comfortable as evening dress? I'm in them now.

Yesterday at a football match a little man—a Rifleman—whom I didn't know from Adam, came up and told me he had been in the digging party at Warden with me, and has been out three months: we discussed old acquaintances, and he was most friendly, though I don't know his name now. I'm very bad at names.

It is far more interesting here than at Epsom or Minster. With these people and methods the work gets done, and it is, for the time being, quite reasonably hard work and not too stupid.

Now I must close, hoping this finds you in the pink, as it leaves me. Have I told you that expression, which occurs in two out of three letters from the men?

December 12.

Your letters nearly always come in exactly at teatime, which is right, as one can set and read them at once.

The last two days have been slopping. We fell in at 8.45 for a route march and inspection by General Plumer, and before we started were dripped by a regular thunderstorm. Then we meandered about for three hours before finding the general by the side of the road, where we splashed past him, my job consisting in giving 'Eyes left' at the critical moment, which I did without being prostrated with fright. But these smart inspections seem out of place in the middle of war. I think the whole Brigade marched past, if not the whole division. In the afternoon watched a football match in several hailstorms. The R.B.'s ended by winning the divisional final, having beaten Londons, Buffs, and Royal Fusiliers easily. We are going to have a cross country run on Tuesday, and I'm afraid my platoon will not win, as it has rather a tail in the running line.

Today being the Sabbath Day, I'm doing nothing, and don't propose to. Fine and cold.

I continue to like my sergeants, but find it rather a bore and very absurd to have to lecture on subjects of which I know nothing and have no practical experience.

December 13.

Today we had a company inter-divisional match which again C Coy. won, and a shooting match for snipers, which the R.B.s won, so the regiment does very well. This afternoon I made my whole platoon run a race round the two mile course, and came in second myself (14 minutes; the first man, Cpl. P., taking 13½)—not so bad for the oldest gentleman present, as it is very hilly. The whole platoon got in under 19 minutes, which beats the time done by other platoons, at present. How we become sporting! I shall soon be an authority on sokker snips.

Yesterday afternoon I got M. and I. on to the range and let off a rifle (for the first time) and didn't do so badly, happening to hit the target before either of them. Rifles are less alarming than I imagined, and at any rate I now know how to load them and what a safety catch does—useful knowledge in war-time.

Tomorrow I lead forty shivering reinforcements to be gassed at some village near—it's rather a sensible idea for accustoming recruits to the thing, but I trust it will not make us all sick. The helmets themselves smell like one o'clock. This is just a short note—more perhaps after being gassed tomorrow.

December 14.

I was successfully gassed with my forty men. The gas helmets are a little smelly, but you don't notice the gas to speak of, though it was whizzing out of the cylinder as we passed down the trench. True, we were only about two minutes in it, and I doubt if it was all proper gas, though it smelt beastly later on when I got into some far-borne fumes after the show was over. The worst of it was that it fixed itself on my clothes and now I smell like an operating room full of ether.

This afternoon I went for a walk with T.[5] He is a very good sort. He is said to be very cool and gallant in the trenches.

Our weather is distinctly better, frosty at night and quite bright by day. I sleep directly at the foot of a window with the panes nearly all broken, and in direct line with the door, so I ought to be getting very much hardened.

December 17.

By latest arrangements we are to be here for Christmas and three or four days after, so I don't suppose the trenches will be reached till 1916 at earliest.

It's rather quaint in this army how one is surrounded by inglorious heroes. One of the most troublesome men has a Russian medal for gallantry, and I heard yesterday that another who bags one's cigarettes and things ought to have had the V.C.

December 19.

Two letters from you since my last and sweets from Richoux the best chocolates I've tasted from anywhere for ages.

I've just been appointed Mess President; I'm going to try and amend it by slow degrees.

I might have become Coy. Bombing Officer, if I had been keen.

---

5. Captain Geoffrey B. Tatham, The Rifle Brigade.

M. had been appointed and didn't want the job; and I offered to take it but without much keenness, as it means going off on a course and having to learn the whole job in a week, which I detest; also leaving my platoon just when I'm beginning to know it. Otherwise I wouldn't have minded—I don't think there's any real choice of risks, and the fact is I don't think I am very brilliantly quick at learning any of these quasi-engineering feats.

I still greatly think the war will go well, and everybody out here is very cheerful.

December 21.

Not very much time before post goes, and the reason is that I have become O.C. of C Coy. as well as Mess President for at least eight days, as T. has gone on leave and I am the senior subaltern. Consequently you might have seen me on a horse this morning leading the coy. on a batt. route march, and I have work and interruptions by the hundred—most of it, of course, absolutely novel. I haven't the foggiest idea as to whether I have the unfortunate Riflemen (who appear before me on charges) shot or admonished, and in vain, while in England, I tried to get someone to tell me. However, I ought to learn something in the course of it and cannot do much harm, I imagine, in a rest camp; and if I get strafed, it really doesn't matter. Not my fault if I know nothing about it. Don't worry if I'm short in letters, I really shall be rather busy.

December 23.

Just another line and a half in great haste. I really am rather rushed, for in addition to the ordinary things an O.C. has to do, I have the Christmas dinner to arrange for, and the point is that we must have 200 plates, tables, and dishes for 200, and, if possible, a piano. All these things ought to have been arranged for weeks ago to make sure of them, and were supposed to be, and now not two days at most to go, they are none of them forthcoming; and I send out parties in all directions to beg, borrow, or steal them in a place the size of Puckeridge or smaller.

Also I had to send off I. to inspect the trenches we go into in the New Year—for two days—and a servant who almost declined to go, as it's not much fun being in the mire and shot at for two days just before Christmas merely as a fatigue. Otherwise we are going all right—no thanks to me, as the thing runs very smoothly, and provided I assume an air which is unjustified, they seem to imagine that somebody really is in command.

Spent half an hour last night in vain trying to persuade the farmer and farmeress to lend us their crockery for the men—but not they. If I were fluent enough to be daring in French it might possibly have been done; but they are not very generous, I fancy.

Just as I had finished your Richoux sweets some more of them came from O. H. [6]—much to the pleasure of the mess, which likes them.

I suppose I shall revert to subaltern and the ordinary course next week meanwhile you won't mind short letters, will you?

Christmas Day is going to consist of a vast dinner for the men—ducks and pork and plum puddings, and oranges and beer, followed by a concert, all in a barn.

The R.B.s have won every competition in the division and so are highly pleased with themselves.

December 24.

This is the third day I have had no letter from you, but I know it's not just that you haven't written, because nobody else has had any letters either.

C. has at last got into the nearest town this afternoon, where he is going to buy Chinese lanterns, candles, and those sort of etcs. I sent the coy. out this morning by platoons to pick holly, and they seem to have depleted the countryside pretty well. Tables are still a difficulty, and I have commissioned a sergeant and a French-speaking corporal to call on the *curé* and see if he can raise any by his authority.

There was to have been a field day today in which I should have had to lead the coy. in some intricate attack, but luckily it poured and the thing was put off. Not but what I believe it's quite easy to give orders on these occasions, provided the men are skilled in carrying them out.

Yesterday I rode over to a lecture at —— on the trenches we are to occupy. The lecturer was some colonel I believe his name was H. If so, he was a youth Frdk. and I were at school with, but I didn't recognise him and the room was too crowded to

---

6. Oscar Hilton, M.D., of Northwood, an old school and Oxford friend.

get close. Heavy rain going back and the animals galloped most of the way.

There are various changes being made in the batt. T. will be in command of C Coy. instead of second in command, etc., etc. This all sounds very military, doesn't it? and other people are mostly desperately keen on their positions. I fear I am too old to have any military ambition; at the same time, it is decidedly more interesting to command than to be commanded—so perhaps I had better aim at being a brigadier, say.

Boxing Day, 1915.

After three days of no letters I got five from you on Christmas Day—about 6 p.m.—and one from my mother, and one from yours.

I hope you saw V. [7]—he seems to have been in luck about Christmas. I've forgotten his batt. and address, so can't write (I suppose I could, but I haven't). I hope nobody will try to make me learn signalling.

I feel we don't need a confession of sins at present so much as of our stupidities. Perhaps that comes from seeing all these patient and gallant youths about, so cheery in what they all know is for them a daily risk of their lives.

By the way, the chocolates from L. have arrived. Richoux pack beautifully, and they are the best possible chocolates.

Now, about Christmas here, which was fairly amusing and will be more so to look back upon, I expect.

We sent C. into the town, and he brought out on a mess-cart chocolates and crackers and plates and cigarettes, which made a very fine show. The C.Q.M.S. is quite a brilliant decorator, and turned out the barn in great style with masses of greenery, and the lamps hung in festoons with Chinese lanterns between.

There were Services in the morning and a football match at 12—won by 11 platoon of C Coy.—and dinner began at 2. The C.O. came round and made a speech, and we gave him port, and all drank to the health of the Coy., and then they set to on pork and geese and plum puddings, and kept it up with a concert till a late hour. Our own dinner didn't arrive till 4 p.m., after much strafing of the servants.

At 7 the C Coy. officers had to go round to the sergeant's mess,

---

7. Lieut. J. H. Vaughan, M.C., Royal Inniskilling Fusiliers. See Introduction.

and I had to make a speech and drink half a tumbler of whisky, followed by champagne. They were all cheery. Then we supped off a magnificent pie sent out by T. from the Trinity cook, and at 11 p.m. the farmeress came and besought me to turn the servant's party out of the kitchen where they were making a frightful row. I routed them out and they sang songs under our windows, and finally retired. Heaven knows how many men turned up at the correct hour at their billets, but I believe drunks and absents are overlooked on Christmas Day. All sorts of officers trotted in at intervals, and on Christmas Eve we all went round to each other's houses and wished each other well.

I don't fancy a certain amount of drinking can be helped, and they don't do much in the ordinary way. I retired to bed at 11.30 and didn't get up till 9 this morning, so had a pretty good sleep.

We haven't heard definitely when we move. I will write as soon as I can again.

December 28.

This will be a sleepy letter, as the Field Day came off today, and I spent from 8.30-4.30 leading C Coy. to the attack, and sending orderlies and signallers, and sergeants and subalterns flying in all directions except (probably) the right one. I don't think we did any worse than the other coys., however; and these sort of attacks always seem a gorgeous mix-up; and on the whole I thought it as easy to be an O.C. as a Rifleman. Now T. has returned from leave and I revert to 2nd in command, without, I think, having given myself away too much, and having had some useful practice.

Got a letter from you on my return, and had a hot bath and shall go to bed in a few minutes. Yesterday we had an alarm that we were to be inspected by Haig (C.-in-C.) but it didn't come off.

There is still nothing fixed about our move, and even our destination is altered by rumour daily. Sleepy I am.

December 29.

Just a line afore I go to bed—to tell you that we don't seem to be moving for some days. Inspection by G.O.C. tomorrow.

December 31.

I don't think there is much news—still none of our departure or of our destination.

I have just been strafing my servant, who is also the chef, over his cookery, with result that we are getting superb meals as a mess, and he is looking after me individually much better too. He said nobody had criticised his cookery before, and he had cooked for seven years for the Guard's mess. I said I had no doubt that he was a *cordon bleu*, but some evidence of it must be forthcoming.

Still the Village. January 3, 1916.

I came back from a long route march through much mud, followed by a long lecture on some new trenches, to find a letter. Of course we are bound to be in the trenches pretty soon now, but that's what we came for; and I believe the R.B.s are expected to hold the least choice ones as a rule. Even so, the risks are not much more or less, I suppose.

Did I tell you we were dealt out steel helmets a week ago to wear in the trenches—frightfully heavy but supposed to be good against shrapnel.

January 5.

This is a beautiful morning and I hope is going to be fine for our move. The prospect of going into the trenches is still rather unreal and dreamlike, but I suppose one will know about it at no very distant date. I wish I had finished some more poems. Perhaps when one gets into rest billets behind the lines there will be rather more time. I don't know. There are many things to learn and one has to be as wide awake as possible, and writing pomes makes one rather absent-minded. Rather a sad accident has happened in my platoon—one of the best riflemen in it, an old soldier (as soldiers go now) went for an escapade at night with another man, and in the dark they both fell over a chalk pit and my man was killed, while the other broke his shoulder. I used to have him out to show the recruits how to handle a rifle, and I should think he was worth any two at rapid fire.

There's not much news. We've been routing about quite energetically and I think the men must be pretty fit. I am.

January 6, 1916. Another place in France.

I got two letters before moving. I was rejoiced to hear that you were in the pink as this leaves me at present, seated on my valise on the muddy floor of a small hut at which we arrived at 6 a.m.

this morning, having started at 7 p.m. the night before. It's not the trenches yet, but may be when you get this.

The start from the rest billet was rather picturesque. A dark starry night, the batt. in fours on the muddy road, singing and shouting goodbyes to the villagers, captains on horses, and pack animals jogging behind down the endless French avenues. We entrained about seven miles away sat—rather thick in a beestje carriage, where I fell asleep about six times and was joggled awake by the sudden way they brake the French trains when they are going at top speed. The men on trucks on the floor, which I fancy was quite as comfortable as the seats we were on. Then dismounted at a place that has been shelled and still is at intervals, tramped through heaps of filthy streets, very dark and muddy, but the sky between all quivering with light from the Very lights on the not very distant Front.

Not much noise of guns, which seems to go on mostly by day. The effect was (when we got into the open country) of the fireworks at Henley seen across a flat land like the Sheppey marshes. Constant passing of horses and waggons and troops on the road; but only an hour before we got to this place of liquid mud, where we slept on the floor (after some cocoa) until about 11 a.m., when we had breakfast. I was very glad of my fur lining as our valises did not arrive until after breakfast, and we slept as we were. I slept very soundly myself and wasn't really cold, or if I was I didn't know it.

Apparently we shall continue to mess in the trenches, which are said to be fairly dry. Those we were to have gone into were waist-deep in parts and so isolated that in the fire trench we should have had to get meals when we could by ourselves. So that is an improvement.

It's quite an animated scene outside—mule carts and horse carts and men on horses and mules all splashing about in the mud under a very sodden sky, which looks as if it were going to rain buckets shortly.

I was going into the nearest town for the afternoon with T., but the order allowing officers off has been cancelled, so I'm staying here instead, a-scribbling to you.

It's absurd the amount of things one carries on the march. I had a pack and two haversacks, glasses, revolver, smoke helmet, and goggles (you're supposed to carry two) and map case all strung about me; and a steel helmet ought also to have been slung to the pack, but ours went by mess-cart. I walked in my long boots and changed into my rubber boots.

Getting dark and tea beginning to arrive.

Dans Les Tranchées. January 9, 1916. (Sunday.)
I got two letters from you last night, so that the trenches are not so bad as they might be. I marched the coy. up to the trenches with L, as T. went up earlier in the day to prospect. Very interesting—along a dull, ugly road that is already historic, I suppose, through towns that have become famous through being reduced to dust. In one of these all of us were dealt out gum-boots, thigh-high and wet through, which is what happens in the army when the object is that you shall have dry feet, but I fancy there is the excuse that there aren't enough of them, and one batt. has to get straight into those left behind by the batt. that has gone out. By this time it was dark and safe to march through the shelled area, which we did, wading through pools of mud and water, and holes eminently calculated to sprain your ankle. The coy. ahead had one man shot through the leg by a stray bullet, but we had (and have) no casualties so far. Since arriving about 7 o'clock p.m. on the 7th I have had about six hours' sleep in 48 hours not enough. Some of the men have had less, I fancy, and that in mud holes: unavoidable.

The difference from what one expected in the trenches is that these are so filthy and dilapidated- looking; not regular trenches and nicely arranged barbed wire as in Sheppey, but crumbled up barricades in the middle of what looks like an earthquake combined with a snowslide, with ancient rusty scraps of wire hanging in festoons here and there, but pretty effective nevertheless. Everything gets blown up at intervals and inextricably mixed, clothes and tins and dugouts and every mortal thing you can imagine. Otherwise they are roomier than anything at Sheppey. Since arriving I've seen almost all the things one reads of—aeroplanes being shelled in every direction, rifle fire, and crater mines being blown up and all the rest of it, except an attack or heavy shelling of our lines, I'm glad to say.

The first night and day were fairly peaceful—though our R.E. (a Canadian) wrecked the German mines late in the evening, and the earth shook, and we all stood to in case a crater was formed and had to be occupied. But it wasn't.

Today, being Sunday, opened rather more characteristically, I suppose. Having retired to bed at 2 a.m. in a sort of little dugout, 2 ft. 6 high—room for one with one's legs sticking out a trifle—I was hauled out at 5 a.m. because the wind had changed and a gas attack was possible. We stood about in gusts of rain till 7 a.m. when I again retired to bed and was wakened by the Boches sending over rifle grenades, nasty buzzing things that make a noise like an enormous hornet, and I found I. just outside, ducking because he expected one on his head. They sent over twenty (you can see them coming and dodge if you have room) but did no damage, and I had breakfast and went on duty from 10 a.m.-2 p.m. During this you trot round and chat with the sentries and take an occasional glimpse in a safe direction and listen to the patter of bullets and find out if anybody has heard or noticed anything, and so on.

Meanwhile our artillery started shelling the Boche; their F.O.O. coming into our front line to get the range, and they began to shell back. This went on for some time, at the end of which I went to see if the platoon was rubbing in anti-frost bite, whereupon a biggish shell fell about 15 yds. away and I had to retire into a very safe place we have, with *one shoe off and one shoe on*, so to speak.

Then back to lunch, and now I'm off, and writing to you, but still exceedingly sleepy; while guns go on overhead, but not much at hand.

The men seem wonderfully cheerful and good-natured about everything; but, of course, childishly foolish in some ways. They will fish water out of some filthy puddle, throw away their socks and do anything the fancy takes them that is reckless.

The mud is difficult to exaggerate. I am crusted with it already, and have a large rent in the seat of my breeks, and haven't washed. Otherwise, I don't think they're as bad as I expected, though there are faint sickly smells and things that take some getting used to. It is extremely interesting in many ways, and I suppose when one becomes experienced one may be some use. I believe T. is extremely good—very cool and conscientious and forethoughtful, and I doubt if we could have a better captain.

It's quaint dodging by oneself at night round dangerous corners and chatting with sentries you don't know and can't see about nothing in particular. Last night three cats were playing about in front of our parapet in the moonlight.

By the time you get this we shall probably be out again in reserve and luxury; so picture it all over for the time being when you get it. I haven't been unpleasantly cold yet and am in the pink.

Our cook-house, which is also the servants' dugout, is opposite our 9 x 3 mess-room dugout; and there you see either five servants snoring or the chef sitting over a brazier taking things out of his pockets and dropping them into the saucepan for our consumption. He sent up some tea which smelt so violently of dead cats that we couldn't touch it in spite of being very thirsty. Water (pure) is a difficulty.

Don't worry if letters are delayed. They are erratic, and I may at times be too desperately sleepy to hold a pencil. Explain this to my mother. I'll try and write more when we get into reserve.

I think I'll try and get a mug of water to wash in and shave now.

January 10, 1916.

Just a line to say that I'm safe and well. Also I had six hours' sleep last night, which is a great improvement, and I shall even do some more this afternoon. Nothing happened later yesterday, and today has been pretty quiet, and I've been watching German working parties in the distance, and an unknown piece of railway. There must have been something on early today, for about 7 a.m. a terrific row on our flank waked me and I believe went on for an hour, but I was far too sleepy to take any interest in it. It's a beautiful day. More sleep—so I must come to an end. My chief hours are 9.30 p.m.-1.30 a.m. and 9.30 a.m.-1.30 p.m. The night part is rather long and dull, though one has some interesting talks.

January 11 or 12 (?)

Just a line to say that we go out tonight into reserve, which is a perfectly safe place. A certain amount of strafing on both sides going on. I would write more but am overcome with sleep again, having had little last night owing to giving my bed to an officer who came in yesterday. It was too jolly cold to sleep elsewhere. Having a fairly interesting time. Too sleepy for words.

January 12.

Here we are in the ruins of a very historic town in some shell-proof cellars, where I even had a sort of bed last night—and the time to lie on it. In fact I had 9-10 hours' sleep, and having had practically none the night before (when I was also frozen stiff) I feel distinctly the better for it, and ready to write quite a long letter. I hope I didn't give too bad an impression in my first letter. It's no use pretending they are pleasant, as many people probably console themselves with thinking. It isn't the filth or the wet or want of sleep or general discomfort or chance of getting a bullet if you walk unwarily, that is unpleasant; it is the shells and shells only, and when they say it is a gunner's war, they mean the gunners have all the fun and the infantry all the horrors. There they are, somewhere miles behind, and they open fire—when it suits them, more or less—on the infantry trenches where, it may be for hours at a time, you squat, not knowing if the next one is coming on top of you or not.

There are various noises, of course, which I expect you have seen described: Those I like least so far are—1, a sound as of the loudest thunderclap you have ever heard going off in your ears; 2, a noise as of the whole of Harrod's Stores falling in with a sudden crash. I don't think it's just my finnickiness or the novelty of it that makes them alarming: in fact, some people say that the more you've had of them the less you like them. I was standing yesterday morning next to a Buff officer who has been buried by a shell and been out since the beginning, and I don't think he liked the shelling that was going on any more than I did. But no doubt some men are better suited for the sort of strain it must be than others. We are said to have had a very light time—only three casualties in the coy.—and we are out now for some time.

I rather think that one can acquire some sort of philosophy about shells in course of time the fact is that it's no good expecting them to hit you. They probably won't, and if they do one knows nothing of it.

The advantage of being an officer is that you haven't very much time to think about yourself whether you want to or not.

Without artillery the trenches would seem quite peaceful and pleasant, and it is pleasant to see the old hands going on cooking their dinners stolidly with the shells crashing round, though they can't like them. The recruits seem to have taken their first experiences very well. But then the older N.C.O.s can be very useful in consoling them, and this, I should say, makes for the greater value of the regular battalions as compared with the others.

T. is exceedingly good in the trenches. He barely slept at all and didn't particularly seem to need it—that's the thing I shall find it particularly difficult to live up to. I never did like the earliest dawn!

January 12. (To his mother.)

Am at present, and for some time to come, behind the firing line in shell-proof cellars, which one subaltern says he would like to live in for the rest of his life—after seeing the trenches. Truly, nobody need think the trenches (at any rate the worse ones) anything but disgusting; but there is a great deal of fascination in them, and the men are extraordinarily interesting and good-humoured, and cook under fire; and they get on the whole a worse time than the officers in the ordinary way of accommodation. Our new ones have the advantage of old hands present to back them up, and the disadvantage of having more dangerous trenches to occupy.

It's all very odd and rather exciting—when on duty at night one goes about alone for hours up and down deserted trenches with sounds of firing in all directions and the Boches within listening distance, and flares going up at intervals through mud nearly knee-deep, slipping and sliding in every direction in the dark and not quite certain at first whether one is trotting straight into the German trenches or not. The landscape is exceedingly desolate ruins—and shell holes wherever you look—and the only cheerful thing is the sun when it appears, and the men, whose cheeriness is unending.

Still the Cellars. January 13.

I am sitting in the mess room cellar, which is about 6 x 10 ft. and holds the officers of two coys. The space is sardiny and the cold icy. The difficulty about writing is that there are so many details and so little time to describe them. Last night, for instance, I sat here with the others and we had the brigade machine gun officer in discussing the position of the guns, and the C.O. and the adjutant discussing the trenches, and all the officers of A Coy (B. included) chatting and laughing, and I got to bed at 11.30, and had a good sleep till 9.

Today I inspected my platoon and then wandered about a ruined place and picked some *daphne mezereum* and rosemary. Tonight at 10 p.m. I take a working party up to the trenches and return about 1 or 2 a.m.

—— told me as we left the trenches that he would give anything to be back in Sheppey, and he was one of the youths who was wild to get out. They certainly don't leave many illusions of the Romance of War—the more credit to the people who have stuck it a year or more.

14. Got back safe and sound at about 12 midnight. There was a high and furious wind blowing most of the time—very cold—also the chance of being machine-gunned, so the men worked like buffaloes and we got through in no time.

Today has been slack and luxurious, sitting over a charcoal brazier in the cellars, eating and dozing. Now we are bound for our rest camp.

Still the Rest Camp. January 17, 1916.

I seem to get your letters very regularly, if I don't get one one day, I get two the next.

The camp is rather dull and cool, but one gets plenty of sleep, which is a good thing.

Yesterday I did practically nothing but censor letters and inspect the platoon and have a small greasy warm bath. Today there may be a digging party, but I doubt it.

January 20.

I wrote a small scrap yesterday and must try to make up this time.

2 hours later. Have been rather hustled after all, inspecting platoon, censoring letters (some of them write a dreadful lot and in any case thirty letters take some time to read through), also writing crime sheets.

Our shed in which we live is, is as T. said the other day, the sort of place where you might possibly put your garden roller in peace time, and now, by an irony of fate, we have been given a small stove for it, but no fuel, and when we go out and hunt small damp chips of wood, they smoke us out.

I know my letters aren't very consecutive, but that's mostly an attempt to be too conscientious. If I told you we walked two hours from the trenches to here I suppose it would be giving some sort of information, though very little.

Since writing I have taken one working party up to the trenches again from 3 p.m.-12 midnight. We went miles and miles in artillery waggons—perfectly open springless carts (holding twelve men)—which, when the horses gallop, reminded me of being on the elephant in pursuit of the leopard. Your spine just gets bumped to bits. The work is rendered less dull than it might be by the fact that the Boches turn machine guns on you at intervals, when you have to lie in the mud. I'm glad to say we had no casualties, though the regt. next had eight the same night.

Coming back I produced a tin of Edinburgh rock; after passing it round my cart we tried to pass it to the one in the rear. It was rather like holding a carrot in front of a donkey's nose. The outrider of the four horses couldn't quite get up, and galloped and galloped his team till he eventually did. Nasty misty moisty night it was.

January 22, 1916.

I'm so sorry about Frdk., and I fear he will feel it being knocked out so soon. I hope it won't prove dangerous and that he'll get well slowly.

The Rifle Brigade seems to have been rather strafed lately. We have had four officer casualties—none in C Coy. A Coy. had a bad time on a digging party the night before last. Hullo, must leave for post.

Rest Camp. January 22.

Partly owing to playing bridge the last few nights, which I can't very well refuse, there being just four of us at present, and partly because the post has taken to going off earlier in the morning, I've rather scrabbed my letters to you, and they have been short if frequent. Now I may as well begin a longer one, though there's not much news. I. and I started on a peaceful country walk this afternoon and had to turn back because the beastly Boches started shelling the road just ahead of us, which was rather unusual cheek at this distance from the firing line. The day before we walked in to ——, a town which is fairly complete for these parts, to do some shopping.

The country is exceedingly flat, prim, dull, and miry—camps everywhere, and the roads, which would ordinarily, I suppose, be as deserted as the Ware to Puckeridge road is, almost as crowded as Oxford Street with artillery waggons and limbers, mule-carts, motor-lorries and omnibuses, despatch riders and troops all bustling along through the never-ending mud. You get splashed from head to foot *en route*, if you walk, but we managed to get lifts both ways (six miles) from motor vans which joggle you along in the dark at a great pace. The town itself is mostly turned into small shops selling tinned fruit to Tommies, and other rubbish; but we had chocolate at quite a decent confectioner's, which has been there evidently from the start, and got back for dinner.

Sunday Morning. I'm camp orderly officer today and have just been the rounds of our camp. There was a frost in the night, and today the sun is shining brightly through a slight mist; and I am sitting by the stove in our hut (we've got some fuel for once).

January 25.

We're still here till the end of the week anyway, and I'm afraid we're going to do things like coy. and batt. drill to improve our discipline, when lots of real work yells to be done. The men haven't all had a bath yet since before going into the trenches—and I'm pretty scratchy myself after two hot baths.

Yesterday I went to a village hard by, and sat in a tub under a hot water *douche* for about three-quarters of an hour. It was very pleasant. We then had tea—buttered buns at a hut rejoicing in the name of the Officers' Club—not bad—if the buns had been hot, but they weren't!

I hope Frdk. is going well. I haven't heard from him yet, and imagine it is a good deal worse than he makes out. Personally, I would rather he didn't come out again, being too good.

It frosts by night and gets nice and bright about 10 o'clock. Much nicer than damp mug.

Thursday, January 27.

There is not much news. We are doing stupid things like battalion drill and so forth. Yesterday I marched the men eight miles to a bath and back—their first since they started from the rest village. They also got their first clean shirt. Today we had a feint alarm at 4.30 a.m., and tumbled out in the dank and dark for one and a half hours in fighting order. Now 6 p.m., have just had my hair cut and here I am writing.

We expect to go into the trenches the beginning of next week, but don't count on it. No digging parties this week. How is Frdk.? I haven't heard from him.

January 29.

I like the handkerchiefs you send. Washing is very fitful. Sometimes my servant does it, and sometimes a neighbouring farmeress.. The results are very shady—but it's useful for handkerchiefs and such. My towels get blacker and blacker under his laundering.

I saw a letter in the *Times* the other day advocating that the sandbags should be coloured instead of white. It would be very difficult to find one that wasn't the colour of the Flanders mud once it has been disembarked. Of course in summer it would take longer.

You wanted to know about the rest camp, which I thought I had described. Well, it consists of a large field or series of fields (there being no hedges) churned into mud—no grass—board walks 18 in. wide through it and huts and tents in rows. We have a hut, and the men huts or tents, according to their luck.

A broad ditch runs at the bottom of the field and out of that our washing water (and a good deal of the water for our tea, I fancy, and the men's tea) is fetched. Rats run in every direction at night, and some people chase them through the slime with electric torches and sticks. The huts are as at Shurland, only smaller, and mostly with mansard roofs, so that you can only stand upright in the middle. *Voilà!* I am sitting by myself in ours at present and have been most of the afternoon, T. having gone up to see the new trenches and the others having an afternoon off.

Sunday. T. came back last night and said the trenches are not so bad as they might be. We shall be there off and on for a fortnight, so you will get rather shorter letters.

I had a hot bath yesterday in I.'s bath, and just as I was getting in, a gas alert or alarm sounded and all the gas helmets had to be inspected, and as I was the only officer at home, so to speak, I had to bustle through the bath and do them.

The water inspection is like our experience at the paper mill when the military visited us. Strict orders that the men drink only the water supplied. Practice, to drink out of any shell hole they see. The water supplied isn't enough or often enough. Of course it is nearly always turned into tea, which, with inoculation, I suppose, prevents the consequences that might be expected.

I read an amusing account in the paper of Friday of a visit by seven influential recruiters to the firing line. The spokesman described how they came under shell fire and fled to dugouts, where they waited hours. But they found the dugouts dry and airy and nearly all carpeted. T. suggests that they must have been taken to Boulogne or somewhere, and the shell fire was a bomb party practising bombs. I don't know whether that sort of nonsense is useful or not; after all there is something to be said for the truth on most occasions.

My servant is doing rather better, but he is an old humbug. Told me he was no longer young—getting on for 40!

Rest Camp, Sunday 30.

C Coy. is stopping back after all for a day or two more.

Rest Camp, February 1.

I am so sorry about Frdk. It will be a great blow to him, I know, not because of the climbing or anything of that sort, but because he'll hate not to be able to rush about on other people's behalf, and will, of course, not be able to see himself in the heroically wounded light.

I don't think it's going to be any good my telling you I'm likely to be in the trenches soon or otherwise: at present I'm still here with the coy. and may go up for a day for some time to come. So you'd better just think I'm in the best possible place. We're across the road from the old camp—in what was hdquarters— a much finer hut, and I have a bed—sacking hung over boards—which I must say I like much less than the floor as it sags in the middle, which the floor doesn't. No doubt it's less draughty, and as it has started to freeze and be cold of nights, I dare say the bed is on the whole an improvement.

January 27. (To his mother.)

Many thanks for the magnificent parcel of biscuits and rocks and socks and all the other things. The whole mess rose *en masse* at the Edinburgh rock and pigged it. It seems very much a thing to have now and then. But you mustn't send so much at a time. We simply can't eat it, and eat too much in the effort. So economise, my mother, and help your country and your son at the same time.

The scarf from Raymond and Meriel [8] is really very useful; I mostly wear it round my waist in the evenings.

Rest Camp, February 3.

Just a line before we go up to the trenches. Only three days at a time. I will try and write each day but don't count on it. Not always easy to write and not always easy to send if you do.

Trenches, February 4.

I don't know if this will get off today. I came up with the rear last night, and the blighters shelled the road as we went, one about 100 yds. behind, another in front and off to the left and right—'cannon in front of them,' in fact—but not bad. And all the old hands are ready with stories of how they came along with shrapnel bursting over their heads in the old days. The nuisance was not knowing whether the next is going to be in front or behind.

Several other regiments got off the road and stopped, but the R.B.s marched on—not, I may say, without my consulting my sergeant, as I fancy I should have stopped myself, and taken shelter, though it's the wrong thing to do unless the shelling is very heavy. The trouble is to know what is heavy and what isn't. However, we arrived quite safely, and I have the satisfaction of knowing that this is about the worst trench that even some of the sergeants have been in. More for its general unpleasantness than for anything else. You can easily step in over your thigh-boots in mud; I'm writing in a dugout in which you can't sit upright and through which there is a trickle of water; the stench in parts is too appalling for words, and we have been having shells right over our heads, luckily doing no damage, for the last four hours, starting at breakfast.

If you move by day you have to go double. Anyone who finds it 'ripping' is very much to be envied, if he exists, but I doubt it. T. suggested the people you mentioned must be with one

---

8. Raymond and Meriel Vernède, son and daughter of his brother Arthur, of the I.C.S., mentioned in the introduction.

of the armies that have never been in the trenches. And you must remember that gunners probably don't see one shell to a thousand they fire.

However, we've had no casualties as yet, and I dare say shan't. To tell you of the advantage of this trench—one gets much more sleep, as one simply can't move about much; and my feet are warm with a pair of thick soles in the gum boots and three pairs of thick socks.

The view from here is rather quaint. On our right front is a wood with every tree struck by lightning, as it were, and the ground below blackened too. This afternoon has turned fine, after rain all night, and I have been watching the snipers sniping while our guns have begun to pound their trenches in retaliation, and you see volumes of smoke and a German trench fly into the air with a crash. I must say it strikes me as only less horrible than the English ones doing so; but it always bucks the men to see our guns getting to work, and they will stand any amount of pounding themselves for the sake of it.

Trenches, February 5.

All is well, except that I've rather gone off my feed in this filthy place. It's largely due to the smell and dirt of the food. Our dugout really is a floor of mire which absorbs anything dropped in it, and is composed, I should say, largely of other people's rotting socks and bread crumbs! And one wanders about over the knee in quagmire, never knowing when you're going deeper. Fearful row, guns going all the time. We've had no casualties except two men shot by snipers, one killed—the first in C Coy. since I joined—which is extraordinarily good. And this man T. had warned to keep his head down only five minutes before. One calls it carelessness, but the fact is, after you've stooped till your back aches, it's almost beyond human nature not to straighten up occasionally.

I went out with a wiring party in front of the trenches last night for about an hour and a half. T. went himself with the men—he's very nice in that way, so I could not but offer to go too. It sounds more exciting than it is. I mostly got mixed up with the wire in the dark, while one of the corporals did all the work; and we weren't fired on, except by stray bullets, and put up quite a fair amount. The old hands don't mind a bit, but the boys don't like it. We come out tomorrow.

Better close before the mud out of my hair or neck falls on this. Haven't washed, haven't shaved since coming in. Nor has nobody.

Sunday, February 6?

I am very well and fit but I suppose I have just found out what it can be like. We have been heavily shelled for about two hours, and one sat there with intervals of seconds, it seemed, not knowing where the next would come. The Boches have just left off for the day, I hope, as, though the casualties were not heavy, it was enough for everybody's nerves. Several men are suffering from shock—shivering and quaking and having to be carried off on stretchers. I'm sitting beside a bad case now—he can't even move. The marvel is that he came out alive—he was one of four in a dugout, and was pulled out uninjured, the rest being killed. I don't want to meet anyone who's had a ripping time out here.

By the way, this man has my scarf Raymond and Meriel gave me. I wish you'd send me another like it—thick wool, loosely knitted, about a foot wide and three yards long—the longer the better.

T. is splendid under this sort of thing. I wasn't as bad as I expected. I was in our dugout to begin with with two Buff officers and got a stone pretty hard on my tin hat, after which I proposed we should move out, which we did, and the dugout was knocked in a little later. Sat behind the parapet with the Buffs trying to find a safe place, but there wasn't any available. Found a man horribly injured in the face, with the C.S.M. who had just escaped. Tried to give him morphia, but couldn't manage it, so went for stretcher-bearers, who attended to him.

Boches have just begun shelling again—confound them after half an hour's interval. Will send this off if we get out safely. We move in about three hours—none too soon.

Monday. Arrived here safe and sound in support trenches about 3.30 a.m. after the most unpleasant day—very nearly—that I've had. I still think it's right that war should be damnable, but I wish everybody could have an idea of how beastly it can be.

The Boches shelled us twice yesterday after I wrote, but only for a little, I'm glad to say, as everybody had had enough, I think, and several of the oldest hands said it was the worst shelling they had ever been through. Our casualties were remarkably small considering that wherever you crouched two or three shells seemed to split over your head every second. We had only five killed and about a dozen injured. T. sat most of the time with a wounded man across his knees, and the man said he knew it would be all right when the captain came along: which I thought was rather nice.

One of our best sergeants was killed—a very nice man who was rather a friend of mine, though not in my platoon. I think the men are wonderful and awfully good to one another. The C.S.M. was knocked senseless by the same shell that injured the man I mentioned, and when he came to, dragged him into the dugout, to which I traced them by a pool of blood. Even the chef, when I went for the stretcher-bearers, dashed out and leapt an open part of the trench where it had been crumped in to go and help, which I'm afraid will render me weak-minded towards his cookery in future; the shells flying as hard as ever. It's an extraordinary sensation—every portion of the trenches seemed to have shells exploding over them and you were nearly deafened by the near ones. I really was in a great state of funk, but I'm not sure that it's avoidable. The least sensitive of the men, I fancy, are strung up to the last pitch, and I doubt if even T. was as cool as he looked, though looking it is all the battle under the circumstances.

C. was our only other officer there and he was very cool, and pulled the living man out of the smashed dugout, which was a terrible sight. I would like all praisers of war to be under that sort of fire for a day, and if any remained, they would have less to say for it. The Buff youths were young and quite cheery, though they would ask me where to go, which I wasn't at all competent to tell them, and had to make them try several places without finding any that was really of use. At the end of it—about 5 o'clock—T., C. and I ate cake without tea and waited for the regiment that was due to relieve us. The latter arrived about two or three hours after time—a thing that can be singularly annoying under those circumstances, as the Boches began shelling again after we should have been well away, and I thought it was all going to recommence for another three hours.

Luckily it didn't and I got off with my party about 11.30 p.m.

for a five mile walk in thigh gum-boots and all our packs and things. I don't know when I have been more hot and exhausted. Rather over halfway luckily we came to the place where we hand in the gum-boots—an enormous dark building where they gave us hot soup (it tasted of tea and oxo mixed—in muddy cups!) grateful and comforting nevertheless. During the last half of the way we passed a man who'd gone lame from another platoon and I dropped behind to give him directions, but couldn't find him in the dark, so went on by myself. Rather eerie in the dark in unknown country with the sound of the guns in the distance.

I was very glad to get in at 3.30 a.m. and find hot tea and a bed. Have washed this morning—first time for four days!

Outside there is the most peaceful scene I have seen for weeks—green fields and unstruck trees, though the brutes put a few shells over here even, yesterday.

I couldn't get this off yesterday as there was no posting during the shells, but it will go this afternoon.

I feel rather doubtful as to whether I should tell you quite the unpleasantest side like this; but I think it's rather good that nowadays, when women have so much influence, they should not be fooled with the rosy side of things only. I don't think I've exaggerated and I don't think I'm using my imagination. At any rate I'm willing to bet that not one of the men but would have given a good deal to be out of it.

Wednesday, February 8 or 9.

Couldn't get you a letter yesterday as I slept most of the time after a fatigue party up to 2.30 a.m. and then had to hustle to another at 4.30 p.m. Got back at 2.30 a.m. this morning. Really rather boring—dripping wet—covered with mud—shelled at intervals, and so on. Will write more soon.

Wednesday, February 9.

We aren't up again for some days, and I don't suppose we shall have another day like Sunday for some time to come. I hope not. It seemed impossible that we should get off so lightly. I suppose they put over twenty shells a minute on the average. I sent you a line today to catch the post, which, having slept from 2.30 to nearly 12, I hadn't time to make longer. It was a horrible wet night, and I led them slightly astray—not in the general direction, but taking a longer road than I need have done, which annoyed me rather, and ending up about a quarter of an hour from the spot without being sure where I was. However, I found a general there who lent me an orderly for the rest of the route, and seemed very amiable, and we got in about half an hour late. It didn't much matter, and came from depending on a sergeant who said he knew the road instead of making sure of it myself, which in the dark wasn't too easy. As it happened, I went a very safe way and we never met a shell, going or coming, though we got some where we were digging.

You've no idea what it is like taking 100 men through an unknown bad trench at night. Sometimes you're on a board, then well over your knees in mire, then you trip over a wire or climb over a portion that has been knocked in by shells, or you come through a tunnel or out into an open quagmire. Everybody ought to sprain their ankles ten times over in the course of three hours of it, but nobody did last night. It's quite a strain in itself, apart from the shells, and the whole job took eight-and-a-half hours. I think the men are fearfully good about it—awfully slow, but they stagger along, grousing a certain amount, but generally cheerful. I believe as you become a veteran soldier you can tell almost exactly when and where a shell is going to burst, which is an advantage in that most of them aren't going to burst exactly where one is standing—not that you could do anything if it were.

At present I haven't the foggiest idea where they're coming, and can't even distinguish between ours going off close at hand and theirs arriving, which gives me a sort of double share of the artillery effect! I fancy it's the same with most new folks. Of course during a strafe like Sunday's nobody can tell—there are too many flying too rapidly in all directions at once. I don't wonder the poor Injuns didn't like it. The best men get rattled after a certain amount of it.

It's very curious, I think, that without one's paying any attention to it in peace time, some of the brainiest people of all countries have been inventing these infernal weapons, which can and do—besides merely killing—inflict tortures at least as bad as anything the Chinese invented.

I've got a night off tonight, which, after two successive nights, is a considerable boon and blessing, and enables me to write properly.

There are so many ways of getting done in while taking the utmost precautions that I don't wonder the men get absolutely reckless, and care no more about rifle bullets than they do about fleas. Think of the way they go off into the dark along a road which they know is swept by shrapnel and walk on through it without apparently turning a hair.

Friday, February 11.

I am very fitly, thank you. It was the awful smell that made me feel sick the first few days in the trenches, but I was already much better before they started to strafe us, having kept away from food for a bit.

Today I've been sitting in the dugout, doing nothing but doze over a very funny coke brazier, which, however, has kept me warm. We don't go up in the front line again for a day or two and then only for a very short time. We ought to be out in so-called rest almost by the time you get this.

I led a fairly easy carrying party fatigue last night—got one shell to our right which blew across the road, but nobody was hurt. A bit of mud touched my coat in passing, which indicates the pleasures of these roads. Got back at 10 p.m. instead of 2 a.m., which was a nice change.

It's been a most slimy day—dismal Flemish rain—a steady stream of it, making puddles everywhere.

I didn't tell you of a letter I censored from one of our sergeants to the mother of one of the men who were killed. It really was one of the nicest I've seen. He said—

> We found your son in the ruins of the dugout, where death must have been instantaneous. His head drooped forward a little, and there was a very peaceful expression on his face as I took him by the hand for the last time.'

Then he went on to explain how popular he had been with his platoon, and how he had fallen fighting for his country, and enclosed some snowdrops 'picked just behind the lines.'

[To F.G.S.]

In Support. February 11, 1916.

My Dear Fred,

I do hope it continues to go well with you and you will manage to get back soon and cheer England up. We had a distinctly hot time a few days ago in the front line—two hours of what everyone agreed was about the fiercest shelling they had known. Extraordinarily few casualties considering, but it is a cruel business. Even to see men suffering from shock, flopping about the trenches like grassed fish, is enough to sicken one, and some of the face wounds are terrible. They were splendid—most of them will leave any shelter they have got to go and help one of the wounded and they remain cheerful to the last.

Nor is it the sort of heedless gaiety I used to suspect them of, but a gallant effort to make the best of things and not let their morale fall below an ideal. Stretcher-bearers dodging about among shells—some of our older N.C.O.s cheering up the grenadiers of a service batt. who had got rattled—a latest draft youth who never took his eye off his loop-hole during the bombardment (so his corporal told me)—these things are rather good. But anyone who hereafter shows a tendency towards exalting war ought to be drowned straight away by his country.

Since then we have gone into support, doing fatigues along shelled roads at night—not a very cheerful occupation, though here again the men are wonderfully good-tempered and cheerful, and march on in the dark without apparently heeding the shells.

Am slightly choked by a coke brazier in a dugout upon which the dismal Flemish rain drips incessantly which makes me aware that I'm not writing a particularly happy letter to an invalid, without being able to reform much.

Saturday—or probably Sunday—and I think February 13.

It's a fine day after a very muddy and sodden one. C. and I are still in support with a portion of the Coy. and don't move up till tomorrow; then only for a very short time. Had a whole day's rest yesterday and about ten hours' sleep—not bad. No news beyond that.

My servant has gone sick and I have a new one. I think he will be good.

In Rest again and very fit.
Wednesday, February 16.

I haven't had a letter from you since Sunday and I haven't been able to write you one, and I have had a time, of which I'll tell you as much as seems lawful. I think I wrote on Sunday morning saying that I wasn't going up into the trenches that day, but was going to carry some rations. Little did I know. We set out in the dark to meet the transport—about forty of us—and the transport was late at the rendezvous by about an hour, and when it did arrive informed me that rations were not to be taken up till a message came through from the adjutant. So I withdrew my men off the road into a trench one of the sergeants by luck found, and some shells proceeded to come over. Then I met the doctor outside his dressing-station, and he told me that there had been heavy shelling most of the day and his colleague had been wounded at the door of the dressing-station—right back—and he was afraid there would be casualties. The walking cases began to come down the road as we waited—a weird sight—bandaged men staggering along in the moonlight.

Presently I received a message to say we were to go forward with the rations, and found the Regimental C.S.M. waiting to conduct us in a great fatigue. Our two companies up had been heavily shelled all day and we were to relieve them—message I ought to have got before I started, but which hadn't come through.

So there we were without our packs, our coats or our gumboots, going into deep slime for a couple of days or so. We went forward with the stuff; I shouldered a huge sack of coke myself which I could hardly lift, and the others were almost equally laden, if not quite. As we went down the road, bang went some shells just ahead of us and in the rear, and we all flopped down and I shoved the sack in front of me, not that it would have been of any use. We waited till they stopped and then went on to find a four-horse waggon just ahead with two horses and the driver killed by one of the shells. Got to the trenches without casualties and found T. waiting to lead us up. My dinner and bed gone for the night. We got up by slow degrees and took over from one of the other coys, who had lost very heavily.

The Boche restarted almost as soon as we got to the Coy. H.Q. dugout, and there I sat the rest of the evening, and in fact all night—a very strange scene. A place smaller than my study at home into which plopped crowds at intervals to take refuge from the shells. All sorts and conditions, from the C.O. who had come up to see how things were, to a Scotch doctor hastily sent for with loads of stretcher-bearers. Later, a sergeant from another regiment—suffering from nerves—dashed in, having abandoned his digging party, of which he felt sure none remained, though only one or two were hit. I gave him a kola nut and sent him off; and engineer officers turned up, and officers of other batts., and the post, bringing quite the best timed parcel I've had, from my mother, containing a cake, gingerbread, dates, Edinburgh rock, and a pair of socks.

The socks I put on over the others, and stuffed myself into some killed or wounded man's gum-boots which I found were full of holes. The rest of the things we and a lot of others lived on for the next twenty-four hours, during which we hadn't a drop of water—only whiskey. As a matter of fact, I had a cushy time, comparatively speaking, as T. insisted on placing the riflemen himself and M. did the bombers. It appeared that the trenches were very nearly non-existent, the casualties large, and C Coy. had the pleasant prospect of sitting in what holes remained for some time. The sappers deepened some holes for them during the night, but before morning one of the sergeants I brought up was killed and several men had been buried. It was impossible to stir during the night, but in the early morning T. went round and extricated the half-buried.

Most of the next day the Boches shelled again and it grew so heavy in the afternoon that T., M., and I—the only officers up—I. having been taken off the day before with bad shell shock—retired from H.Q. to a sort of drain pipe under the road, where we stood doubled up in water over our thigh gum-boots for two hours. (The other coy. officers had stood the day before like this in the same place for six hours, and I don't know how they stood it.) Shells that burst near roared through the funnel and nearly blew one off one's legs. (It was in there that I. had been knocked out by the shock the day before.)

Then the water rose and we cleared out, not relishing the idea of being drowned as well as buried, which seemed possible, as one shell just overhead made the whole place shift.

I made sure the Boches were going to attack at the end of it, and said so to T., who doubted it; but as it turned out they did actually give the signal for the assault, and began to get over. Meanwhile P.B. at Batt. H.Q. far back, thought we had put up a signal for help (which we couldn't do, wires being all cut) and he wired through to the gunners, who presently put up so terrific a barrage that the Boches instead of coming on bolted back—very luckily for us; and at the end of an artillery strafe of some hours, when night arrived, we were told that we should be relieved that night. They say the Boches suffered very heavily. I hope so, to make up for ours.

Really the men were wonderful, as always. There was C Coy.—lads of twenty, many of them—planted out in burrows for thirty hours, plastered with shells—no communication—T. wouldn't let anybody stir by day. And at the end of it only two posts had broken at all—in one of which one was killed, three buried and unable to stir, and the others suffering from shell shock; and in the other they had all dug one another out two or three times before they gave way—besides having three wounded. Then we had the same scene as the night before—reliefs arriving and the wounded being brought down. M. bandaged and I administered laudanum and kola nut for hours.

Then Tatham went off and I moved the coy. off in a hurricane of snow and icy rain. I'd been wet to the waist for about twenty-four hours, and I imagine the men were wetter, and I had no feeling in my legs for about two hours. They put whizz-bangs over us at one point in the open, but we got back to the support camp in the end, just at daylight. I sat up from 6 a.m. to 12 drying my drawers over a brazier (while the others slept) without any trousers on.

Later at night we had to move again here, and I was left to bring the coy. with M. We had to come across open country. Just as we started a terrific bombardment began on both sides, and in a tearing wind and rain we ran right into the Boche barrage and had to bustle through it. My idea was to try and find some shelter, and one of the sergeants positively urged it, but Sergeant C. said, 'No, sir, the best thing is to get on,' which accordingly we did. I knew Cousens was the better adviser, and we got through without any casualties and arrived here soon after midnight—wet through again after a most weary trudge. This morning we—the batt.—were hauled out of bed to receive, I believe, the general's compliments; but he was detained at the last moment, so we didn't. But I believe the whole brigade is to be patted on the back. [9]

---

9. This bombardment took place at Hooge, as appears from Sir Douglas Haig's dispatch, dated 19 May, 1916, in which the batt. is mentioned for its conduct on this occasion.

9 p.m. Divisional orders have just come in, patting batt. on back for its behaviour during this strafe. Several people are to be recommended for D.C.M.s and so forth, including Sergeant C., Corporal A. of my platoon, possibly M., who helped some wounded down under fire. A. was the man who shot down the first advancing Boches, who, if he hadn't been at his post watching, might have started an entry for the lot.

I wish I felt really fit to lead these sort of men, I haven't had enough of it to feel really useful.

We're out again for some little time—I can't tell you exactly how long.

I don't know if this sort of account is interesting. It could be much more so if I could explain the sort of positions, but I have to avoid anything that could be construed into military information, and so I rather mix it up. It's extraordinary how one doesn't feel the worse for this sort of thing. I don't know when I've been colder or wetter for twenty-four hours: my teeth simply chattered with cold in that drain pipe, and sitting without your trousers for hours in a dugout on a winter's day doesn't sound salubrious. But I am very well.

Thursday. Hope to get a bath today after a fortnight of being plastered with mud from head to foot.

Rest Camp, Friday, February 18 (?)

Yesterday we paraded for the G.O.C. Division, who made quite an eloquent speech, if rather inanimate; said the batt. had added a new laurel wreath to the Rifle Brigade and set a splendid example to the batts. who had already benefited by it, under the hardest trial troops could endure, *viz.*, concentrated shell-fire over many hours. It rather amused me to read in the paper next day an account of several little artillery engagements on the —— front, which the men quite welcome as a change from the monotony of the trenches. Blithering idiot. If he had ever seen what remained of a coy. coming out shattered and wounded and drenched and hungry, to tramp for hours through a snowstorm to some place where they can recuperate. Or if he had ever tried even ten minutes of fierce shell-fire.

It's true the men stick it and make little of it, once it's all over; but the stoutest of them would probably give anything to be out of it at the time. Isn't there any imagination in those who stay at home that they can stand that sort of bosh in a leading London paper? I don't know why I'm being rhetorical.

The brigadier, who followed the G.O.C., merely said, 'R.B.s, I'm not eloquent. I only want to tell you how proud I am of you and how pleased I am with you'—which the men seemed to prefer to the more elaborate oration.

I went in with C. this morning and had a bath—the first for over three weeks. I have never been so piggishly dirty before—my hair plastered with mud like a Papuan's; and I'm not clean after an hour's scrubbing in hot water. Tomorrow I take two platoons in to be bathed and shall have another myself.

Have a slight sneeze and sniffle coming on, but you can't wonder at it, can you?

T., who draws not bad cartoons, has done one of me standing doubled up in the drain pipe, holding up the skirts of my Aquascutum out of the water—with a large shell in the act of coming through! He entitled his drawing, 'The only place where Vernède could not go to sleep.'

C. and I decided to recommend T. for a distinction, so we went to the C.O. about it and he informed us that he had already decided to send in his name for coolness and gallantry; so we hope he will get the D.S.O.

The stupid thing is that, as one realises out here, these honours go to the higher command as a matter of course and sometimes evade the lower to avoid giving too many away. War is very like Peace in that respect.

Rest Camp, February 20.

Not much news. There never is in these rest camps. We've had a fine day today—cold but bright, which is a nice change from the dismal Flanders weather. T. and F. have gone off on leave and I am left in charge of the coy. for the time being with C. This isn't the same rest camp as the last—perhaps a trifle less muddy, but otherwise very simbly, and we live in a damp hut with a smoky brazier and are not supposed to move about much. I am sorry letters have been taking longer, and I'm afraid you will have had to wait several days for my account of the trenches; but you mustn't ever worry. You see, one is absolutely cut off at such times from posts. Your guess was about right as to the whereabouts; but you see we came off very well on the whole.

The corps and army commanders have also tendered their thanks to the batt., which shows we did something, I suppose.

I think there will be very fierce fighting for some time to come—both sides, I suppose, are fully armed now; and there is bound to be some up and down; but don't let anyone make you downhearted. The men are endlessly gallant, and the higher command is bound to learn in time. Anyway we rest here for quite a long time probably and watch aeroplanes go over and get shot at. I have not seen one hit yet by either side. The papers are so complaisant over every little success that they are almost bound to be equally downhearted over every failure—don't believe them. Only believe that we shall win in the end.

I'm afraid I can't begin to think of leave for a couple of months more.

As to your question about quartermasters: some of them do go up occasionally, not to the trenches actually, but to what they call a 'dump' on the way there, and so far they undoubtedly run risks. Every road out here is liable to be shelled, and so far everybody takes his chance. But the man who takes chances all the time is the infantry soldier in the front trench of the worst sectors; and I don't think England can do too much for these little riflemen when they get home, if they get home.

February 22.

Am in the middle of a violent sneefle. As luck will have it, I've got to go with the other O.C.s and explore some trenches to-night not for going into, but so as to know them when we do get into them. It would be quite interesting if I hadn't such a sneefle on, but I dare say being out all night will cure it; and I shall have my scarfs handy.

I'm lying in my valise to write this at 6 p.m. and I thought I would get a doze till 10, when we start, and it's decidedly warmer in the valise than out. These dark, damp huts with nothing but a smoky brazier for a few hours a day are well calculated to make one sneef, even if I hadn't had twenty-four hours or more of wetness in that drainpipe trench. I am sure decent comfort between whiles is what they want, and what neither we nor the men get in any sufficient quantity.

9.15 p.m. Have dozed a certain amount and eaten a large meal, so can't be very bad. I expect I'll be back tomorrow in time to add to this before the post goes; but will put it into an envelope in case not.

23. Expedition all off at last moment, so that I got to bed all right and feel considerably better this morning. Nasty snowy day, though. Last night at 10 p.m. it was rather a fine scene—white snow on the ground freezing, and a moon that looked as if it had been crumped by a large shell.

Rest Camp, February 24.

Just a line to say my sneefle is fast disappearing. We're just moving to a new rest camp. Had an interesting day yesterday, which will tell you about in next letter. This is in haste to catch post.

February 25. (To his mother.)

It's bitterly cold, freezing hard and our hut is more like a funnel at the N. Pole than a residence—no door, and two holes instead of windows, and a very little coal-dust to make a fire with. We're all in the same boat, more or less, but it doesn't make it any warmer!

The batt. had a lecture on discipline from an old general to-day—oh, lor, some of these old boys would haul up St George on his way back from fighting the dragon in order to rebuke him for having some mud on his armour.

Saturday, February 26.

My cold is much better going,—in fact, as fast as you can expect in this benighted country, which at the moment is under several inches of snow. We've got a door to our hut, but still no windows so far, so we are still draughty. I ought to have a little more time for the next day or two, as D., who is senior subaltern in the batt. and belongs to C Coy., has come back from leave and naturally takes over the O.C.ing till T. returns.

The only thing I can think of wanting is a pair of gloves as I've lost that good pair we got. Any sort would do as long as they are very large and woolly or otherwise lined. I use them not so much for warmth as for protecting my hands in the trenches. You pull yourself along like a monkey, and in the dark may lay hold of barbed wire, pointed stakes or sheer mud; or a combination of the same.

We had a lecture in discipline yesterday from a very bigwig—it made me quite sick. I am still altogether up against that aspect of the army—which I believe to be only a pale imitation of Teutonic methods, and if carried out rigidly, a mistake. However, it's their say and they will have it, or try to have it.

I don't think I told you of my walk with the acting C.O. and the other O.C.s to look at some other trenches. It was through a rather less desolate part of the country—sloping and green instead of smashed-up mud-holes; and we went near one of the recently captured trenches. Called on an old general at one place, and he asked the C.O. if he knew these trenches. The C.O. said, Yes, the batt. had been there before; whereupon the old thing just roared with laughter and said, 'Yes, but the Boches have got them all now!'

He was, however, not a bad old one—only cheery—seemed to know about things and be reasonably optimistic. We came back the last five miles in a six-horse artillery limber, and I don't think I've ever been so jolted in my life. It seemed a fairly good cure for colds.

February 28..

There's very little news. The snow has all gone and it is steadily sploshing with rain, and we're in the same rest camp as ever, and my cold is much betly but my throat is rather sore—to be truthful—but then so is everybody else's, I think.

I asked you for gloves, didn't I? Two pipes would also oblige. I've just broken the last again. That's the trouble out here.

I'm afraid I can't hold out any hopes of leave for a long time.

March tomorrow, so I suppose winter is thinking of coming to an end. I shan't be sorry. It's very difficult to keep oneself and the men fit in this sort of thing, and there never was a bigger lie than that colds are unknown at the Front. The absence of one is the rarity, I should say.

March 1

I somehow fell asleep this afternoon instead of writing to you, and now there is no time before post goes.

It is a beautiful day—the first for weeks.

Have just seen a Seaforth Service Batt. go by to the pipes—to the attack, I think. Good-looking men.

T. is just back.

Rest Camp, March 1.

I sent you off a small snip to catch the post, and now I don't see why I shouldn't start a longer one. T., who has come back from leave rather ill—cold, I fancy—is asleep on my bed, C. reading, and a not bad fire in the hut, which is fairly peaceful. When we shall move I don't know—probably suddenly and soon. There are a lot of things in the air, and I wish I could always tell you what little we know and expect; but we mayn't, and anyhow it's just as well, perhaps, as they don't always come off.

I'm rather annoyed about leave and the time it will be before we can even think of it—apart from the chance of it being stopped altogether. I can't help thinking that married men ought to be given preference, because there are two people to be considered; and also, I think it should start at the bottom instead of the top. More decent somehow for a C.O. to see his juniors off before he goes himself, and I don't think this is just because I am a 2nd lieut. However, it doesn't strike them that way—quite the contrary—and the men, of course, get much less leave than the officers. There, the sole excuse is that they are less used to it, make less good use of it, and so on—in which there is something, though not a great deal. Also, of course, the transport difficulties would crop up. I think myself the answer is that the officers should go less often. One didn't join to get leave.

I rather foresee a time (after Peace) when people will be sick of the name of the War—won't hear a word of it or anything connected with it. There seem to be such people now, and I see numbers of silly books and papers advertised as having nothing to do with the war. It's natural, perhaps, that soldiers should want a diversion, and even civilians; but I rather hope that people won't altogether forget it in our generation. That's what I wanted to say in the verses I began about—

Not in our time, O Lord, we now beseech Thee
To grant us peace—the sword has bit too deep—

but never got on with. What I mean is that for us there can be no real forgetting. We have seen too much of it, known too many people's sorrow, felt it too much, to return to an existence in which it has no part. Not that one wants to be morbid about it later; but still less does one want to be as superficial as before. I fancy this comes from hearing —— say, that the army will be the place to be in when peace is declared—no work, all leave and amusement. I don't think it will be or should be, and I'm sure it's a mistake to suppose that times ahead are going to be gay and easy in any case. The sword has bit too deep. He's only a boy and a very nice one and doesn't mean a quarter of what he says, but I do wish these nice and high-spirited youths learned as well as dared.

Ever one here seems quite cheerful about Verdun, and rumour says that the French have done very well. It's quite likely, I suppose.

Am at present endeavouring to learn the Lewis gun, as we're all supposed to know a little of it. Like all machines, it seems to me very mysterious, though Lindsay[10] would probably know all about it in ten minutes. I think I should be less stupid at knowing good positions to fire it from, which is, I suppose, more the officer's job.

Bombs are fairly simple, though beastly. In fact I imagine they have made the war more cruel even than the artillery.

March 2. Fine day just turned to rain. Still don't know when we move. Nothing special on.

Still Rest Camp, March 4.

It is the most revolting weather again, snow and hail and rain alternately, and we are very lucky to be out of the trenches. You mustn't picture me suffering hardships, even in the trenches. It's only what you might call discomforts as long as one is well and unwounded, and really this hut has been much better the last two or three days, owing to more fuel.

Why we haven't gone into the trenches is that we are or were in reserve for an attack you probably will have read about. Luckily it was very successful and we didn't have to go up. I told you of the Scots marching up the road to the pipes. They were on their way to it, and the following day they came back—detachments with Boche prisoners—rather picturesque, and very conscious of having done well.

T. was much taken with my fur lining, which I lent him when he retired to my bed; it certainly is very nice and light.

I am just off to try to get a bath at a camp near—haven't had one for about three weeks, and am too dirty for words.

---

10. Lindsay B. Fry, an engineer, my brother.—C. H.V.

Rest Camp, March 6.
We go up about two days hence to some different trenches, supposed to be a great improvement—or are rumoured to be so. Have been very lucky to be out during this awful weather. Have been digging drains this morning (physical drill at 7.30!) in the snow and take the men to bathe this afternoon.
We only go into reserve anyhow for some days.

Rest Camp, March 7.
It snowed last night, and wet snow which prevents anything being done, which is one advantage, as the ground is a mass of icy puddles. I hope it will improve before we go into the trenches. I am very well—slight sore throat, but everyone has them.
There wasn't any need to worry about that attack which we were not wanted for, as it went exactly as planned.

Rest Camp, March 9.
Beautiful day after hard frost the ground really almost hard for the first time. Just to say we got up; but C. and I shall have a cushy job for next few days—making dugouts in support. Should be very safe. No time to write today.

March 10.
I started off yesterday with two very nice letters from you and two platoons, and marched five miles in five hours to get to this place, which might be the middle of Plashes Wood, with flares going up and guns crackling in the distance. C., who had gone ahead, had vanished without securing a dug-out for us, and I meandered about till Heaven knows when, looking for one in the darksome *forêt*. Eventually he turned up—midnight or so—and we had chocolate and whiskey (the only foods available) with D Coy., who are also here, and then re-hunted for a dugout till we found one, where we lay extremely cold with the snow drippling around till the servants arrived with a blanket for each of us. Would one, for choice, sleep in a dugout in the centre of Plashes Wood with deep snow and deeper mud all round, and some dripping thro' the roof, with one army blanket to cover one? Beestje cold, and as everybody started with a cold, it should be a Spartan cure.
Was on duty from 6 a.m. to 8 a.m., and after that we set our platoon making dugouts. If only one could keep one's feet dry it wouldn't be bad—quite picturesque—work easy and no shell-

ing, bullets occasionally hit the trees overhead. This really is a wood—living trees, and there are other woods round, quite pretty. I have given your mother's scarf to Corpl. A., and found him sleeping in it last night when I looked into his dugout. He seemed fearfully pleased with it, as he might be. We are going to mess with D Coy., at their request. For comfort I would much rather mess alone, as our two servants could and would look after us very well, but the invitation was well meant and I dare say a change of society is good.

March 11. Couldn't get this off last night and didn't get a letter from you.
C. has been ordered off to a course for a fortnight, so I shall have a dugout and two platoons to myself and shall dig with them. I did some this morning and felt warmer at the end of it. The snow is melting fast. Am just sending off a line to my mother to ask her to make Cording send another pair of knee gum-boots, as mine have been lost, and they are fearfully useful in wet weather.

March 12.

It is a most beautiful day—the first of Spring, balmy and even hot in the sun—quite the nicest day I've spent in Flanders, in spite of the fact that I've restarted a cold in the head. It seems impossible not to have one. As soon as it subsides, something starts it again—usually wet feet, which are unavoidable. Still it is nothing but a cold in the head, and everybody has one.
There is an artillery strafe going on—not in this direction, I'm glad to say; but the guns are popping away like mad, and people on either side getting killed. We are, as it might be, in Hanging Wood, our front line where our well was, the Boches at Plashes.
The ground from our front line to here is mostly dead, so that the Boches can't see anything: hence they have *Taubes* out all day trying to see what is going on. Whenever one comes over our sentry whistles and we stop work and take cover. I think they are bound to spot us, for the air is brilliantly clear, and the wood still quite leafless, but they don't seem to have done so up to now. Our guns always shoot at them; and it is a pretty sight, their aeroplanes like silver moths dodging between the white puffs of shell smoke in a blue sky.

The wood must have been quite a pretty one and isn't bad now. I sit in my dugout, largely underground, and round the corner is a bomb store, then a field dressing station, H.Q., more stores, and dugouts all along the rides. Everywhere there is evidence of the Tommy's thriftlessness—sacks of meat stuffed into some corner to rot. If they could teach them thrift instead of smartness, it would pay.

Our dugout building is going well, and they will be the best I have seen. The men work very well. And yet here we've been in this wood a year, and these will be the first decent dugouts in it; those already up being sheer waste of labour. Just outside the wood there are the remains of a Boche aeroplane. E. and I went out to visit it yesterday, but sped back again as there were too many stray bullets about. In the distance you can see ruined and shattered farms and villages—skeletons.

Last night, after about nine hours' work (starting at 5 a.m.), I played bridge with D Coy. till 11 p.m. It's extraordinary all the people that pass through on business—machine gunners, sappers, F.O.O.s, trench mortar gangs, digging parties, doctors, generals, stretcher-bearers and the wounded, who are brought down to the dressing station next my dugout. Two men of D Coy. were both shot through the chest by a sniper this morning: one walking down quite cheerfully. I really think the men are cheerful on being wounded; it shows what sort of a war it is. You wicked thing, reading my letters to strangers. Just remember that most people don't approve of hearing of the realities and it is not the thing to relate them. On the whole, a very decent feeling, I think. Moreover, most of the thrilling acts of the Front are written, or at any rate are said to be written, by members of the A.S.C. or R.A.M.C., or some other denomination that lives mostly miles behind the firing line. And relations of soldiers may know this, so don't give me away too much.

Now I must go out to D. for my tea. I am very comfortable and quite well really. I believe I stay here another week at least: then they say we rest and go to a much better part of the line.

March 13.

Another beautiful day and the cold again rapidly going. I trotted about the woods on duty (also chasing rats) with a pleasing D sergeant, till 11 p.m., after which —— and —— came and sat by my fire till 12.30 or so. They insisted on knowing my age, and guessed 32, so I must be ageing visibly, but the truth almost agitated them, as something pertaining to their grandfathers. Both nice lads, desperately keen on being out of it. It is hard luck, I think, spending your youth at this sort of thing. However, we thought one another sporting!

My new servant has a wife and family—looks 20. I've just seen a letter in which he says he is pleased to say he is servant to a very good officer. Meant me to see it, of course. I must say he is an enormous improvement on. the last, and has none of the old soldier tricks.

Our expert builders—pioneers as they are called—are rather after my own style of carpentry, and would craze Lindsay. They never saw two pieces of wood to fit, and if they want to measure anything, they'll tie a piece of stick and a piece of string together to measure by. Why they can't be taught their job properly I can't think. They get things done, but fearfully clumsily and never by rule or method, and any suggestion of making a dugout comfortable they resent. I was absolutely snubbed by Cpl. —— this morning, who said, 'What we looks to is protection from fire.'

I meekly said, 'If you can get comfort too, why not?' But he only sniffed.

Same Place, March 16.

Last night, I'm sorry to say, I had a man wounded. We were collecting bricks at dusk from a ruined farm near, to roof our dug-out with, and as the men came in they would stand on top of the dugout. Bullets fly mostly overhead at night, but several came jolly near, and I ducked, as I still cannot avoid doing, and said to Sergeant C. that I thought they were lower than usual and the men ought to clear down. He said, 'Oh, no, sir, they're over the trees.' However, I said to the men they'd better stand lower anyhow, and they'd begun to do it when flop went one of them, and Sergeant C. had the grace to say, 'It seems as if you were right, sir.' The man had got it in the eye and head, but I believe not seriously, and we got him down quick. He himself thought someone had thrown a brick at him and was rather annoyed. Probably lose his eye, poor man. But it was lucky no one else got it, as we were in a cluster of about five or six. It wasn't aimed, of course—only a stray—but I don't know that I should consider that if I were hit. These N.C.O.s, like C., absolutely scorn strays, but I think that's the mistake of being too valiant. Cpl. —— is more or less head of the dugout party.

They are babies. He's supposed to be foreman, and works on one dugout while another cpl. has another party doing another. He will not explain what he wants done to the others till they've put up a lot of stuff wrong. Then he makes them pull it down. I think it's to prevent their party going along as quick as his. However, I encourage the other party to disobey him, and they're both going very well. You'd think the measurements for a good sound dugout would be standardised; but no, we have to invent our own as we go, and there are at least fifty useless ones in the wood that wouldn't stop a peashooter.

Same Place, March 18.

Only time for a line, as I'm moving my platoon to another spot close by, said to be cushy. Move down to rest in three days.

Sunday, March 19.

The gum-boots arrived in the middle of last night, and are excessively nice and useful, as the damp remains in spite of very balmy, pleasant weather. I am still in a wood—rather a nice place and safe, I think, as the Boches aren't supposed to have spotted it, and it's not front line at all. It's a small post which I hold with my platoon, and we're going to sleep by day and work by night improving it. Have quite a decent dugout, with my servant hard by in another; Sergt. C. and Cpl. D. a little farther away—both good men. We ought not to come in for any strafing at all, and I hope we shall not.

Some sappers have just shown themselves on the skyline about 200 yds. away and been *whizz-banged*, some wounded. Some of the men are hopelessly careless.

The enclosed two letters from Marchetti [11] and Knowles respectively are rather sad, aren't they? He was a very nice youth, and I always thought it particularly sporting of him, being Greek. He was quite intelligent enough to know the bloodiness of it all, but as I wrote to Knowles, he probably would have thought it good enough. You might keep Marchetti's letter in case his people care to have it, as it must have been about the last he

---

11. 2nd Lt. A. Marchetti, killed in action 15 March, 1916.

wrote. I'll try and send them a line.

I also enclose a letter from the wife of a rifleman to whom I wrote on the death of her husband. She's got me mixed up with T., who, I told her, got her husband down and looked after him.

I enclose a letter from the R.N.C.O. anthologist.[12] I'm rather glad to know an authority on navy matters likes *England to the Sea*.

I got two letters from you in the middle of the night as I came in from perambulating my wood. It was bright and moonlighty, and except for the ceaseless crack of rifles, a pleasant hour to read them. What a sharp one you are! I've been trying to conceal about the deerskin waistcoat for ages. It was one of the first things stolen at the rest village, before we started for the trenches, which I was keeping it for. Taken from the bottom of a bag by someone. A sad loss, but luckily the weather is now such that one isn't likely to think of such things for months to come. I've been almost too warm the last day or two.

The only drawback to this place is that there's no water in it, and so far I have not even washed my face; and I am also reduced to rum in my tea instead of milk, which is also absent. Not at all bad—tea and rum—and it's extraordinary how the men delight in it. It's almost enough to melt a teetotaller.

The chief interest here is watching aircraft and not letting them spot you. It's rather pretty seeing a squadron in the sky all among the puff-balls of smoke. Yesterday I saw one of ours hit, and it was most exciting to see if he could clear the wood and come down safely. He did. But only just. Hits seem very rare, considering.

March 21.

We go out tonight to rest—it is rumoured—for three weeks. It really has been a very cushy time, and I've rather enjoyed my private command and the building work. The guns of either side are popping away over us, and we lying doggo in the middle, so to speak, though why we haven't been spotted I can't think. There was a Fokker over us most of the day yesterday, and

---

12. Mr. Geoffrey Callender, who wrote asking to be allowed to include *England to the Sea* in an anthology he was editing for the Royal Naval College, Osborne. (*Realms of Melody*, pub. Macmillan and Co.)

I spent the time watching him through Mr Clarke's glasses.

Had about five hours' sleep the night before last and seven hours last night—being waked about seven times in the course of it. It's extraordinary how one gets used to going to sleep again: at least I do, whether it's midday or midnight, I'm glad to say; and I don't feel at all sleepy, which is just as well, as on these moves one may not arrive till 2 o'clock in the morning.

Have had lunch since writing the above, cooked by my servant. He is not a chef, but really the food supplies are always very good, even when the *cordon bleu* deals severely with them. Now and again one pops out to see how near the shells are bursting—an aid to the digestion! A blackbird sang in an oak last night, as in one of my pomes. I notice several of the men write home to say how they enjoy the birds singing. It is a nice change from high explosives.

Yesterday I had —— in to lunch. He's a machine-gunner nowadays—not attached, but wandering about the Division with his guns. He's a nice youth, far more intelligent than most of them, but very simple. He corresponds, moreover, with my ideas of a gentleman, which all Regular officers do not by any means. He's a good judge of character too—a thing I find most of them blind about. They recognise their like and rejoice in the young apes, and that is about all. Of course their like is pretty good; but what they want, and what England in general wants, is an acknowledgment that the less conventional folk are not fools or criminals.

Same date. Still in the wood. A little later.

I seem to have become a tremenjus letter writer, while waiting here to be relieved; and besides a letter to you, which I fear won't get posted till tomorrow, I've written to Frdk., Oscar, and Arthur, [13] and now I'm beginning another letter to you again. Not that there's anything to tell you—*spunk* go the bullets in the trees and a machine-gun runs like a swift typewriter, and the flares go up and sich is life. Oh, and a bomber bombs too in the distance. Shan't be in bed till 3 a.m., I guess, and was up at 2 a.m., and also at 5-6 a.m. this morning. There's toil for you—but as a matter of fact there is little to do or to worry one here; and keeping awake a good deal is the hardest part of one's

---

13. See introduction.

job. —— has already gone off with my kit. The servants travel separately with a small handcart. I think I must try and break him of a habit of loudly whistling as he brings in the food. I think it's shyness chiefly.

March 21, 1916.

[To F.G.S.]

A wood in Flanders. Subaltern visible in dugout. I write with the shells going past from either side, we being safely out of it in the middle of a wood. We go down tonight to rest for some considerable time, and unless shelled on the road should be asleep in our beds behind the lines somewhere about 3 a.m. It's really been a cushy time since the last strafe.

Rather sad about Marchetti, isn't it? I got a letter from him one night to say he had joined the — Batt, and one from K. the next to say he'd been killed instantly while taking up his first working party. I liked him. He was intelligent and cheerful, and to die for a country you admire, though it is not your own, seems extra gallantry.

I think some armchair criticism by somebody who has been out should be most salutary. I suppose one is bound to get a biggish residue of confirmed shirkers in a country that has been taught to hate militarism and has not been taught to realise war. As for peers—they will be peers, I suppose. Nothing beats me more often than the fact that not only peers but whole classes of men have never even heard of the things which you and I think are the things. I doubt if —— ever heard of Henry James, for example, but he breeds West Highland terriers enthusiastically enough. We at least acknowledge the existence of West Highland terriers.

I wish we were rather more open to ideas. I'm thinking of shell-proof dugouts at the moment—their value and the absence of them for no ascertainable reason, except that we are so happy-go-lucky. They go with the Henry James, almost, and the way you wear your cap-badge with the West Highland terriers. And war is war, and the amateur view of it wrong. There should be no amateurs of war—there, at any rate, the Boches are right.

These views are prompted by some mud blowing over from the last shell, and may not be as pondered as they should be.

Anyhow, I'd best come to an end for the present. Do hurry up and get well, Fred.

March 22.

Arrived after a peaceful but most weary walk at 3 a.m. Bed at 4. Heavy bombing at 4.30, for what seemed hours. Go farther from the line tomorrow.

Rest Village, March 24.

We've got here, all very tired, after doing about ten miles in eight hours! Snowing again, bust it, but lucky we are here, quite comfortable. I have a bed by myself in a farmhouse, and we mess in another. Gum-boots invaluable in the snow.

March 25 or 26.

I sent you off a scrap yesterday, and I don't rightly know that I've got any more news for you today. We really are rather in luck to be out of the snow in quite a comfortable farm, and it's to be hoped that by the end of the month, when we move on, it will be spring again. Said to be a very cushy sector. I told you I had a bed—very comfortable in a small brick-floored room off the farm kitchen. I get hot coffee in the morning, which is rather luxurious; and the people are cheery, which is pleasant, when you are thrust upon them.

March 27.

Heard last night that my leave starts on 29th, which means that I shall be back some time on 30th. I don't go into the trenches in between, so there should be no question about this—except for the ordinary intervention of Providence.
I get seven clear days in England apparently.

Sunday, April 9.

Here I am back again where I told you, and things seem to have gone fairly well, though two of D Coy. officers seem to have managed to get slightly injured in the time. I got back rather brilliantly, really. Neither of the others turned up, and the crossing was excellent, as I wrote in my card from Boulogne, where later I saw the *Sussex* just below me with the whole of her stern blown off. Didn't leave till 7.30 p.m. and arrived at my first possible station about 12, but only woke up to find the train about to move out, so got out at the next one, which anyway was nearer.

Pitch dark and no knowledge from anybody as to where the batt. was, and another youth of the brigade and I got the R.T.O. cpl. to find us beds, which he did in a cottage opposite—quite good bed and breakfast at 8 a.m., and pay '*ce que vous voulez*,' after which we got on to a hay waggon, meandered along the road till I met a transport corporal, who told me where the batt. was, and took my pack for me. Got in about 10 a.m., and was able to laugh at the other two old soldiers who had not applied at the War Office, had started the day before, and had wandered about all night trying to find the batt., which is at present out of the trenches in support. It's a beautiful sunny day, and if it weren't for the noise of guns would be a very nice day for trotting about.

Monday. Couldn't get finished for the post, which went off soon after I arrived. Another beautiful morning. I have a hut to myself. My little blighters mostly seem to be flourishing. We don't go into actual trenches for several days, but have working parties—nothing like so bad though as t'other place. The wood is beginning to look green in parts and the sun shines. The land is wonderfully tilled—more forward than ours—the women, I suppose, doing most of the work.

The Trenches (in reserve). April 12. It's just slopping down on to the hut tent arrangement in which I set in a wood, and the damp is very considerable. So, however, is the peacefulness, which is a most pleasant change from the part of the line we used to be in. You'd hardly realise here that you were in the firing zone, except for an occasional noise of guns, and at the end of a few days we go back into camp again. I've never had such a quiet working party as I conducted the night before last—two shells a couple of hundred yards away and that was all. I dare say it was a good thing to start in a really bad bit; and I don't think I exaggerated it as a newcomer, for —— was saying yesterday that even last winter—the first winter—didn't compare with it from the point of view of unpleasantness, even allowing for the much longer time they used to spend in the trenches.

I don't think there is much news—we haven't really done anything and I expect we shan't.

Horticulture has begun among the troops, and consists chiefly of digging up violets and cowslips and sticking them in the roofs of their dugouts, together with a suitable inscription and a few boughs of palm or something similar. I'm not quite sure that I'm able to admire it, but it serves to amuse them, I suppose, if it does nothing else.

April 13.

Got your first real letter last night. The sun is shining at intervals this morning, though I'm afraid it's going to rain again. Nothing at all to tell you since yesterday. D. has gone off to his staff job and T. and I are alone in the wood, M. occupying a post elsewhere, C. having been lent temporarily to another coy.

Now I must censor some platoon letters and then go and see some work the men are doing. It is most peaceful here and I hope will remain so. Don't go properly into the trenches until the end of next week.

April 14.

I had another peaceful working party last night, though further along the line I'm afraid one of our coys. got it rather. Raining again, bust it.

April 15.

The working parties seem most peaceful so far, and quite pleasant nights.

April 18.

We have got back to rest camp, arriving last night; but it doesn't amount to much—the same working parties and a good deal further to go. The Boches have been rather more active with our trenches too, bust them, but it can't be helped. Also I get the job nightly, being the only subaltern left in the coy. at present. Our casualties haven't been many though. One of our officers had a very lucky wound yesterday—shrapnel burst right over him in the trench and he was only hit twice in the hand—once right through the palm, the other knocking a finger nearly off. That really is lucky, and he went off very well pleased with himself.

Must finish this quick as there's much work in the rest camp.

April 20.

Today is bright and windy and, I think, threatening snow. I never saw such a *pays*. It poured all last night—hail and hurricane. Luckily I had nothing to do either by day or night, and played bridge after dinner.

I cannot quite chuck my cold—it's no worse, but remains muddy, and this morning I distinctly feel a slight sensation of what might be lumbago. Comes from sleeping in draughty floors in this yowling weather, I suppose. Very slight and nothing to worry about.

I'll try and give you a plan of day's doings next time, if there are any doings. But really and truly they are very dull. People roll into your hut and roll out again. I got up late for breakfast—censored letters and read a short story book by O. Henry, who is really very good had lunch and a bath in the afternoon hot shower bath in a dirty little hut—more reading—dinner bridge. A lazy and luxurious day.

Good Friday, April 26.

Yesterday I wrote you a fairly long and, I expect, a fairly dull letter, at the end of which my back became so lumbagoey that I had to call in the Medicine Man, who rubbed me with something and put on a mustard plaster, and this morning it's a good deal better, though not quite gone. It makes one feel about 95—to be put on in two pieces at an angle of 45 deg. I suppose it's these beestje winds and lying on a draughty floor. T. and I dined together—it being B.'s turn to take the working party, luckily, as I could not have done it.

Then I got into bed with my hot bottle (used for the first time, and very pleasant) and read *The Woman in White* till about 11, when I slept. This morning it is fine, but cold and windy, and I think detestable. I fancy we go up on Easter Sunday, by which time I should be all right again. I haven't 'gone sick' once yet, and don't want to; I prefer to leave it to the Babes and not have it attributed to my venerable years! Which it isn't, as, at no age, did cold and mud agree with me.

Easter Sunday

It's fine after about three days' incessant rain, and my back is distinctly better, though somewhat weakly in parts still. Also the cold is better today. Some warm weather would probably make them both vanish. I've really hardly been out of this hut since the first day, as my back was not conducive to walking about, nor was the rain; and so my news really and truly is limited. D.

and C. both returned yesterday; so now we shall have our full complement of officers in C Coy.—six, in fact.

A lieut., named Butler came to dinner—quite an amusing man—I believe he's a Fellow of St John's, Oxford, but didn't cross-examine him—one of the clever family of Butlers. He intelligently talked a lot of nonsense.

Bother, I've been interrupted, and now there isn't much time to write before post goes. I know there were several things I wanted to tell you, but can't recall them.

Easter Monday.

Just a line from the *tranchées*, which are exceedingly damp—but, so far, very quiet. By the time you get this I shall in all probability be out again, as I have been selected as the next victim for the Technical school, which, I think, I told you about. This means being away for a fortnight, roughly, learning how to form fours, etc. The C.O. almost apologised for sending me, and said if I find it too impossible, would I let him know; but he thought it might amuse me. I said if it was to be regarded merely as copy, perhaps it might.

So there we are, and the only consolation is that you needn't worry for a fortnight. Back nearly well—cold much better. It's not a special insult being sent to this place—an officer has to go about monthly from the batt.; it's merely fatuous, and you're liable to be pounced on if you've seen the doctor, as I had for my back. I am too sleepy to write, having only had two-and-a-half hours last night.

April 26.

Rode over to this place yesterday from the trenches. Lovely day today but am so sleepy from the trenches and having a day of exercise that I'm hardly awake enough to write coherently. Back practically cured, and cold very near it. I have a room in a farmhouse (rather like our larder): the other fourteen officers in tents. I think it will be fairly amusing and good for me, perhaps, because I shan't be able to think I'm more incompetent than the subalterns of other regiments—judging from those present. Will write more tomorrow. Here for a fortnight—far from the strafe.

Thursday, April 27.

Still nice weather, but almost too sleepy for words—and early rising and many parades; that's all my news really and truly. There's a rum collection of temporary officers here—some very pleasant. I don't think there's anything they teach one that I don't know about—which fact I'm rather glad to know, as never having been to one of these places, I thought I might be even more iggerant than I am. I sleep very peacefully in my farm bed, and we take our meals in a hut together. The rest of it is rather like Dotheboys Hall—winder—W-I-N-D-E-R—go and clean the winders. We are a rum people.

I feel quite youthful, however, as there are several gray-headed officers at the school. I can't write to you—am very well—it's just slipsiness. I rather fancy our trenches were strafed a bit yesterday, but haven't heard details.

April 28.

Still nice weather. We are working very hard all day, doing all military lore in a fortnight in the most muddle-headed way.

Sunday, April 30. Still at School.

You have been minged in letters from this place, but the effect of being lectured all day is extremely soporific, and so is the weather, which continues very nice. The day before yesterday your parcel arrived. The cake I shall start at tea—it won't last long with twenty of us!

Now I'll tell you about yesterday as it was rather more newsful than the rest of the week. Started with a run, then lectures (the British Army ought to wear a bumble bee as a cap-badge!) then lunch; then walked into the nearest town with the sub-commandant. A good-looking man, very like a pirate-captain to look at. In the town we met the two youths I mentioned as being pleasant, and had tea together in a tea shop at 2 *fr.* each, if you please, for a very minging tea; then went to have our hairs cut, and with great difficulty found a little Belgian barber in a small side street, who undertook the job in a back sitting-room with a pair of shears such as tailors use to cut heavy cloth with.

From there made for the only two baths we could find. Keeping two small zinc baths is a regular occupation in this sort of one-horse town—they are planted down in the sort of shed the Standon barber shaves his clients in, with two women to fetch the water in pails, and a queue of British soldiers waiting to plunge in at 1 *fr.* 25 each. Not unprofitable either!

Then walked back—had dinner and went early to bed, hoping to sleep till about 10 a.m. today. Instead, the Boches chose to gas us. I'm rather pleased to have had a mild taste of it, as apparently gas attacks are to be expected all the summer when the wind is favourable. What happened was that at 12.45 midnight I heard a terrific bombardment open, followed by the gas alarm signals, in the distance, which is considerable. Being very sleepy and fairly sure that we were not gassable here, I went to sleep again, hoping it was not the R.B.s getting it. Twenty minutes later I woke to hear someone shouting 'Get on your gas helmets at once,' and to find my room full of gas, which was pouring into the window and not, of course, going out again.

Bustled into helmet, which is very difficult to adjust properly to pyjamas, and heard the captain in the next room—coughing and choking and calling for another helmet. Took him my reserve one just in time, I think. His servant was crouching on the floor in a great fright; and the pirate captain was cheerily dressing in the next room—all the doors opening in on the one room. Bustled out as soon as possible in pyjamas and Aquascutum and stood about in the night air while the gas blew by.

Of course it was exceedingly dissipated when it got here, but it took twenty minutes to float by, and was quite unpleasant, especially in the house, and shows how vital these unpleasant helmets are. I got quite a headache in the twenty minutes, besides breathing like a grampus. Found a farm hand wandering about without one, but the commandant assured me that these Belgians have all acquired them, mostly by theft from our men, and will risk going about in the gas without them just in order to get another from some charitable person!

Nobody suffered here—except from want of sleep—as we stood to for four hours after that, the men playing football from 3-5 a.m.; a thing which I am sure would annoy the Boches if they could see it. We hear this morning that the attack was a failure—and mostly on our left—but apparently a good many people and cows have been gassed including some in the next farm.

As I say, it's just as well to have tried it mildly like this, as it leaves one none the worse and considerably wiser. It was an extraordinarily bright idea of the Boches, and the first use of it must have been exceedingly ghastly for us.

Am very fitly now, and the only nuisance is that my eyes are still tiresome and the right one will see black spots at intervals.

May 3.

We've had a beautiful warm morning followed by a thunderstorm, which has made it cooler. I shan't mind how hot it keeps.

It's funny being up here—in sound of the guns and within reach of the gas—quite safely and listening to interminable lectures. The line of country through which the gas passed is rather curious—the clover blackened and killed as if by a hard frost—75 *per cent*, of the cows knocked out, and so on.

Some of the lectures, by experts, are interesting, and we had a most excellent first-aid lecture—quite the best I've heard on that subject.

(To his mother.) April 30.

I'm afraid I've been a very bad correspondent since I returned from my leave, and don't think I've ever thanked for the very nice parcel you sent. But somehow coming back to this existence put me off letter-writing, and now I'm at a school some way behind the lines doing a sort of general course. The school being here, somebody has to be sent from each battalion in the division every month, and it came to my turn this time. The weather is very nice, and, of course, it is healthier than the trenches; otherwise I think I prefer the latter, as I fear I never did like schools at any time, and find them as boring as ever in my old age. However, it's rather a different sort from most, and last night, or at 1 a.m. this morning, we were gassed in bed, and had to struggle choking to those smoke helmets and hustle out in our pyjamas. The Germans certainly do have some nasty ideas.

I think there are some pretty hot times ahead, but don't get worried by newspaper reports or lack of letters.

Now I think I'd better drore to a close, with much love to my best of mothers and all the others. I think I'm beginning to agree with Dr Watts, that we were not made to bark and bite like dogs.

May 4.

Am here for another week, and then I believe the batt. is out for some time, so cushiness is ahead.

Saturday, May 6.
I have put you off with minking scrabs. It's still most beautiful weather, largely wasted sitting in a stuffy hut listening to balderdash. However, it is very nice and I hope it'll continue. C Coy. won't be in the trenches for at least ten days, I suppose, though there may be a working party or so to take up towards the middle of next week.

Sunday 7.
The Irish business is rather sickening. It makes me disgusted to see these papers going on with their party politics over everything. Personally, I greatly doubt if any government of any sort is going to finish this war. The army is going to do it by its intelligent giving of battle, and I wish there were more intelligence. Still, there's probably more than one thinks sometimes.

May 9.
Just a line to say I've arrived back at the coy. in a wood out of which we go almost at once into a still quieter place. Rode back from the school yesterday in a pouring rain at the end of my examination, which did not strain my brain excessively.
T. is on leave and D. just going. We don't seem to have had many casualties at all, and the batt. did not get that gas which we did.

May 12.
Here we are in a rest camp, and I got up at 9 and had a hot bath and shaved and dressed outside in a beautiful summer atmosphere, which made it the pleasantest rising I've yet had out here. I rather fancy no *tranchées* for some time, but one's never quite sure about that.
I'm going to borrow a horse if I can and ride in to —— this afternoon, and buy myself some boots.
This camp is a series of huts side by side on a hill, and you see everybody all day. I have already chatted with about twenty officers and men this morning.

May 14.
The country here has changed extraordinarily in the last month—all the leaves out and the trees flourishing again. The day before yesterday I rode into the big town near here through a village about the size of Puckeridge that is mostly ruined

by shells. It was strange to see babies rolling about among the fallen bricks and mortar, and old women sitting out in the sun beside the remains of their cottages. How these old people must hate the Germans, whom they have seen twice bringing desolation upon them.

This morning I started at 9.30 a.m. with two others to inspect a place the batt. might have to go to in an emergency. We went by muddy lanes and tracks (it rained nearly twenty-four hours yesterday) and emerged on the place, which is a field full of orchids and forget-me-nots in deep wet grass—rather pleasant and peaceful—though it wouldn't be if we had to go there as a batt., for the Boches would probably do some shelling. Then we came back by the main road through rather a pretty little country town that has also been terribly shelled. There was a big girls' school at one end of it—half in ruins. I don't know when that happened—whether it was at the start of the war or not, and whether the *demoiselles* had to flee hurriedly along the roads as did so many other folk round here.

All the small shops in this sort of place have been turned into small grocery shops for the Tommies—and you see announcements like 'Coffee and Chipps,' or 'Egs—Milk—Buter—Chipps.' Chipps are, I suppose, potatoes, and always seem to be purchasable. You see Tommies sitting with their legs dangling out of top-floor windows—windows as once was—and guns nosing out of barns, and an armoured car, perhaps, half sunk in a flower bed, waiting for the Push.

Fine weather makes the country far pleasanter—it's stiffly laid out in avenues of trees like the maps they use at Hythe, and it certainly makes war seem more fantastic and unreal.

Got back, had lunch, and then a hot shower bath. The shower-baths consist of a place quite as small as the Billygoat's house, in which there is just room for two people to stand together, and you generally have to wait half an hour to get in.

The old soldiers whose time is up are rather annoyed at being compelled to serve on—not unnaturally, perhaps—but it is obvious that they cannot be spared, being each worth several recruits. I can't write interesting letters. The sort of enforced slackness plus the idea that you must not say anything the censor might object to, rather dulls me.

(To his mother.) May 14.

This is my wedding day. I went for a longish walk through muddy lanes and shelled villages. The weather has turned wet again, otherwise the country would be looking rather pretty—all the trees in leaf, and orchids and kingcups and forget-me-nots blooming in the meadows. In fact, it is looking pretty—in a formal way and where it isn't ruined. Some of the hedges, for instance, have autumn tints instead of spring ones, caused by the gas passing through them.

Yesterday I went for a ride to the largest town in the neighbourhood—again through shelled villages where babies still sprawl among the ruins. The Company gee has taken to stumbling of late, bother him, otherwise he is a fine powerful beast and jumps well. Of course on *pavé* especially stumbling is a great nuisance.

Are you keeping fit? My sister will want to collect a Red Cross fund for herself if she does much more severe work.

May 17.

Just going up—a beautiful day.

May 18 (I think).

It's a perfect day and I'm seated outside my dugout in shorts made from my breeches cut down, shirt and gum-boots, not to mention tin hat and tie.

My servant is really very good—quiet but most useful and attentive. He has just baled out about ten buckets of water out of my dug-out (below the floor) and he does this about twice a day. Just as he finished, two Riflemen came up and were disappointed to find none left as they wanted to make tea with it! Apparently the bottom of my dugout is also a drinking water reservoir. This is quite a good dry trench. I was up from the time of arrival till 4 a.m. this morning but have the rest of the day to sleep in.

Have already seen this morning the brigadier, I., D., a new *padre* attached to the batt., who is a brother of A. B., and several other people who have been up through the *tranchées*. Very quiet, I'm glad to say only aeroplanes being strafed overhead. T. said he went to the trench exhibition in London when he was home on leave, and found he had never seen anything at all like it before. Some old soldiers apparently show people round, and while he—T. in mufti—was explaining the workings of a Lewis gun to a friend, an old gentleman said crushingly, 'If you'll kindly allow this soldier' (pointing to an attendant) 'to explain the gun, we shall all benefit by it.'

******

I think this is the 20th May. It's still beautiful weather, and if the Boches would cease whizz- banging it would not be unpleasant sitting in the trenches. At the moment I've retired to my dugout, which, I think, is *whizz-bang p*roof, and two martens are trying to flutter in at the door. I don't know if they've inspected it in my absence and decided they would like to build there. The frogs—green ones—are yulling from a rather stagnant pond just behind, and birds are cheeping around. Cpl. A. has just gone by carrying some timber for a gas-proof dugout which he and I are constructing by the aid of our united brains. This is a few minutes later, and the Boches have left off *whizz-banging.*

Since lunchtime I have been listening to L, chatting about 'Intelligence,' in the company dugout, and falling asleep at intervals. When he got up to go off, I pulled myself together and came over here to write. Not that I have very much to tell you. Oh dear, I've got to shoot off to censor the men's letters. You needn't picture strafes at present.

Monday, May 22.

I am still rather sleepy from a seventeen hour day, started by being on duty from 2.30 a.m.-7.30 a.m. In the course of it we got a few *whizz-bangs* over—only a very few slight hits—and in the evening the unfortunate M. tried to blow himself and two other men up with a rifle grenade—none of them serious, however, luckily. It was a case in which I might almost be accused of the evil eye, for at the moment I was standing with Sergeant B. about 50 yds. away, saying, 'I dislike rifle grenades. I always expect them to blow up everybody round and I never expect them to blow up the Boches.' Which happened the next instant; but, as I say, it was a lucky business on the whole.

Having started at 2.30 on Sunday morning I came off at 3.30 a.m. this morning and slept till 12, when some bumping on the next line woke me. Still beautifully warm, and I go about with bare legs and shorts, which isn't bad in May, is it? On the whole, this is a very nice trench and simply doesn't bear comparison with Hooge, so far as I've seen it. I am very fit—and the eyes very fairly good.

Here in the early morning one sees jays and pheasants and lots of smaller birds, and green frogs, and heaps of rats, and a semi-wild cat occasionally. I imagine wild life is on the increase, because the No Man's Land is becoming rather jungly, and except for the shells, of course, very peaceful. So is the country immediately behind the trenches.

One of my platoon, who was always writing home to say he was in the thick of it (when he wasn't), has been hit slightly and will be enormously happy, I think, to go home with tales of the peril.

May 23 (?).

Another scrab, but I have such long nights somehow—only three hours' sleep last night that one dozes off most of the day and is not, as you know, particularly brilliant! S.—of the Buffs—whom I met at the Technical School, came up last night and spent last night with us. I had coffee with an artillery officer at 7.30 a.m., breakfast with S., lunch with D.—all visitors to the trenches. It's a heavy, still day—very quiet, a thunderstorm due, I think.

T. has gone off (temporarily) to the Divisional Staff, but I'm afraid they'll keep him when they find out that he is good.

We shall be out by the time you get this for several days—almost double the usual.

May 26.

Just a line from camp. Very damp march. Breakfasted at 11 today and post goes at 12. Nice weather again after very sloshy night.

May 28.

As I have had a whole night in bed, being the first for about ten days, I ought to be able to write more than a mere scrab. The weather is very pleasant and the honeysuckle is coming out in the wood, and yesterday I picked a bunch of yellow irises, buttercups, and a lot of new young red foliage of oak and sycamore. The only drawback to being out of the trenches is the quantity of working parties, which are a bore, but *roll on*, as the Riflemen say.

A.B.[14] has been appointed to the O.C. ship of C Coy. in Tatham's absence.

A youth in my platoon who was in the —— wrote in a letter I had to censor that he wished he was back in the —— as the batt. was a washout, all wrong. I had to send for him and ask if he thought it a polite thing to say of his batt., and discovered, of course, that he resents the stricter discipline. I tried to explain that it wasn't done for fun entirely, but to beat the enemy, but I'm not sure if I convinced him. Discipline is an infernal bore. There is no doubt that some of the new batts. are not particular enough about really vital matters, and the men don't of themselves seem able to distinguish what you must be strict about and what you mustn't. If only one could reduce discipline to its absolutely necessary elements and insist on those only, we should be nearer the ideal.

D. goes off on a gun course today which will leave us short again, with the corresponding extra work. I don't know why they can't keep an extra subaltern or two when there are such hundreds about.

Tuesday, 29 or 30.

Rather stupid of them to send —— to the —— but it is the sort of thing that happens. If anybody gets hit they are quite likely to be sent out again to some different batt, which I think is a great mistake.

I didn't have a working party last night and had another good sleep instead, but there seems a fair amount doing this morning, which does not leave me very much time to write before the post goes at 2 o'clock.

Mr Faviel—a copy thereof—is being passed round the batt. with an inscription (by the D youth, I fancy): 'To all officers for information and necessary action,' which is one of the Orderly Room phrases attached to reports.

I feel as if I wrote you the dullest letters and can't help it, and Frdk.'s statement that my letters are the most interesting reading he has at present is an unblushing lie, unless indeed he reads nothing else, which is quite likely.

Still Tuesday.

I wish I could write you nice letters like you write me; but

---

14. Captain Andrew Buxton, The Rifle Brigade, killed in action, June, 1917.

when I take up the pencil I seem to be just as dull as when I don't, or duller.

The sun has come out and it's not a bad day. Working party tonight, blow it, as I don't amuse myself much digging in the dark, though I like it by day.

31. Working party no bad last night—fine night told off the sappers successfully. Another party tonight, bust it. I'll have to finish this tomorrow.

June 1. Have to send this off in a hurry, and I meant it to be a long one, but was out till 2 a.m. and busy this morning. Have you seen the batt. mentioned in despatches?

June 2.

I had to hustle off a letter yesterday which I had meant to be a long one, as there was not much time left. We spent the morning dodging shrapnel which the unpleasant Boches put over what should have been our sequestered spot. Both B. brothers and Brown were nearly laid out, being within a few feet, and we were all within a few yards. The *padre* had one bullet put through a letter he had just written to his wife and found another in his surplice. Souvenirs! In the afternoon I went for a ride on the coy. horse, who skidded on his nose for about twenty yards on the way back.

Luckily I had just decided that he was going to fall, so managed to jerk him up again. It's a troublesome trick in a fine horse otherwise. He used to belong to Prince Arthur of Connaught. After tea I started a trench in which to get if any more shrapnel came along; also had my hair cut, but no digging party at night.

Today we move—not exactly into the trenches, but not far off.

Our guns are making a horrible row, deafening one, which accounts for the spasmodicalness of this.

Did you see the new C.-in-C.s' despatch (in the papers on Tuesday last)? It's not very exciting, but it describes the attack at Hooge and the batt. is mentioned. The list of those mentioned looks long, but as a matter of fact there is only one other in our division mentioned, so it is an honour of sorts. It's still beautiful weather.

June 4.

It is my birthday. It's a little cooler today but not bad, and as a matter of fact the nights are the more important, as that is when we work. There is very much to do, which I like, as it's less boring to have work, and we also have some small excitements—were *whizz-banged* yesterday and had a great artillery display last night—over our heads almost entirely. 'Noise, noise, noise!'

My servant is on leave and I realise how good he is now that I'm doing with somebody else. Cpl. A. has been made a sergt., and we are perfuriously putting up really good dugouts together. Some shells are coming over, bust the Boches! The noise puts me off.

Still June 4.

I am ashamed of my scrabs, though it really is a little difficult at times, what with candles and other people jabbering and slipsiness and such—not to mention being an idle letter writer at the best of times.

The weather has turned suddenly muddy, bust it, as it's very easy to be too cool in the trenches even in summer.

June 5. Not much done yet and very near post time. It's turned Aprilly today sharp showers and sunshine.

June 7.

Peaceful day for me today—Brown being on tonight. I got to bed at 3 a.m., having trotted about since 9 p.m. yesterday. The men are working very well and the only trouble is that we don't stay long enough to finish things properly.

Yes, awkward about that Boche gain. A place I sat in quietly for four days with my platoon was, I believe, heaped with dead bodies—ours and theirs.

I suppose the navy business was much better than it seemed at first, and at any rate there wasn't the glib boasting that takes off from some of our other efforts. The main disappointment is that they didn't, and probably couldn't, deliver the sort of blow that might really have hastened the conclusion of the war, for I suppose if Germany had lost her fleet, she would have had to resign the more absurd of her pretensions. The proportion of killed is rather awful: otherwise the casualties are no more than the armies lose in a day's fighting that practically goes unrecorded.

June 9.

This will somehow have to be a scrab, as we have been working all the morning instead of last night, which was very wet. Two *padres* just come into the dugout and the jabber is incessant.

June 10.

Out today—a mild showery April one. Got to bed at 3 a.m. to the sound of distant firing, and am not as vigilant as I ought to be when writing to you. We had a fairly exciting day yesterday. Some aggravating gunners, two of them colonels, who ought to have known better, came into the trench unbeknown to us and began observing over the parapet by day—a thing we have been at the utmost pains to prevent our men doing for days past. Just as we found them there, dancing happily about with field-glasses and things, the Boches spotted them too, and opened with *whizz-bangs* and H.E. Quite hot for half an hour, but nobody hit luckily, though the trench was bashed in in parts—the annoying thing is that they have now marked it down as a suitable target. In the evening I had a man hit by a machine-gun and had to roll rapidly down a steep bank in the dark to avoid it myself. Still, it's a very nice change from the last place, especially when one thinks of what is going on there now—of which we only get the light in the sky and the heavy boom of the guns.

June 12.

The weather has turned to a horrible wet cold slop and it's more like November than June.
One sees a few roses in shelled gardens climbing among shattered bricks, and the wild flowers are rather numerous in the parts where nobody dare go to cut the hay, and it's too dangerous to pasture animals. Yes, Sgt. A. has got the M.C., and also Sgt. W., and some of the others may get it for Hooge yet.
The naval news seems to grow better daily.
I think Howard [15] is justified in his grouse, but, of course, it is even more so in the regular batts. and the plums are very strictly preserved. I think before the war ends, the system will have to be altered, or we shall find ourselves working on the odd and probably disastrous view that three months at Sandhurst is

---

15, Sub-Lieut. Howard Fry, Howe Batt., Royal Naval Division, killed in action, November 16, 1916, my brother.—C. H.V.

more valuable than two years at the Front. However, we generally do end by surrendering our cherished stupidities before it is too late.

June 14.

I hope you aren't getting this awful wintry weather. Here there has been heavy rain for about four days on end, and we are extremely lucky to be out of the trenches for it, as it is even stopping work at present. I had one night of it till 3 a.m., the last one-and-a-half hours returning at a walk in a limber—all the men wet through long before—and I don't want any more. The country is so wet that when I rode with D. to a gas lecture we got our horses in up to the chest and had to leave the road for 100 yds. or more, where it was hopelessly bogged—about 10 ft. deep. That was yesterday afternoon. This afternoon I have been talking 'gas' to the platoon, and told them that if any of No. 12 ever got gassed they would be put on a charge—which pleased them, I think.

1 p.m. It's clearing a little and much I like the sun. The *padre* has just asked me to go for a ride with him, so if I can get a horse this will have to stop.

June 15.

It hasn't rained today but is beastje cold, and I shall put on my fur-lining for working party tonight. We go and return in a lorry, which makes it a lot better for the men, who always hate to have a long march thrown in. Yesterday I went for a ride with Padre Buxton. We had a very nice ride for three hours. I rode a pack animal—rather a nice beast, sturdy, but with a very hard mouth, like most of them. No stumbling, however, which is a great advantage. We had tea at a nice French shop and were joined by the doctor, who rode back with us. Then we changed our time at 11 p.m. and are now the same as you again, I suppose—an hour earlier.

B. has (temporarily) taken on the bomb squad which was offered to me, but I rather jibbed at it. It means leaving your own platoon and also dealing with weapons which I know I should be absentminded about at intervals, and I don't altogether believe in being turned on to any mortal thing, whether you're suited for it or not, merely because the authorities don't try to find out who is suited for what, though one doesn't like to refuse if it lets someone else equally unwilling in for it. However, I did offer myself as victim before, and let B. have it this time, as he said he didn't mind in the least. They probably have forty trained bomb officers waiting at Sheppey, forgetting things as fast as they learn them!

There seems to be next to no news of the Salient in the papers. The Canadians seem to have had a lot of casualties. But everyone is very cheerful over the Russian news, and the war, as usual, is going to end in a month or two. I'm afraid leave is going through very slowly this time, and it's very hard luck on the men. One sergeant was telling me yesterday that he's only had four days since war started. It's not economy, considering what a strain it puts on everybody, and I don't think people realise that this is a war where for the first time almost there is no rest from risking one's life and limbs—least of all, of course, for the rifleman.

I suppose there are bound to be many and violent happenings this year (not that I know of any).

June 17.

The weather has turned fine again, which is rather pleasant, but on the other hand we had one of these middle-of-the-night alarms, gas helmets on, prepare to go up, and all the rest of it, amid a terrific noise of guns, which makes one fairly sleepy next morning. Nothing came of it except sleeping in one's clothes. Also yesterday we had an accident by which one of our best sergeants lost his life. Poor youth, he was a very brisk, well-made, gallant young sergeant, and I remember thinking several times when I happened to be watching him in days past that it was particularly unpleasant to think of any one so splendidly built being knocked to atoms by some of these devilish machines—as I saw him yesterday. He was telling me a few days ago that he was going to apply for a commission. It's very sad, and I don't think one gets used to these things.

Everyone is very cheerful about the war at present.

This is written in snatches of a very fussy morning.

Sunday 18.

I really am rather hustled today and didn't have much time yesterday. Went to Sergt. ——'s
funeral—about three hours—very impressive the C Coy. of-

ficers acting as chief mourners came back and had a working party till 4.30 a.m. this morning, since when I've mostly slept. Trenches to-night, so I'm glad I slept most of the morning and had a hot bath; but I've very little time for writing. I've still got to make up accounts—I must stop. I shall probably have more time the next few days. I hope so. Nice weather again.

Monday, June 20, or else Tuesday 21.
(Really Wednesday, June 21!)

I got two lines started to you yesterday, and do feel as if I were treating you badly, sending meagre scrabs instead of the long letter I thought might come. But the time I expected didn't come either. We're fairly quiet but excessively busy, and this is the fifth night I haven't been to bed till 3.30 a.m. to 5 a.m., which is too late for me. Coming in was very boring. We had a gas alarm the moment we were up, but no gas—against which we are taking great precautions.

D. is a nice youth, I think, but, of course, being quite fresh to it can't be expected quite to pull his weight for a few days, and, anyhow, we are short handed again as C. is taking over another job temporarily.

A.B., when he sees a meal approaching, dashes out to look at something and comes back an hour later, and you may be thankful if he hasn't dragged you with him! But he's very intelligent and pleasant.

My friend Shafto of the Buffs has got the M.C. for a very gallant deed. I heard this from H., whom I met in the dark on a working party last night. A very pleasing lad.

Very few shells so far, but it's been beestje cold—almost freezing at night and a sort of sunless blight by day.

Why —— gets ten days' leave I can't tell. I wish I could.

June 22.

Got to bed at 3 a.m. this morning—on duty 7 a.m.-10 a.m. and 11 a.m.-12. Shelled for ten minutes then. On duty again to-night 7 p.m.-2 a.m. and from 4 a.m.-7 a.m., and probably shan't get to sleep between. So you may imagine I am getting fairly sleepy. This isn't so much grousing as explaining why letters are so muddily small, but you'll forgive it, won't you?

Out when you get this. Possible change from this part. Mostly quiet except for ten minutes this morning by very heavy shells which rather daze me. Man next me was shivering and quivering the whole time. Nobody hurt. We are exceptionally busy. Last night I was wiring in front for about three hours and had a party of men cutting the long grass with sickles—mostly on their stomachs. Rum scene in the moonlight. I always did detest barbed wire.

I am desperately afraid that this smidge or another equally scribbly smidge will be your birthday letter.

June 25.

I'm afraid even three lines really are quite difficult at present, as even if I wrote them (and we have been terribly hustled lately) they aren't always possible to get off. It's a beautiful day today and we are at ——, somewhere quite safe at all events.

June 26.

The men are all splendidly cheerful at present and it does one good to watch them at play. It's raining again after a fine Sunday. We are at the same safe place, I think for some little time. We are living in great luxury—strawberries and cream.

June 27.

It poured last night and nearly flooded us out. No news.

June 28.

I do hope that letters are not going to be stopped, as you suggest. I should think that is only one of the many rumours that get about.

It's just hopelessly wet. We're still at the same place. I had a gallop round a fine big field yesterday and then played rounders and then wrestled with A.D.—we each won one round; after which, I am thankful to say, he had sprained his thumb, as in the second one he fell heavily upon me and weighs about fourteen stones.

June 30.

A letter from you today, which shows the posts haven't stopped this side at any rate.

Had quite a pleasant day working party yesterday behind the lines, and played rounders with the men in the evening. Pulled out of bed in middle of night on false alarm, then back again. Today cold but fine. Shall probably go into nearest town after tea and have hot bath.

July 1.
Your letters keep coming and I hope my letters keep going. Good news today. I expect you'll have heard of it. Not in yet for several days. Weather beautiful.

July 2.
It's a beautiful day again today, Sunday, and we shift a bit, but our nearest town is still the same as when I was last on leave, which, I think, is not giving away military information.

Yesterday I inspected a flying place with C., and if we had got there an hour earlier might have had a ride, which it seems rather absurd not to have had hitherto—not that I think that I should take to the things at all.

The mess gets on very well together. A. D. is so merry and cheerful that he is invaluable at most times. He spends his time seeing that his elders' ties are straight. He is our only boy, and the great value of boys out here is that they can be so much more mercurial than other people—which the men like, being babes themselves. The whole army is a collection of brave babies.

I suppose for the next few months there are bound to be doings.

This is a hop country and the hops are 15 feet high and rather pleasing. Beautiful sunset last night.

July 3.
Beautiful weather and the news seems good so far.

July 4.
Weather fit, self fit. Nothing doing here much. We had a coy. photograph taken at the last place and I will try and send you a copy.

My servant has gone sick, I am sorry to say.

July 5.
Heavy rain yesterday, but good night's rest. Lots of rumours flying about, but nothing substantial. Very quiet for us so far. There is a small Bilien goat in the camp here which wanders into the huts to eat things. Rather a pingly one but not bad.

I saw a passage the other day which I expect you know and like. It's something about '*Be brave and endure for the Lord will protect you until you have finished the service that He requires of you*'—

something like that, rather fine and suitable for a soldier.[16]

July 6.

Another fine day. Had a rotten time last night. Brown and I took up a working party and some fools of gunners started shelling the Boches, who retaliated while the trench was full of our workers. Result very unfortunate, including the wounding of another of our best sergeants—a horrible wound in the thigh. Brown quite good and cool—self quite good and cool. Went down with sergeant and stretcher-bearers at the end of it—an awful trek for hours—got him off about 4 a.m. and myself to bed at 5 a.m. Lots of men do awfully well on these occasions, but there should not be any such. No time for more. The poor sergeant was engaged—has been out nearly two years and will surely lose his leg if not his life. He was awfully patient going down.

July 7.

Just a line to say very fit. Nasty muddy weather again. Much sleep last night. We really get our news from the papers, so you hear before we do. Sergeant A. has been made platoon sergeant of 11 platoon, which means I lose him, I regret to say, but I still have the best N.C.O.s.

July 8.

I am so sorry to see Huddart has been killed. He was such a nice fellow and they seemed so very happy together. I suppose it was in the advance.

It's a beautiful day, and I'm sitting in the remains of a huge cellar of a farm not far from the front lines. We got here yesterday after being shelled for about half an hour where we were at the farm. The old farmer's wife and a girl-hand spent the time trying to drive their cows into a shed—mostly under shrapnel fire.

I never saw such coolness and stupidity. Of course whenever a shell fell near the cows scattered, and the women, after a shriek, chased them and got a shell on the other side. Meanwhile the British Army crouched under a wall, sensibly enough. Two cows and a calf were hit, and I expected to see both the women laid out, and shouted in vain to them to leave the cows. They

---

16. He sent the reference later, *I Chron. xxviii. 20*, saying, 'Not quite as I thought, but very much.'

simply would not.

We marched up here through a very bullety area; but once arrived, it's rather nice, and I have the best dugout I've ever had, very nearly shell-proof, I should say. There's a moat and ruins of barns and cellars amid which we live with the shells planking around and a continual rattle of machine-guns at night. Two Australian officers came in here an hour ago for a drink—pleasant simple souls from Gallipoli and Egypt.

Spent the morning with Brown counting the contents of a dump. I may send back some more kit sometime, if we move, so don't be surprised if you see it arrive.

July 9.

It's another beautiful day, but no letter from you. But praps I shall get two tonight—about 1 a.m.—which is when I get it here. There is a moat below my dugout with green frogs in it. I don't think I have any news. I take my platoon out at night to work in gum-boots in a very muddy ditch, much sniped; but we rather like it as we are on our own without the assistance of any R.E.s, who are always tussome.

This afternoon we had a few shells, after which I took up my N.C.O.s to see our ditch by daylight; and we crawled about on our stomachs in a hot sun and got quite warm, which is very pleasant. Brown, the two Buxtons, and I are the only mess in this particular ruin, but I have entertained on whiskey and soda-water today P.B., K. (adjutant), O.C. A Coy., M., and several others. Sich is life. D. complained of our absence of leave—quite rightly, I think. One in 8-9 months is not really fair. However, the men get less and grouse very little.

Tell my mother I really will try to write soon. It's bad not to, but I got so sleepy with night work and don't want to get really short in case one had to make an extra effort.

July 11.

I got your last night's letter about 4 a.m. this morning after what was an interesting night and for some people a very exciting one. C., with two other officers, led a raiding party into the Boche trenches. The party had been training down below and came up in the moonlight to where we are, as it were, among the ruins of Plashes farm buildings, with blacked faces and labels on their backs—to help recognise one another in the dark—and armed with *knobkerries* and axes and any weapon of their fancy, and stood about till the light, or rather the dark, was right for the fray. Cpl. ——, a great hulking savage child, pressed into my hand three packets of woodbines as a parting gift (in case he didn't come back) for a friend of his. They were a fine collection of cheery, excited ruffians, picked volunteers, and went off amid many good lucks.

Meanwhile I had to get two platoons into a trench we had been hastily digging in case the Boches retaliated with a heavy bombardment, which they did. I sat with them there for about one-and-a-half hours while the ground shook and crash followed crash. Then the raiders trooped back, having done very well. They got into the Boche trenches, the Boches fled, and they burgled their dug-out and rushed back with only one or two casualties. Unfortunately one of D Coy. officers and one of our very best stretcher-bearers were killed after they'd got back into our trench, by a *minenwerfer*—very bad luck.

Then we had the raiders back in our dugout to have drinks, all of them with different stories of what had happened and how many Boches they had killed, and adventures in the wire, and the nature of the Boche trenches. Then the casualties arrived. I fancy I got to bed about 7 a.m.; but I was too sleepy to be sure. Slept till 2 p.m., and am so far having a peaceful day. I don't much approve of these raids—you take too many risks to achieve a doubtful end. Still, it went all right, which is satisfactory.

Tell my mother not to worry. I don't suppose the Push is very much worse than anything else really, and so far we are not in it.

July 10.

Another nice day and I did get two letters from you at about midnight when coming in from digging. No news at all—the general outlook seems good, doesn't it? I have just lent Frdk.'s rifle[17] to E. to do some sniping with. He is a very fine shot and stationed at present where sniping is possible. Poor youth, he has two brothers wounded this month, and one may be killed apparently, but he doesn't know.

Must stop at this point.

---

17. A telescopic sighted rifle lent him by Frdk.

July 12.

I enclose two photographs—one of the coy, and one of 11 and 12 platoons, taken at a farm we were at, some way back, a fortnight ago. I have pointed out the leading lights.

I am sorry to say that Say, one of the men hit on the raid, and once a corporal in my platoon, has died since, leaving a wife and two children. He was a very fine fellow. K., who brought him in, said Say implored him not to do it lest K. should get hit. The doctor, too, said he was one of the best patients he had seen. It seems to me the children of such a man should have every chance. He was very cool and quiet-mannered, and would have done extremely well, I think. Last night Brown had another of our corporals shot through the heart—also about 22 and married, with children.

There is an awful waste of our best men just at present; but I suppose it can't be helped.

July 14.

I send you a letter pretty often though I have no news to send. I fear one batt. got badly hit and you will see some names shortly.

I meant to write reams to you, but I have to chuck it right now. I'm going to try and answer your letters later.

July 15.

Our part here is lined with *minenwerfers*, and Cpl. D. and six men nearly got laid out by one today. A tiny bit fell on my knuckle about 300 yds. away, but one gets too many souvenirs of that sort to keep them.

I think the idea of being censored makes me so dull.

Sunday 16. Now I shan't get a very long letter written after all. Had a rather exciting carrying party last night up a road full of *minenwerfer* holes and got in, changing camp, at 4 a.m. As a result I have just got up for lunch instead of breakfast and the post goes at 2.

Here we are, back in the farm where the women herd the cows among the shells. I'm with Brown in one of those bivouac covers, very nice in nice weather, but somewhat damply in Flanders.

July 16.

Another working party tonight—probably till 5 a.m.—so that

I don't suppose I shall wake up in time to write you much of a letter tomorrow, as I intended to do, not expecting the party tonight. I do not like being up so late, especially along a bullety road, but sich is life. Haig is reported to have complimented the division on the way it has worked and been bombarded up here, while the strafe goes on down south.

Nice of Vaughan to write. I am glad he was left out of it. His batt. must have had a specially bad time, having to retreat—always the worst part.

We are in the same hut as a fortnight ago, C and D officers together, the same gramophone tunes going (but one officer less—the one who was killed); everybody the same, except that war seems more in the air, and they talk of how to spike guns and such things. I think there is going to be little rest now for any one till the war has taken a different turn for the Boches. It's a strange atmosphere, artificial in a way—the zest to kill and all that, but necessary, I suppose. I wish I could get up more of it.

One of D Coy. sgts. has been recommended for a V.C.—Sgt. Smith—he was twice wounded in the second line on the night of the raid, and went twice through a barrage to fetch stretcher-bearers—quite good work.

July 17. Got home at 3 a.m. after all. Two separate bullets between Sgt. E. and self, who were walking side by side! We both looked at t'other to see who was hit. However, no harm to anybody at all and slep till 12. Tonight there should be a boost on and I am hoping to watch it from a high hill. Will tell you if I do.

Sgt. M., the one I took down the other day, has written to Sgt. E. to say he's going on very well on the whole, and asking him to thank me for my attentions. Nice of him, as he must still be very bad, I should think.

July 18. Thought I would keep this a second day and tell you about the strafe as seen from the hill. As a matter of fact I was rather disappointed. It was a fine night (after the hottest day we've had) with the moon drifting behind tiny clouds, and a dozen of us sat in the open watching shells burst—ours a couple of miles away and some of theirs just behind us. Tremendous noise, of course. We set fire to two houses behind the German lines within the first five minutes and they did not retaliate effectively. The red flashes of the bursts and the crashing sounds were rather terrible, but did not compare with the same when you are marching beneath them, I thought.

Today is bitly cold. The news still seems good. Just post time. No letter from you, perhaps two tomorrow.

July 19.

Just a line to say I'm very fit. Three letters arrived for me from you today. Please thank my mother for her parcel when you write—all the things were good.

It's a nice day again after a dull one. Much shooting in the night.

July 21.

It is a very nice day, and so was yesterday, though on neither, so far, have I got a letter from you. However, I expect some today. I expect with all this fighting going on there simply isn't room to carry mails in trains and steamers. We are sitting once more as in the photograph—what next I don't know, and as there is supposed to be an extra strict censorship, couldn't tell you if I did.

At present C Coy. is rather annoyed. You heard about the Paris review of troops the other day. Well, the 3rd R.B.s represented our division at it, and our best N.C.O.s represented the 3rd R.B.s and went off expecting a tremendous good time. Instead of which they were barely let out of barracks the whole time they were there—with the result that they took French leave one night and went to a box at the theatre and were all put on a charge when they got back. Some reprimanded and several reverted to the ranks exactly when their value might be inestimable. Discipline! Here were these men just come out of a raid and with two years' fighting behind them, kept as if they were prisoners. The consequence of it all is that we are short of N.C.O.s and have to appoint young or inadequate ones to take the place of these tried ones. It isn't good enough. Oh for a little elasticity in the army.

I do hope you are getting this nice weather. I think it will make the waiting a little less depressing.

July 23.

Here's the post going off at a moment's notice. It's fine weather and I have a new servant, my last one having got his discharge.

The new one is a Manchester guttersnipe called 'Ginger'—you would love him. Looks about 15 and has been out about fifteen months—unutterably cheeky. He offered himself for the job. I'll try and write a proper letter tomorrow.

July 23.

I sent you a small scrap today because the post corporal, who is a silly little very mournful wisp of a man (who also cuts hair and sniffles over you as he does it), chose to send word at 11.15 a.m. that all letters had to be sent off at 11 a.m. And I was only down late after the third most maddening night of mosquito biting.

Before I forget, I have sent back Frdk.'s rifle in the case together with my MS. book. We never know now where we shall be next, so the less kit we have the better.

We are in a rather nice farm with a nice old farmer who congratulated me on the beauty of my French accent, which was rather tactful of him, as the accent is the only possible merit of my French.

—— seems to have lost heavily. I am afraid these newer batts. lose more heavily even than they need, for experience at this game is the only thing that counts for much, it seems to me.

By the way, until this strafe is over, I don't fancy anyone hit would be kept here over twenty-four hours. Everybody seems to go back like lightning. It's strange how warlike the air is—every night the noise of heavy bombardment: the roads crowded with troops, rumours flying in every direction. And all this land in the meantime is ripening to the harvest—corn getting yellow, the hops climbing sky-high, the hay in cocks, and broad beans six feet high. Today was a beautiful day—a hot sun and a fresh breeze. Brown and I walked into —— to buy things for the mess basket: we purchased from a charming French maiden, and sent our goods back—five miles—by two orderlies, one my new servant, Ginger.

July 28. (Really 26.—C.H.V.)

It may be the 28th or not, but I'm writing in bed just before snoring off and I'm rather vague about it.

It's still rather nice weather—in quite a different part from the last: in fact, we seem to be on the move, and I suppose someday shall get to the centre of things: but for the next six days I am on a bayonet course (!) in order to qualify as a batt. instructor. This rather amusing, with the greatest battle of the world going on, but like us. C Coy. had to send an officer and only Brown and I were available, and Brown wasn't keen, so I offered myself, though I'm afraid some physical drill is included, which I detest. Five hours' bayonet fighting a day for a week ought to make me rather fit, and, as you know, I rather fancy myself with it, but shall probably want to correct the instructor most of the time.

Last night we spent in a train till 2.30 a.m., when we started to march twenty miles—stopped for breakfast at 5 a.m., after which Brown and I, alone of the batt., bathed in a rather nice river just below us. It ran about five miles an hour and one could only just prevent oneself from being carried down. Cold but rather nice in the middle of a long march. Got to our destination about 12 noon, and I am in bed on the floor of a very small farm in a kind of Collier's-End village—the farm kept by a very ancient and smiling Frenchwoman, who is horrified because B. and C. insist on sleeping in the garden.

My French is getting terribly bad and fluent, and I bargain for hens and cream and make jokes in French. I had about twenty minutes' chat with a charming, dirty, small girl of about eight, who wanted to sell me *gateaux*, but was quite happy to talk instead. She told me exactly where we were going—which was more than we knew ourselves.

As usual, not being able to describe things exactly puts me off, but it can't be helped.

It's rather amusing how the modern Malbrouck (like A. D.)—*s'en va-t-en guerre*—with John Bull, London Opinion, a pound of chocolates, a bag of greengages, and the utmost light-heartedness, on the seat of his compartment beside him.

Did I tell you that —— has been made adjutant?

And there are people like —— and ——, men of 30 and 35, with every intellectual distinction and the habit of command and organisation in the batt., and yet baby boys who have spent four months at Sandhurst have to be tried first at what is not the simplest job in the world. However, I'm not girding at things—though I do think it will take longer to win while we go on in that way.

Must sleep now.

27(?) Thursday(?)

I believe there are extra stringent regulations about what is put in letters at present, so I feel rather as though one is not at liberty even to say it's a fine day, which it is. I ought to be getting rather fit with eight hours' bayoneting a day, and I think I am; but am also rather annoyed with the instructor—a sgt. major of some other regiment who is rather impertinent. I don't know how I shall get on with him as the days roll by, though it's absurd quarrelling with anybody but Boches at present, and I shall endeavour not to.

A funny little rosy-faced midget of a Frenchman rolled in today to say that some of our men had stolen his espalier apples, and I had a long conversation with him in a sort of French, and the *padre* gave him some almond toffee, and he went off after shaking us by the hand warmly with the statement that he should consider the apples as a 'souvenir' for the troops. Poor little man, they were apples that would weigh a *livre* each and last till March.

Some of the French people can be very annoying. I discovered a very good *vin ordinaire* at an *estaminet* in sealed bottles; and some very bad in unsealed bottles. I bought the sealed bottles and returned them empty at their request. Next time the servant was given the sealed bottles I had returned filled with the inferior wine.

We have rather an amusing staff at present: ———'s servant is a musical comedy star of sorts and quite amusing. He came to me last night and told me that Ginger—my little guttersnipe—had had toothache for three days and nights and wouldn't say anything about it, and would I see to it. So I sent Ginger to the doctor, who pulled out his largest tooth before breakfast and then gave him M. and D.—which means carry on with your usual work—which meant a long day's march in the sun. Some of the army doctors are awfully inconsiderate, I think. The poor little wretch hadn't slept for three nights apparently, and anybody could see that he looked ill as a result of it. Luckily, Buxton let him off for the day; but he gets told he's too sentimental.

I must to bed—I had breakfast at 8 a.m. and it's 11.30 now—

very late!

Frdk. is absurd about the paid job. He ought to know as well as anybody that in war more than in most things people can't be paid according to their works, and it's therefore excellent if somebody who really has got the capacity gets some sort of reward for it. However, nothing will persuade him, I suppose.

Saturday, July 29.

I am afraid my last letter will be rather late, as this is the third time in a fortnight that the rat of a post corporal has told us one time for collecting letters and then taken them at another. And now I have nothing to tell you. It is still very beautiful weather and we are still here, and I am still bayonet-fighting. Haven't quarrelled any further with the sgt.-major, who is more respectful in his manners, and am getting very fit. I breakfast at 8, bayonet-fight from 9-12 and 2-4, and then feel considerably sleepy, apart from having letters to censor, which takes a long time and is rather dull.

The back gardens of these cottages are about half an acre large and well-stocked, but very weedy. Of course they sell us vegetables at high prices.

Brown and I are just setting off to a village three kilometres away, as we have the afternoon off, and this will have to close as Brown wants to start early to catch the cashier and get money out of him.

Will try and send something better tomorrow.

July 30.

It's Sunday and a most beautiful day—very hot sun and very nice air, and I am sitting in the garden all by my lone, as the batt. has gone off on a Field Day, and I, being supposedly on a special course, am taking advantage of the fact that there is no bayonet-fighting today to do nothing at all. So that I really have got time to write.

The country round is rather nice—the village in a steep valley with a stream half the width of the Rib through it, marshland on one side and parkland on the other, rising steadily to a kind of downs which, not being too well cultivated at present, are full of wild flowers. Several of these I haven't seen before—especially one or two campanulas—new to me, but I dare say not rare.

The men have a bathing pool or two in the stream and like it much. The British Tommy is like the pig—just as clean as he is allowed to be.

A. D., who is a lively youth, spends his time scrapping with me in the mess, who spend my time trying to persuade him that if he hadn't been to Eton and Sandhurst some glimmer of sense might remain with him. He's really not unpleasing at all.

Just had to move into the shade of an apple tree out of the sun, so you see how warm it is.

The Paris episode has died down now. They simply could not afford to lose the sergeants. Of course you have to bear in mind that the older soldiers take these things philosophically as being the army all over. The trouble is that there are not going to be old soldiers for very much longer—only old officers, and the new wine will be forced into the old bottles by the old Sandhurst system because that system has been artificially preserved by rapid promotion, which prevents it from suffering the normal casualties.

Do you see the lad Anderson has got the Military Cross for a raid he did? I thought he would show himself pretty competent and gallant.

I am almost as hot as if I were in India! The old lady next door has just told me it was too hot, but I said 'No.'

Very distant but continual noise of guns.

It is quite extraordinary to see the sort of military articles and sketches that go down in some of the papers. I saw one on soldier servants in the —— by someone who stated that his servant even built a dug-out for him when he went into the trenches. A decent dugout takes about ten men to build, working several hours several days; and the idea merely indicates that the writer has never been out of England. The same with half these reported conversations with the men back from the Push: they don't even suggest the sort of attitude the men take towards the whole thing. And the undoubted gallantry is far too much insisted on in order to cover up the shortage of organisation and forethought that so often goes with it. I don't want to seem critical, but one does want to let it out sometimes, and I know you won't mind listening.

These courses such as Howard has embarked on are rather quaint. Of course, it's the same with me at present. I ought to be handling my platoon instead of learning the bayonet; and the other officer learning it is a regular who has had about fifteen years of it before, I suppose, but the instructor must have a class, so off you go to it, whether you are expert or not.

Naturally, there are some new tips. I don't happen to agree with most of them; and it will be rather like having to instruct the men to cut their balls at tennis instead of driving them—a painful duty.

August 1.

I wrote you two lines this morning and just missed the little post-corporal, who announced that he was taking the letters about five minutes before he took them, and then scuttled off down a track through thistles 10 feet high, like the white rabbit. I sent my servant in pursuit, but he failed to catch him; hence this letter, which may be a little longer but not much. I'm writing it in my valise in a tent on the top of a bare hill by the light of a very flickering candle. Eric [18] not far off I dare say. It's really hot weather now: men fainting by the way from heat, so you may imagine I'm rather well suited by it. We're not in anything so far. It's very difficult to write by this bougie. Guns in the distance. I must say goodnight now, I think, and see if I can add a line in the morning when I believe we go early to bathe like the Spartans.

2. No time. Just going to bathe.

August 2.

Just a line to say still no news. Not a bad bathe this morning in the river, somewhat coloured by the rest of the battalion. I am on a court-martial tomorrow. It's a picturesque place this—many troops in view—bands, concerts, football going on, and in the distance the crack of the guns. I must stop now.

August 3.

Still another beautiful day and still nothing doing. I spent four hours court-martialling—no deserters, I'm glad to say; but I did not enjoy it for the same reasons as Frdk. used not to at Sheppey. Tell him he might do a very useful work revising the Army Code and the general powers committed to the casual judge. There are some sentences that may be necessary, as a matter of

---

18. Capt. T. E. Le Blanc Smith, M.C., R.F.A.

course, and the question of guilty or not guilty seems seldom difficult, but when the punishment varies between a month and three years in prison, and the decision is left to amateurs of justice, somebody is sure to suffer.

Sgt. —— has not been well and I find he was laid up last year with some chest trouble (caught from old French lady where he was billeted) and warned by the doctor to 'look after himself' in case consumption followed. As if a man could look after himself out here. It seems strange in so splendidly-built a man, and one of the added horrors of war.

A captain in a Scottish regiment is coming to dinner. It's just about to come on the table, made of old ammunition boxes, in the open, on the side of a down. Beautifully warm—band playing—five-course dinner—sunset in crimson dust, and always the infernal crash of the guns.

August 4.

I have no news to give you. Nothing doing. Practised an attack before breakfast; spent the morning teaching the Coy. the latest style of bayonet-fighting; had a ride this afternoon among barbed wire and trenches with Brown, who was thrown by the coy. horse; tea; lecture by the G.O.C.; dinner; went out with Buxton to watch a great strafe that is going on; came back; corrected platoon letters, and am now writing to you.

My mother's parcel has arrived—very welcome—also the gauze netting; just at the moment the mosquitoes are off, frightened by the guns, perhaps! But it will be very useful if they return. The noise is very distracting.

Must sleep now. The baynit course isn't keeping me back at all. It's sort of extra.

Sunday, August 6.

At the moment of writing I am a-setting in my valise once more, and two *padres* are sitting on the next valise having supper at 10.30 p.m. after a round of services. The Buxton Brer and the Methody parson, a Cambridge man. It has been a nice day, very hot sun but cold wind: everybody is peeling under it, and one's knees in shorts are quite painfully burnt. I started the day by bathing with the coy. at 7.30 a.m.—somewhat cool; a Brigade church parade at 10; after lunch, sleep; after tea a long walk with Brown and the doctor; then dinner and correcting

platoon letters; then writing to you, then more sleep.
I am sorry to say the doctor has sent Sgt. —— down, strongly suspected of consumption. It's awful to think of in so fine a fellow. I saw him just before he went. He has promised to let me know how he goes. He thinks he'll be back in a couple of days, but the doctor says not for this war. I would rather have lost half the platoon, but it can't be helped.
Still nothing doing. I teach the baynit and we practise digging and such things. I got a letter from Frdk. Nice of him to write. Please thank him. There isn't a lot of opportunity for letters, though I expect he would make them if he were in my place. I wish I could tell you any news of interest, but I canna.

August 7.

No letters for two days but I know that is not your fault.
It's still the hot windy weather that takes all the skin off you by day and is rather icy at night. I taught the baynit this morning and threw some Boche bombs this afternoon, and then had a swim in the river. I really think I should not be bad with the baynit (which we call the sword) if only I had not a slight rheumatic in the left shoulder which will not quite go away. Advancing years? or sitting in the mud and snow at Hooge?
This is rather a picturesque spot: I wish I could tell you about it, but I may not. It's rather stupid.
I must say Goodnight now.

August 9.

No time to write to you today, but am very fit. I got three letters from you yesterday. Will try to write more tomorrow.

Thursday, August 10.

You would be amused by the place in which I write this—a small scoop in the side of a trench, like a rabbit burrow, to which I've retired after a somewhat disturbed night in the bottom of a trench—disturbed only by rain at 4 a.m. after which I wandered about till breakfast time, getting damp and fearing greatly that the fine weather has gone for good. The night before I was in yet another place—resembling a hare's form more than anything else. I made it myself out of an old shell-hole with a hurdle on the top, covered with wild mustard and old sandbags to keep out the dew. Bitly cold it was, too, as nowadays I carry all my goods on my back in my haversack—plus the *Aq-*

uascutum strapped to it. Not even a pack. I think I am about as Red Injun in colour as I ever have been, including the knees. No. 12 platoon is not in luck at the moment.

I told you about Sgt. ——: next day a corporal recently appointed was taken ill and sent down; and yesterday, while I was instructing the platoon in the bayonet, a fat shell pitched about 30 yards away, and knocked out Sgt. D., breaking his leg below the knee. It was luck having only one man hit a little nearer and the whole platoon might have been; but, of course, he is a great loss—the only really good N.C.O. I had left. The doctor thinks he won't lose it. He shed his gore all over my only pair of bags as I was helping to carry him in, and there's no water to wash them in. Sich is life at the moment.

Later in the day I had an endless walk with C. through a trench—three hours we took—eating dust all the way, through awful smells and every form of abandonment, from rifles and tin hats to dead men. Oh dear, I don't like war.

The flies are disgusting and the mosquito netting is very useful. I'm afraid I envied Sgt. D.

No more at present, and don't picture that we're having a bad time—we're not—so far it's only rather disgusting.

★★★★★★

I think it must be Friday, the 11th of August, and I am lying in my scoop again at 3.30 p.m., whence I move very shortly. My schedule for this afternoon was lunch at 1; write to you 1.45-2.15; bath at 2.15; sleep 2.30-4; tea at 4, start at not much later. As usual, things cropped up and have done me in. The postman arrived and departed about 1.45! Buxton has gone up; Brown has gone sick; and messengers have been arriving with messages, effectually preventing me from sleeping at all, and it's now nearly teatime.

On the other hand, it's a fine day again: I have had a magnificent hot bath in half a small tin of water; and your letter has arrived. Also" one from Frdk. , enclosing Vaughan's. I'm afraid we've missed for sure this time: having just reversed our locations, and I've been seeing the things he has and *vice versa*. I had a most tussome working party last night: was given a guide and a map reference; didn't trust the guide going up, and took my own way to the map reference. On arriving found that though I'd got to the right place, sure enough, the reference had been

given me wrong! Meant another two hours' work for everybody. Got into a shelling and had three men hit (all very slight, I'm glad to say) and one with a sprained ankle, from dodging shells. Allowed the guide to guide me back, with the inevitable result that he lost himself and us; then struck across country and very luckily exactly hit our trench. But not enough sleep quite. Still, it's a beautiful day.
I'm glad you like t'other poems.

August 12. Must send this off—no time to write more. We are working despritly hard—very little sleep. I'm afraid letters are likely to be very irregular at present. Don't be worried by that.

August 14.
I dare say Eric is quite near, but one simply hasn't time to find out, and we might be only 100 yds. away without knowing it. We are having a fairly peaceful two days after two fairly hot ones. I got about three hours' sleep in forty-eight—constant shelling—fearful smells and working like navvies. Did about double the ordinary infantryman allowance myself. The flies are disgusting now. I think the platoon is getting rather friendly at last—had about half a dozen of them chatting to me during the shells, when they most want a little consolation. My Buff friend, Shafto, was killed, I think the night after I had the carrying party, in much the same place. Quite the best man in the batt., I should say. We got off very lightly.
I can't distinguish sunburn from dirt on my face now. If I rub too hard the skin comes off; and if I don't, the dirt remains on! Vaughan's letter very amusing. I hope Frdk. is really better. Brown is back again, fairly fit, I think.
I am in my rabbit scoop again. My last bed was a ledge of chalk about 1 ft. wide and 4 long, at an angle sideways—not very comfortable! Oh dear, there comes the Q.M.S. for the letters. I must finish.

August 1 6.
No letters for two, three days, so a little flatness. But I hope soon I shall get three or four to make up. The weather has turned misty moisty, which is rather a nuisance when one sleeps without any bedclothes. I tie things like a sock or a towel round my knees and get my legs into a damp sand-bag to keep warm; and really was quite warm last night.

Quite a slack day yesterday and might have for some days. You remember Vaughan's position in the Push? Probably mine would be the same if there were one at any time.

Did I tell you of a rather nice boy in my platoon who writes a family letter daily always beginning

> Dear Mum and Dad, and dear loving sisters Rosie, Letty, and our Gladys,—I am very pleased to write you another welcome letter as this leaves me. Dear Mum and Dad and loving sisters, I hope you keeps the home fires burning. Not arf. The boys are in the pink. Not arf. Dear loving sisters Rosie, Letty, and our Gladys, keep merry and bright. Not arf.[19]

It goes on like that for three pages—absolutely fixed; and if he has to say anything definite, like acknowledging a parcel, he has to put in a separate letter—not to interfere with the sacred order of things. He is quite young and very nice, quiet, never grouses or gives any trouble—one of those very gentle creatures that the war has caught up and tried to turn into a frightful soldier, I should think in vain. I can't imagine him sticking anybody, but I'm sure he would do anything he felt to be his duty. ——'s servant is also another of the gallant lambs. He is a squat little elderly man of about 45—was a comedian of sorts, and looks it—has a wife and five children—was rejected six times by the doctors and got in as a bandsman; then shoved out here into the front line. He sings comic songs and cheers the others and waddles about manfully, but is no more a fighting ruffian than a child of six. Yet he too takes part in the bloodiest battles of the world.

A. B. really is a pleasing and exasperating person. He'll wander in at 11.30 a.m. and ask if lunch is ready. I say 'No, it's only 11.30. Would you like it earlier than usual?' He says 'Yes, I should rather—I'm rather hungry.' So I get the cook to promise it at 12.30 instead of 1, and at about 12.25 B. will stray forth and return about 2.15, and be quite hurt because the lunch is rather cold! But I enjoy it.

August 17.

I did get four letters today.

---

19. The names in this letter have been changed—my husband had a great regard for the writer. He expresses it here and did later in conversation with me.—C. H. V.

I got into a nasty bombardment last night with a party I had volunteered for—80 men and only one hit, which was very lucky, as we had to sprint across the open under shrapnel, besides two hours heavy stuff. All quite unnecessary and somebody's fault, but I don't know quite whose and probably never shall. These things will happen at times. The regimental sgt.-major was with me: a terrific person with a wonderful waxed moustache, and it was very funny to see him peering out of various holes in the ground like a coney. He told me he cracked several jokes with some of the young fellows to keep their spirits up; but I can't say that I heard him, and as Brown remarked, that would have been much more awful to them than the actual bombardment. His idea of a joke would be to say—'Here! You! Put yer cap on straight!'

August 18.

I forgot to answer your question about the small dog in the photograph. It doesn't belong—was only a farm creature of one of the mixed French types, introduced as a mascot. The troops like a mascot in fact, I believe that is why the very young officer is better than the older ones. They like some young frolicsome creature like —— barking at their heels and playing about in their midst. There are two or three lurcher creatures kept at the Transport, but they don't go into the front line much. One big puppy doesn't seem to mind shells a bit.

I am afraid I am in for a Lewis gun course. I suppose other people would like it, so, pig-headedly, I don't. The thing is a machine, and, anyway, like Howard, I don't like leaving the platoon in these strenuous times. The course is, I believe, a week, far from the firing line. At present I am at the Transport on my way, as it were: might be recalled, but don't think it's likely. I asked to be left with the platoon and can't do more.

I don't see any Paris or other leave in prospect for a long time, confound the Boches. I wish I did. I do wish they hadn't done away with leave. The thing seems never-ending without a prospect of it.

Give my love to all and a pat to Meriel and the Bui Hound. [20]

August 23.

I am very fit and well, but I'm afraid you've been left without

---

20. The bull mastiff appearing in the frontispiece.

a letter for five days and I only hope you haven't been worried by it. I might have sent you a Field postcard, but the fact is that I thought that might make you worry rather more, and I hoped that, as my last letter told you I was going on a course, you would at all events think I was in some safe spot instead of the very unsafe one where I was.

Directly after I finished that letter to you I was wired for to re-inforce the batt. in an attack. When I wrote to you that I should be in Vaughan's position if anything happened, I knew something was going to happen shortly. I had proposed to Buxton that I should go up with the platoon instead of V., and that had been arranged; but at the last moment the C.O. insisted that V. should go, as an old and regular soldier. C. was necessary as Lewis gun officer, and the choice lay between Brown and me. Brown was taken because owing to the bayonet course I had missed some attack practices he had had. V. and Brown are both dead now, shot through the heart.

You will see the account of the Push in *Times* of 21st, I went to the Transport with four others when the batt. went up, stayed a night there, and wrote to you on the 18th. The attack came off at 2.30 p.m., and at 3.30 the five of us were sent for to Brigade H.Q. No time to pack anything, a blazing hot day, and I had to borrow the quartermaster's revolver as I'd lent mine to V. An hour-and-a-half's walk to Brigade H.Q., where we heard that things were going very well, but more officers were needed. I sent Ginger back from there, as he seemed too small to stick Boches.

From there we had a three hour walk to the front line. Shells most of the way, and the wounded streaming down an open road between the downs. We passed A. D., hit through the leg, but filled with delight because he was going back to Blighty alive and kicking: then ——, rather badly hit in the shoulder— heaps of bandaged men, including two of my platoon. The men of all regiments, and wounded in every variety of way. To read in the papers you might suppose the wounded were whisked from the battlefield in a motor ambulance. I get rather tired of all that false and breezy representation of a battle.

I've never been so hot in my life as when we came to Batt. H.Q., just behind our jumping-off trench. There we heard of Brown and V. and many others, and from there we went on to join our coys, in the various bits of Boche trench they had taken. No guide, a hail of shells and a sort of blind stumble through shell-holes to where we fancied the new line was. I found C Coy. at last. H.Q. in a 30 ft. deep Boche dugout, choked with dead Germans and bluebottles, and there we had our meals till we started back at 4 a.m. this morning (five days).

In between that time I certainly spent some of the most unpleasant hours of my life. It seems that the batt. had done extraordinarily well and gained the first of two objectives. The second was to be won that night, and next day we were to be relieved. Unfortunately a batt. on our right had been held up and we had to wait for them in a trench choked with our dead and Boche wounded and dying for two days and then do another attack. The men had been in high spirits over the first part, but naturally the reaction was great when they found that instead of being relieved they were to dig in, and I had never seen them so glum. Here again the breezy reporter is revolting. The Push itself is done in hot blood: but the rest is horrible, digging in when you are tired to death, short rations, no water to speak of, hardly any sleep, and men being killed by shell-fire most of the time.

I was given the C line in front of H.Q. to hold with two-and-a-half platoons, and luckily the Boches never really found it, and I had fewer casualties than anybody. I slept in the bottom of the trench, sometimes in rain (in shorts), without any cover and really never felt very cold. Also, though I don't suppose I got more than an hour at a time, I never felt done for want of sleep. C. and Buxton were the only officers left.

The second attack was made yesterday, and only our D Coy. was sent off at the start. C. was to support it if it needed reinforcement. My dear, you never saw anything more dramatically murderous than the modern attack—a sheet of fire from both sides in which it seems impossible for anyone to live. I saw it from my observer's post about 100 yds. away. My observer was shot through the head in the first minute. The O.C. of D Coy. had been badly wounded, and Butler led them on most gallantly. The last I saw of him was after a huge shell had burst just over him (laying out several men) waving on the rest. None of the D officers came back, and very few of the men.

Again the right batt. failed, and this time the R.B. was inevitably involved in it, as far as D Coy. went. We gained a certain amount of France back by digging a trench in front of my bit of line about 100 yds. from the Boches in the dark, lit by terrific flares from the German lines.

After that we hunted for our wounded till 4 a.m. I found S. S. about 50 yds. from the Boche trench, shot through the heart. R. got back wounded in several places. Butler was last heard of in a shell-hole about 10 yds. from the Boches. He was an awfully gallant fellow. The whole thing was almost too bloody for words, and this, mind you, was victory of a sort for us. We fancy the Boches lost far more heavily, as our guns got on them when they were reinforcing.

I'm too sleepy to tell you anymore. The batt. did magnificently: captured many prisoners and advanced several hundred yards; but the cost is very great.

Now we are out of it for days at any rate.

August 24.

I was so sleepy last night when I finished my letter that I don't know what I told you and what I didn't, and I'm sleepier than ever now. I'll try and write a decent letter tomorrow. I got two of your letters in the middle of the strafe.

August 25.

I hadn't time after all today to write. We have been moving behind the lines, where we shall be for over a week, I fancy.

Your cake arrived, and one lieut., remarked it was the best he had tasted since he had come out, and several others said the same.

August 26.

It's one thing to promise a letter and another to get it done, for when the fighting is done, it's not, as the newspapers make out, a rest cure, but fuss and fury and discomfort and hard work.

I don't think I told you the most miraculous part of the affray the other day. One of the D Coy. wounded, dragging himself back to the line I held, heard a shell coming and dropped into what he thought was the nearest shell-hole, but was, in fact, a well 60 ft. deep. Nobody saw him, but a sentry heard him call after a time. The problem then was how to get him out, for the beastly thing had shelving sides made of boulders and old mortar quite loose, so that if you went near it started rolling down and threatened to bury him.

We got him up six hours later at about 3.30 a.m. by means of a pick tied to a wire rope, to which he fastened himself. I was desperately afraid he would fall off half-way up or wouldn't have the strength to tie himself on, but he did. One would have had to go down in that case, but I think he would have been buried from above in the process. At least three men were ready to go after him, though it wouldn't have been a pleasant job for them either. The amazing thing was that he came up—without a bone broken—from a dry well 60 ft. deep.

It's rather melancholy this after the battle business. ———'s brother came over today to hear about him, also ———. You'll see a host of names.

I see the *Times* of 24th says it's the most successful day since the Push started, and apparently the R.B.s are considered to have done awfully well. I spoke a lot of German that night to wounded prisoners.

August 27,

I'm still without leisure. Buxton has gone sick for two days at least.

The troops after their push are bivouacked in an open field with no cover but their waterproof sheets—constant showers—not very comfortable for men who have hardly slept and never ceased working under shell-fire for a week. Some old noodle's fault, I suppose.

My dear, some of the men are too quaint. One lad, whose brother was killed the last night in the Boche trench, came to me to ask how to write to his sister-in-law about it. He had got as far as—'My dear Lil,—I now have great pleasure in telling you that Tom———' and there he had stuck. I had to draft a more sympathetic letter for him. The same on being asked if he would like to help bury his brother said, 'I will, if you like, sergeant.' Yet he was quite upset.

The G.O.C. congratulated the brigade today in the rain; it somehow seemed unnecessary.

Funny that E., D., D., and I, who came out together, should be all left—with only about five others.

August 28.

It's a fine evening and I sit in a tent with a towel over my knees to prevent the flies, which are appal- ling, from tickling them, and am for the moment at leisure, so I must freakly try to write to you.

It's one of the errors of the army that Q.M.S., which is a non-combatant job, is part of the up ward gradation, so that you may lose a good fighting man at a critical moment because he's been made Q.M.S., or you may have an intelligent clerk step out of it to be sgt.-major.

They have got up tents for the men and there's a concert now going on just outside mine. They do pick up their spirits most wonderfully.

—— has just gone down sick. He was frightened to death in the trenches, yet very brave and cheerful, but saw himself there for days after, and the shells coming. I got C. to swop him for the *padre's* servant, who is a fit youth, so that in future —— won't have to go into the trenches, which he's too old for. Forty-five!

9.30 p.m. The concert is coming to an end. The *padre* has got them to sing 'Abide with Me.' It is rather fine—a starry night, the tents all lighted and looking like a lamp-lit city in this niche of the downs. Away to the north one of these murderous battles is raging.

August 29.

I fancy we shall go into trenches for a bit before we rest properly, but not, I think, for an attack.

Tremendous thunderstorm today, which flooded our tent and the men's.

Tomorrow we go for a bathe.

August 31.

No letter from you yesterday. We had a thunder storm yesterday—tropical rain—with the result that all the tents got flooded. Ours being pitched on old horse lines, we spent the day on liquid manure, which does not tend to make things any cleaner—or oneself. In the evening we moved to this camp. I rode the coy. horse till I was stiff with cold, after which I walked. We dined about midnight, and are this morning shifting our tent again.

Buxton still away, but the *padre* is still with us—*i.e.* C. and self—so are flies and other bougs!

I fear the damp won't make the country or the men any healthier, as it washes the dirt about and probably gets into water supplies. I am afraid we shall have some working parties the next few days, but I ought to have time to write to you.

Please order a new Aquascutum; I have lost my other and don't see a chance of getting one out here.

September 2.

A pleasing Blighty one at last, and almost before you get this I shall, with luck, be in *Angleterre* with you a-coming to see me. It's shrapnel through the thigh, and hasn't been pronounced on yet by the medical authorities, who have to extract a bit of iron that didn't go quite through. But as I plunked through the trenches knee-deep in mire for six hours afterwards, more or less, it can't be very bad; and I ought to get back before you can think of coming here. I got it in another show suddenly forced upon us, in which I was in charge of the coy., with C. only subaltern. A shell plumped neatly between six of us, killed Sgt. Oliver and hit the rest in divers ways. It was rather a funny sensation. I thought I'd been bruised. Handed over to C., who a little later got badly hit in the arm. So C Coy., when I last heard of it, is without officers—three platoon sergeants knocked out—two killed—both awfully nice fellows, and A. rather badly hit.

Haven't had a meal since lunch yesterday, and now it's lunch today; advanced to the attack in the full height of an attack of sickness and a temperature up. All the troops are that, but I never expected to be. It was very awkward.

Will let you know as quick as quick.

A chaplain is addressing this.[21]

[*September 7. Telegram from Robert from Southampton saying he was on his way to Oxford where he arrived at Somerville Hospital about 6 p.m.*]

[*December 29. Robert left Waterloo at 11.55 a m for Southampton, crossed that night and reached Havre next day.*]

Infantry Base Depot, Havre.
Sunday, December 31, 1916.

As you will see from the above I am posted to another batt,

---

21. The envelope was addressed and signed 'L. Maclean Watt, C.F.' If these lines should ever come to his notice, I here offer him my thanks.—C. H.V.

which means only that that is the one I go to when I go into the line. In the meanwhile I am here in quite a pretty place among a pack of lads whom I don't know from Adam for the most part. We had the usual quaintness in crossing; arrived at Southampton, where the M.L.O. took about forty times as long over his job as was necessary.

We were then despatched in the rain to a dirty boat (good enough to breed rabbits in) and then told we had just an hour to go into the town and get a meal. When we got back within the hour, we found that the boat was not starting, so all the valises had to be carted to another boat, about a half a mile away, and we got off at 9 o'clock. Crowds of people, some of whom slept in the gangway. I luckily secured a cabin (without berths or door—both had been taken down for some unknown reason) and offered half to a pleasant doctor-captain. An under-steward offered to rent me his own cabin for the night for the small sum of 25s., which I refused, and should like to have the authority to shoot him.

Am quite a believer in Mothersill, as I took two doses and never felt a qualm, though it was rough and many people ill. Breakfast on the boat half-a-crown. Profit about 200 *per cent.*— why? Went off at Havre with the two lads—who insisted on breakfasting at an officer's club that one of them had visited before when taking out a draft—in preference to a French hotel! After which we came here by train. Brilliant criticisms of the French nation on the way by the one lad who has spent one day in France. Am in a hut with a man named Barrett—brother of Roper Barrett and up at St. John's with Howard. Didn't we meet him in Dorsetshire once?

Have a quite excellent temporary servant.

January 1, 1917.

My kit arrived and I slep in the Jigger (Jaeger) blanket and it was very pleasant.

Marched up in the rain this morning and then down again at the terrible hour of 8 a.m. (breakfast at 7.30) which does not suit me. But the idea of making things uncomfortable for the inferior people seems very dear to the heart of those who do not take part in the discomforts. However, it doesn't make much odds for a few days—after which, of course, discomforts become necessities, and for that reason much more tolerable. I don't expect to be here for very long. Am by months the senior subaltern.

January 2.

It has been drizzling steadily for most of two days. Yesterday I went a walk with Barrett and a pleasant Rugby boy. Had *café* at a dirty little *estaminet* with some French soldiers in it. I am going to be inoculated today or tomorrow and shall take a day or two off doing nothing, though I don't suppose it will affect me any more than last time. Food desperately bad on the whole but nobody to worry about it.

January 3.

Have just been inoculated. The doctor, a Canadian, told me that he found men between 35 and 40 couldn't stick the trenches! Am just beginning to get a little stiff from the bougs, but have forty-eight hours off.

Met a pleasant man; he has been in Canada a good deal, and says that when he was very ill he read *Mr Faviel* and it made him delirious for three nights. I don't know if this is a compliment or not.

So far I might just as well have been on leave in England, as I have not done one single thing. It continues to drizzle.

January 4

This is so far the second day of inoculation and I've had no sensations but a slight stiffness of the chest, so I don't think I'm likely to be any the worse for it. As it has been raining steadily for three days I am rather glad to be off all parades and setting in a hut ante-room which, while the bulk of the youths is away, is quite peaceful.

The only annoyance is that I might just as well have had another week with you.

One doesn't feel much nearer the trenches than before, and it's mostly as unreal as at Minster.

I pass the time reading novelettes abandoned by the other officers and chatting and occasionally playing bridge for money! Have lost 70 *centimes*, so far there's extravagance!

2 p.m. Just before lunch Howard Elliott [22] and two other gun-

---

22. Lieut. Howard Elliott, R.F.A., a cousin.

ners walked into our mess by mistake, having just arrived from England. I gave them drinks and gathered you were well. Their mess is almost next door, so I may see him again if we are both here for a few days.

January 5.

I am afraid that after this there will be a small gap in the letters, as I start for the Line tonight.

I have made two voyages to Havre—one yesterday afternoon with B. to see the sea front, which is really rather fine, and one this morning with Barrett and Scoville to have a very good hot bath and *déjeuner*. I believe it takes at least forty-eight hours to get up. Luckily it has turned dry, if colder, and the roads have become roads again instead of mud soup. Howard Elliott has just been in to announce that he is going by the same train—so we may travel as far as Rouen together.

I think our selection of goods for the Front was excellent, and I can't think of anything I want beyond.

Sunday, January 7.

Having started on Friday have arrived at our back lines without a cold, which is rather good. The batt. is in the *tranchées*, but comes out shortly: as a result we have not met any of the important officers as yet. I am very near where I was last time and glad of it, as here the spring should come earliest. I might even come across your *Téléphoniste français*. Shan't be in the trenches for some days.

The scene of writing is an enormous and cold hut containing about thirty officers—outside, a sea of mud.

January 9.

There isn't much news. Have spent two days almost entirely in a large hut about four times the size of our long barn—without windows—and one brazier to warm it. We really are too stupid at making ourselves as comfortable as circumstances permit. This is an out-of-the-trenches camp and should be really comfortable, but no. Outside a sea of mud as far as the eye can see—not so deep, perhaps, as the Flanders mud, but less diversified by buildings or hop poles. A Service Batt. has much less grand notions of comfort even than a Regular one; and personally I should have sacked the staff long ago. The food—wug!

The officers have just turned up—some quite pleasant, I think, the remainder very young and temporary, but all very friendly. The adjutant is a trifle junior to me, I think, in the army, and probably about 20. Haven't seen the C.O. yet. Haven't got a coy. yet or a servant.

The weather is not very chic—bitly wind and rain. I almost think it would be well to send out my old tunic—the one I was hit in.

January 11.

The Jaeger blanket is very nice and I don't know what I should do without it, as it is bitly cold. Had a bayonet practice yesterday and a ride on a most charming small horse, who kept bolting for about twelve miles. It is unfortunately the A horse, not B.

I can't quite see the Service Batt. in comparison with the Regular. They haven't nearly as good an idea of making themselves comfortable, feed and live like pigs, and don't get any work out of the servants. Same with N.C.O.s, I should fancy, but that remains to be seen.

January 12.

Am renewing my acquaintance with dugouts, and such just as bad as ever—and the mud as deep as I've seen it. I like the coy. officers, what I've seen of them, and think I am probably lucky in that respect. I doubt if any of them have been out as long as I have; but that's the way it goes. The coys, are occupied now: a couple of months ago nobody to command them, so I get left again. I don't really mind.

January 15.

Just a line to say very fit. Post just going. Will write more tonight—probably.

January 16.

Can't write very much now. Have a rather beastje sore throat, but otherwise very fit, and the throat is not to be wondered at, for conditions of damp, dirt, and absence of fuel are a good deal worse than any I have seen. Like the people of the coy. very well, and the Front seems very fairly cushy and if only the warm weather would come things would be much improved.

January 17.

My throat is so sore that I cannot eat or smoke; and you know the complete misery that is bound to ensue and how it prevents long or nice letters being written. I dare say it will be better tomorrow if not, I shall have to find a M.O. to give me some cough lozenges. I lay all packed in my valise yesterday, but took a short walk this morning for a change, in about a foot of snow. Not very good for the trenches when it melts. A parcel from Frdk. and May—very fine raisins and short-bread and mints: he must be stopped.

It's very nice of Milliken[23] to want me on the Staff, but no one else does. I think the point is that as long as one can, one can't arrange a cushy job for oneself, though if one offered it's rather different.

January 18.

Back in the large damp hut, still with rather a sore throat, but otherwise going fairly strong. I don't think I should have got this but that the O.C. of the coy. is one of those sort of people who don't seem to mind if they have warmth or not. The consequence is that the first two days and nights we sat in a dripping dugout without a fire, while four boxes of matches went sodden in my pockets and the servants enjoyed two braziers. Then in an excess of energy he insisted on cutting up wet wood for us, so that asphyxiation came very nigh. But he is quite a nice fellow.

There has been heavy snow and I'm afraid a lot of men will be done in by the weather. The fuel allowance should be trebled and it seems instead to be halved. I should say that for discomfort this part of the Front takes the cake, from what I've seen, nor does a Service Batt. know how to look after itself so well as a Regular. Many of the things we do and don't do would make the hair of the 3rd Batt. stand on end.

Tell Frdk. I will write sometime, but find it very difficult here.

January 19.

I am so sorry that letter took so long, but I think they are more erratic from here. Today, for instance, I received three of yours, after getting none. I'm in my valise reading and writing this— still with my throat very sore and my voice practically gone. A valise is the only place, because out of bed it's impossible to keep warm in this barn, with snow on the ground and freezing

---

23. Lieut. H. E. Milliken, King's Royal Rifle Corps, a friend of Sheppey days.

going on; but valises are not good for writing in and I hope you don't find my letters too dull for words. The fact is, the light and the cold suppress me rather more than usual: it is too cold to sharpen a pencil properly. I haven't meant to grouse, but what with being too sore to smoke and so forth, you know that I wouldn't be at my friskiest. I am eating the *crème de menthes* you sent me, which are very good and soothing.

January 21.

I put the 19th on my last, but I think it must have been nearer 21st! Anyway today, which is the next day, is Sunday. My throat is getting better. It is freezing away. The Jigger blanket is just invaluable, and I wear Aunt Fanny's scarf round my head, and between them I manage to keep warm. Sorry —— won't publish my poem *To F. G. S.* Their letter is absurd. A poem is a poem and they don't get one once in six months—still there you are.

Tuesday 23

Just a line to say going very well. No letters from you for two days, but the first parcel of tabac.

January 24.

I am much annoyed because I only wrote you a postcard yesterday and that hasn't been posted. I have been left behind in the damp hut with my sore throat, which the M.O. refers to as laryngitis. It's getting better all the time now, and I get out of the Front line with it, which is not so bad in this awful cold weather. Last night was probably the coldest since the war started—20 deg. of frost, I should think, and a bitly wind blowing, and tonight promises to be as cold. Very miserable for the men, but I believe when they come out we have a long rest behind somewhere.

I slip in and out of my valise for meals! It's much warmer in it than anywhere else—with my two waistcoats (your Jaeger one and the new deerskin one that Lily gave me) on, and my fur lining and my trench coat and my blanket on top, and Aunt Fanny's scarf and Frdk.'s Balaclava helmet on my head. One youth here, quite a pleasing cross between an eel and a monkey; very young, but might be 40—so *blasé*, and wins contentedly at poker. What a race we are rearing and killing,

I think my servant is a very decent sort of youth, and he certainly has been most attentive.

January 26.

Still the hut, but I rather fancy we go out to morrow and that I shall go ahead and get the billets; I shan't be sorry to be out of this as I have sniffled and coughed here for the best part of ten days, I think. Still freezing hard—icicles poking through the cracks in the hut, and a fearful number of men with trench feet. I am really very much better—can speak now which is a nice change for so great a conversationalist.

✶✶✶✶✶✶

But it does all seem to show that we are still more fit for war than for peace, though one had begun to think the opposite.
The posts are most erratic again for 3-4 days I haven't had a letter. The snow may be holding things up, though it barely more than covers the ground in these parts, and really yesterday and today were beautifully sunny and nice enough for a walk— only I found the sharp air tickles me up too much. However, if we are in billets for a fortnight, I ought to find my feet.
Just got three letters from you and a parcel from my mother, cakes and socks. They are most opportune, as sure as I say I don't want anything, it comes in handy.
It is no good wondering why people get things. They apply mostly, I suppose! One could get them, but that isn't the idea. I don't mind saying I would rather have avoided this winter, but it's getting on now.

January 28.

Am in a rest village and have just had two letters from you and a card from your *téléphoniste* saying he shall be delighted to meet me if that is possible. I don't know if it is, but will try to find out where the French are and ride over to see him if there is a chance. I billeted yesterday, bicycling the six miles here with five Q.M.S.s—taking over the accommodation offered, which is pretty bad. The town major is, I suppose, responsible, but the village is very poor and anything is good enough for the Infantry. For the Coy. Messes there were three possible ones and one impossible, which accordingly I had not the face not to take for B Coy. It is a sort of cross between a small cellar and a garden room stone floor with four wire beds—so called—in it; no stove and the wind whistling through the walls.
When we introduced a brazier, the old man and woman who

live in the rest of the house—two quite comfortable rooms—one of which I tried in vain to get them to lend us for a price just to sit in—dashed in and protested that the ceiling would be blackened! As though the ceiling in a place like our apple room mattered. They would prefer us to sit without any fire in this weather. Naturally I put my foot down. I think those sort of trivial prejudices—trivial at any time—should be entirely disregarded, whether they make for *ententes* or not, in time of war. And this is the sort of place where one is supposed to recuperate from the trenches. All part of a bad organisation. The civilians could quite easily be turned out, and should be.

I'm really getting on though, and you mustn't mind if I grumped a bit. You know I always do when I am not at my fittest. As I say, I've escaped the trenches by having a sore throat, and after all, that's something.

I stayed in bed today (as being the warmest place) till 4 p.m. when I arose and went to the baths, not having had one for a month, in fact, since I left Havre. That would have amused you—simply a hut with boards to stand on and showers overhead—a howling draught—a Tommies' bath-house after hours. Officers don't seem to count on this Front! I found the bath corporal in a sort of stoke-hole by a brazier with his mates, and in the stoke-hole I undressed and walked about 10 yds. to the nearest shower. They had no clean towels but leant me two black ones—one permanently black from stains—and therewith I cleaned myself and hustled back at the double, and feel better for it, though, I dare say, no cleaner.

At the moment we have a brazier in our cellar, but the smoke is so thick that we have to open the door wide every three minutes to escape being suffocated. There, I am making the very worst of things and they aren't really so bad.

My servant is excellent, and in time, I think, things will march better. There's no side, which I like.

January 30.

I am getting better and better. I went for a ride yesterday on the coy. mare—a stupid, clumsy creature; lazy too, with enough go to shy at some drums and barge me into a lot of led horses, stampeding about six in front of an old general! I also brought off another feat, *viz.*, bribing a French woman to cook for us while we are here. The others had tried in vain, but I persuaded her; the result was that we started off last night with the best dinner I've had in France in war-time. Tapioca soup, fish, mutton, and compote of vegetables, and a sweet omelette. She is a widow, lost her husband in the war, and has a small girl, and a baby-boy born after the husband was killed. They live here in a broken-down hovel, but of course she can cook ten times as well as any rifleman.

I'm having plenty of sleep; generally breakfast in bed: we all do, as it's too cold to get up and eat it without a fire, and altogether am living in great luxury.

February 1.

Letters seem to be coming a little more regularly. Also it has snowed again and is on the whole a little warmer, especially as we have taken on a sort of small hall at the French lady's hovel, removed a broken stove and got an open fire going. You mustn't think I'm having any hardships: you might call them discomforts, perhaps, but nothing more than that, and really at present I'm getting fitter daily and eating like a pig.

The Welsh boy is very nice, and I like him better all the time. About the question you asked—whether we make better dug-outs? As far as this Front is concerned—No! There are none in some places and very poor ones in others, nor have I ever seen a more uncomfortable part of the line—quite apart from the severity of the weather.

Saturday, February 3.

I think last night was about the coldest we've had, but apart from the cold there is really nothing much to complain of. It's exactly the sort of weather one had at Zuoz—a little more wind perhaps, but if one were skating or skiing, good enough. When one is standing about doing nothing, it is distinctly cool.

Still the rest village and for some days to come.

Don't pass on my grousings too much, or everybody will think me a pig. I'm really feeling better all the time, though sneefs and coughs will not entirely vanish, which isn't to be wondered at seeing that we sit over a bonfire and freeze alternately. The cooking here goes very well. *Madame* reminds me very much of Elise in appearance, but is very mournful-looking. The small girl rather taking and always beaming.

Sunday, February 4 or 5.
I wrote yesterday and there's no news, but I just send a line. *Madame* has now offered us her inner apartment with a real stove in it, so that we now have the best mess in the place. I suppose we made a good impression on her.

The Guiachum lozenges have arrived; please thank my mother for them. I have passed on some to my servant, who, with half the batt., has also a sore throat.

February 7.
Just a line to say that we have moved to another place, where I took over the billets from a fatuous town major full of muddles. The descent from *Madame's* cooking to our Rifleman is considerable. The cold is considerable, with a cutting wind such as we had in Finland. But I am better all the time and found my name had been put down for a cushy job behind the lines—consisting of staying behind and paying out money to the division—apparently on the strength of my having had a sore throat. Not feeling inclined to do the job, I went to the man at present commanding and asked him to select somebody else, which he has done. I don't fancy he knew that I had been out before or knows now. Sich is life in the army.

I have taken to wearing my pony-skin gloves all day and shall soon be as addicted to gloves as any one, I fear. But the cold is sich that you can't feel your hands without.

My throat is much better. One of the officers of another coy. I found today quite speechless and evidently with bad influenza, shifting camp like anybody else instead of being sent to hospital. And it really is most bitter weather.

We have just heard the likelihood of the States coming in. I hope they will, if only that one will be able to treat them as human beings after the war, instead of as shirkers.

February 7 (9?).
We have rather a comfortable hut here, luckily, as the wind is tearing cold. I don't know when I've known it more bitly. We are where I told you and nowhere else, in spite of what somebody may have heard to the contrary. I don't think I shall be able to get to your *téléphoniste* for some time: can't find out where he is yet, but you never know when you may strike any one. This is rather a quaint battalion. I haven't seen a man in the

coy. yet, except by accident. They're mostly away on fatigues somewhere else, and one might arrive in the trenches without having known any of them. Not good. I can't make out who is responsible.

I'm very fit in spite of the cold: one's blankets get all dripping wet at night where one's breath freezes and melts again. A parcel from Frdk. last night. Please thank him when you write. Haven't washed today so far—3 p.m.—owing to water being frozen up and unobtainable. We have been very lucky to be out during this weather, as one can get gradually acclimatised to it and it can't last indefinitely anyhow.

Oh, *Vanity Fair* came in Frdk.'s parcel from Mrs Jenkinson. Very kind of her.

February 10.

Just going up. Very fitly. Two parcels arrived most opportunely—the Richoux sweets from you and a parcel from my mother. The sweets already finished and much appreciated. Last night was, I think, the coldest I've ever felt—in a small hut without a door and the wind raging through. The water left in a glass froze solid inside. I think I ought to be some use, as I don't think, comparatively, they know very much about holding a line.

February 12.

Out again, but have slept so long that I've only time to send a line. Am very fit. It was most bitly in the trenches. I think I've never been so cold. No fire, no dugout, and below zero. But very little shelling.

February 13.

It is much milder and I expect next time we shall be up to our knees in mud. It certainly was most bitly cold; the men dug out lumps of ice to fill their canteens with, and in the early morning the frost settled all over me. I think the men seem cheery in spite of not being smart, which is perhaps the best thing.

There are tons of things I want to tell you but I can't at the moment think of them.

February 14.

Just a line before going up. There's no news. It still freezes fairly hard by night, and thaws rather by day. Except for the wind it wouldn't be bad far better than mud. Didn't have a letter today, but they still arrive in twos or threes mostly.

February 19.

I am afraid there will be a gap between my last letter and this, but the fact is that we don't seem able to send back letters from the trenches, or at any rate don't have it done. Out now, after a fairly peaceful time, though we were lucky too, I think. The cold first, and then mud later, when it thawed, were pretty bad—not so much for us, who had a dugout (Boche) to retire to, as for the men who hadn't.

I found that two hours standing about over the ankles in icy water in ordinary boots froze me up, but was nothing like so cold as last time, when we spent all the time in the open trench. The Boche is very sensible in that way. The whole front, however, is extraordinarily desolate in this weather: pock-marked with frozen shell-holes, every kind of abandoned material lying about, and bodies in ghastly attitudes, just as they fell and were constricted to the ground by the frost immovably until the winter chooses to give up its dead.

I think if everybody could see these scenes, the general horror would somehow find the way out, which ordinary morals and intelligence don't seem to. The time the men have while they live is bad enough; it's pathetically absurd to see them plunging about in the mire, laden to the teeth, falling into shell-holes in the dark, getting stuck fast, cursing and patient, and half of them ill enough to be in bed or hospital in peace-time. I pulled one little man ahead of me eight times out of mud holes into which he had fallen in the course of about 200 yards, as we came out.

Am at the moment in a little sausage-shaped iron hut with room for two, but four of us in it.

Rather amusing this afternoon—a greatcoat inspection ordered. B Coy., as a whole, has mud still wet plastered on up to the arm-pits, but no doubt some brigadier was made happy by knowing that an inspection had been held.

February 21.

No news. Out for some time and quite mild weather, which is very nice for a change.

The gingerbread and all the other things have arrived; and the gingerbread is very good and much appreciated and opportune. And the pipe is very good. The towel came into instant use as a pocket-handkerchief.

—— has got a temperature; —— has bad malaria, and —— a sprained ankle. So that we may be described as a crocky lot on the whole. We are in our most comfortable camp, however, and doing well.

February 26.

Arrived back in camp in the early hours of this morning to find five letters from you and one from my mother. But I am so sleepy still that I can hardly keep my eyes open. I was given charge of D Coy. about an hour before we went (its captain being on leave) and was given quite one of the least pleasant parts of the line I have seen. Luckily, we only had two men wounded, though the shelling was incessant and the noise considerable, and, worst of all, the shortage of water sich that on the last day we had nothing at all to drink from breakfast onwards. It doesn't suit me to be a camel, as you know, and I was fairly tired when I got in, largely from want of drink, though the mud was terrible and many men arrived in the trench without anything on their feet at all! I will try to describe it later, when I'm less sleepy, but some of the things you would like to know are just what I mustn't tell you.

About morphia. The M.O.s out here vary according to their experience, and I've heard one imploring officers to carry morphia. In many cases it isn't to save life but to alleviate agony for those who must die. Look at the case of the man Shafto got the M.C. for going to give some to—blown out of the trenches on to the barbed wire, quite immovable and dying in great pain, and in any part you may see twenty such. This ground is strewn with the dead who might have been eased a little earlier. I quite admit that it's probably a very dangerous doing, but it's worth taking risks on some occasions. It would be best if all officers knew as far as possible when to and when not to give it.

I think I managed the coy. moderately all right. Of course it's not much fun running somebody else's coy. temporarily when you know none of them. Found several lads there whom I used to conduct on working parties to Warden Point in May, 1915. I'm just desperately sleepy.

February 27.

When I wrote to you yesterday, I had just received five letters from you. The same evening three more arrived, so that I got eight yesterday. Sich are the posts!

I'm ashamed when Billy[24] writes about my refusing cushy jobs like that. You ought not to pass it on. It's not valour at all—mere conceit. If I were offered a good cushy job, I should probably jump at it.

I said I'd tell you about the line.

We were to go up in gum-boots, and the authorities carefully provided a large number of size 5, with the result that nobody could get into them; and before we could get large ones two-and-a-half hours had passed and we had to go up in the pitch dark. I've never seen it pitchier, and the first hour was a long succession of splashes as men fell off into shell-holes full of water. I fell off three times myself, but luckily missed shell-holes. We took six hours to do a two-and-a-half hours' walk; and some of the men arrived some hours later without anything on their feet! The trench impassable, and you can imagine how warm they feel at the end of a day or two sitting or standing in that sort of half-frozen liquid mud.

The youths and I had a Boche dugout—the most uncomfortable one I've seen, and as filthy as filthy, and there was lots of works on and very little water and plenty of shells. However, we managed very well, though I was glad to get out of it all. The O.C. will be back today or tomorrow to take over, which I shan't mind, as I don't like having someone else's coy. A very sad thing happened.

An officer just arrived back—had been out before for a long time went out on patrol from my trench, got back safe to his own, and when some shrapnel came over a little later, fell down dead—untouched. I suppose he must have been very wrought up, or a weak heart, or something of that kind. A very good man too, he was.

Who do you think came into my dugout at dead of night and chatted for an hour? Hilaire Belloc—not *the* one, but his son, a very taking youth of about 18, most intelligent, in the R.E.s. He'd come up to site a trench and we chatted of G. K. C. and Bentley. He knew Daly—that nice boy who had been killed

---

24. Mr L. W. Clarke, an old school friend.

at Guillemont—and had been trying to find his grave. I was very pleased with him and thought the R.E.s had got hold of somebody good at last!

The D sgt.-major, rather a nice old boy—an ex-policeman—fatherly and amiable, but considerably lost in the trenches, I think, and would be happier at an island of Charing Cross.

D Coy. O.C. just returned. You must not worry about gaps between letters. It's unavoidable. The thing that alarmed you [Le Transloy] wasn't far off.

February 28.

This is a line-and-a-half letter. I sent you a longish one yesterday and not much has happened since, except that we stood to in the middle of the night for an attack and ate the gingercake, which was very good. I don't know that a monthly toothbrush is required, because it's only very occasionally one has the chance of cleaning one's teeth, and I've still only had one bath since joining the batt. The fact is that it seems to be the maid-of-all-work to the brigade, unlike the 3rd, which was upper parlour-maid, so to speak, and they never seem to give us proper rest. The men barely get down from the trenches before they are up again carrying, sore feet or no. They go sick pretty often, but that's no wonder.

—— is just going off sick, and we shall be three who a little time ago were eight. Of course, the weather has a lot to do with things. There's a raw cold on again now and much mud, but I seem to keep very fit.

Spurling is a very good fellow. I like him better all the time, and if I haven't got coys., I've been very lucky with coy. O.C.s.

March 1.

It's the nicest day we've had out here, from the weather point of view, which is something, and will be more if it continues.

I had a working party last night—a fairly clean night, not bad for carrying in, and very few shells—the only drawback being that there was a mess and we were kept waiting about doing nothing for one-and-a-half hours. Sich is life in the army. I lay in bed till lunch time, and now I haven't a great deal of time to write in. I know my letters ought to be much better and more interesting, but somehow dullness is the thing that oppresses one out here, or at least me, and I haven't the sperrit to rise above it.

Have just written to that officer's wife, as it probably rather adds to her grief that he was not among people he knew at all.

March 5.

Just come back from a tour in the *tranchées*, and as this may go early tomorrow morning, I am sending you a line and a half just to tell you that I am fit. It snowed pretty heavily last night, and the night before was a sharp frost—about 15 or 20 degrees, I should say, which made us as cold as mud, as we ran out of coke.

Trenches very dull and noisy—not many casualties.

March 7.

I feel rather a thneak because I didn't write to you yesterday to make up for the scrabby one of the night before, but the fact is, I had my second bath. You might not think that would prevent it, but as a matter of fact, B. and I, after sleeping till nearly lunch time, set out directly after in search of a bath and didn't get back till dinner and bedtime. We voyaged to the village partly on foot, partly in a motor belonging to an old Roads capt., and partly by a big lorry—about nine miles. The baths were real baths of aged tin, and the water was as hot as hot, and when we got out we both said, we hope we shall get a lorry back, as we felt remarkably feeble.

We did get a lift another way in an Anzac lorry, and also in one driven by a Belgian spy, but had to go out of our way as our road was blocked; and in the end were dropped about six miles from camp. I got better as we went on, but B. got worse—so much so that we had to stop every 100 yards or so to rest him, and I thought I should have to leave him and go and get some whiskey to bring him back. It's an odd result of a bath, but I suppose due to not having had one for a month or more. I certainly felt extraordinarily tottery too, though I think we're both all the better for it today, besides being clean once more.

The weather has turned bitter again—a raging wind which is freezing the ground hard. I'm all by my lone in a hut without a fire, the others having gone to the local 'Coliseum' in the hope, as B. says, that the congested humanity there will help to warm them.

We started your cake today and it's nearly gone already—very

very good.

I might possibly get left out of the trenches next time, as, if possible, we take turns, but so many officers have gone sick or hit that we may be rather short. One youth was shot in the dugout I was in when I had D Coy.—through the thigh—by a man cleaning his rifle. Rather annoying sort of way to be wounded.

I don't think there is much news of our last tour; the last few hours were horribly cold, and you couldn't move about at all; but Spurling is a very good sort to be with, and an excellent coy. commander, my only criticism being that he does too much himself instead of making other people do it. I came down with the sgt.-major, who was an old 3rd Batt. man, not that he's more than 28 now, I should think, but served with the 1st during the retreat from Mons and was full of reminiscences. He's very good, I think, and I think the men are very good and cheery too.

March 8.

It's gone excessively cold again—a bitter, raging, freezing wind, and I'm very glad we're not in the trenches, and hope you haven't got it, as it won't be very nice in the garden for you. Had a short parade this morning and was glad to flee in and set by a smoky but warm fire.

Nothing suggests itself to be written about, though I dare say there may be plenty. I think it's true, as I've just heard Spurling and B. saying, that you can't settle to a letter when you're cold, and much smoke in your eyes doesn't assist. So you must take the will for the deed.

I believe almost for certain that I shall not be in the trenches next time.

March 9.

I would like a letter, not having had one for some days. I'm afraid it's U-boats or something, and will work both ways, and we shall each get bunches when they do come, and the ones you get will be dull bunches. What with having no letters and a jump in my right eye, I feel a little flat; also, it has snowed mostly all day, which is stupid when one had begun to think the spring might be coming. I have been orderly officer today, which meant doing nothing whatever which, considering the weather, I didn't mind at all.

Think this must be finished tomorrow, as much smoke is going into my eyes.

March 10. I have just been to the local Coliseum will tell you more tomorrow. No letters yet.

March 11 (I think).

Probably send you a long letter tomorrow. Am staying down for a court-martial. Have had six letters from you in last twenty-four hours, so am much bucked.

March 1917.

I must write you a properly long letter between today and tomorrow, and answer some of the questions in the six letters I've just got.

This is started in another hut—a little further down the road, where I am dwelling with two officers of C Coy. The weather is full of heavy showers, but much milder.

There is no leave on—not that I should have any if there was. You asked if there were any spring flowers here—the only sign of life is some dull gray grass here and there which has come out since the snow melted. It doesn't look, in this pitted country, as though anything like a flower could ever come out.

Sorry Milliken has gone out again. I doubt if he should have. It's rather annoying the differences. A youth who has just come tells me that his colonel at home was going to send nobody out for the second time until all those who had not been out before had gone. Which seems only fair.

The tunic is very good, but I haven't had the courage to get out of my woolly one, especially as the latter goes over both waistcoats—Lily's deerskin and the Jigger one you gave me.

I am sorry about the poem, but it is rather odd, considering the amount of bosh that is printed, that unassuming poetry should not stand a chance even with the self-considered literary papers. However, I seem born to miss the mark.

I enclose letters from Billy and the Medicine Man.[25] I suppose people do want to know what it's like here, but very few who have satisfied that knowledge would want to go on adding to it. Of course those boys who write home that it's the time of

---

25. Dr. O. Hilton.

their lives may be doing it from sporting motives. I know —— always maintains that people at home should not be informed, and he tells his people that he is enjoying himself thoroughly. That is rather nice, but I'm not sure if it really works.

We are no longer three but five. Hence I am staying behind, but I don't know that one is overworked anyhow. You can't do more than a certain amount, and that is perhaps better than doing nothing in this appalling country.

March 14.

I'm a little shaky about the date, but I rather fancy it's Wednesday or Thursday, and I'm still resting. The weather is storm-like—heavy downpours with intervals of sun. We have breakfast in bed, where we shave and wash (?) and get up for lunch—inspect some rifles after it, and then one's duty is o'er for the day, so that I ought to have time to write. The only remaining difficulties are that one's eyes are usually full of smoke. —— talks his head off in a very interesting way, and as one does nothing at all there is not much to write about. However, I did get off a short scrap to my mother yesterday, and might attempt Frdk. and Billy today.

March 18.

Just got up—11 a.m.—and still in camp, so you see I have been living a life of luxury and ease. Might not have been, because, shortly after your last letter went off, an old magazine exploded in the camp we had been in for days and demolished things. We became aware of it by an awful roar, followed by earth and stones falling in our hut here—half a mile away. The sort of thing that in peace-time would fill the front pages of the newspapers. Crater about four times the size of the one you saw at East church. Sich are some of the incidents while in rest, though to be sure they are not exactly common. One little bugler I assisted to dig out about a quarter-of-an-hour later, said, as he was unearthed—'Ah'm one of the looky beggars, ah am.' He was the colour of this paper and deadly sick, and couldn't stand. They are plucky, most of these men.

I wish the war were nearer a finish. I suppose it will be if they can squash the submarines.

March 19.

Just going up on a very fine day. It's rather contradictious that

——, who likes soldiering, should be made a colonel in Ireland, isn't it? 1 think I should make quite a good Irish colonel.

Getting appointed to Roads jobs, and such, is not usually a compliment. The worst of this war is that the cushy jobs are not the honourable ones, as a rule; though it may be that one cannot stand the trenches. Only a percentage can in this weather.

Field Service Postcard.

March 21.

I am quite well. Letter follows at first opportunity.

March 22.

Being forrard, this isn't writing time, but things are rather different at the moment, as you may see in the papers, and for us at present safer than I've ever known them. Also a groom has come hither, and can take back a letter, so I'm writing one at two minutes' notice, and it won't be very long. Bitly cold; I don't think I've been colder than the last three nights; but the snow has knocked the wind down and made it a bit warmer. We are in a ruined house in a ruined village, and in the far sky is the smoke of many burning villages.

March 24.

Just a line to say I'm out, very slipsy after sich bitly weather that I was too cold even to sleep! Found pipe and pipe-cleaners just when I wanted it; also a very fine parcel from my mother. Things are so difficult to get out here now that these gifts have become extra valuable.

That was a very nice letter your mother copied for me—she could not wish a better.

Very fit, in spite of the cold, and hoping that the Boches are really getting it somewhere.

March 25.

I sent you a snippet last night to say we were out. We had rather an interesting time, and but for the extreme coolth it would have been a nice change.

The newspapers will probably have given you some idea of it, but as usual they are grossly exaggerated and unduly optimistic, though no doubt things are moving forward considerably. We spent some days in a ruined room in a ruined village with snowdrops poking out of the shell-holes in the garden and saw cavalry on the go. Spurling and I also went for what looked like a country walk and got in a spinney rather larger than the one on the way to the Lordship, which the Boches then shelled for half an hour, while we dodged around and around trying to get out. Just as we did, I heard another coming, got under a bank and shouted to him to. He did so just as the shell burst on the road not five yards ahead of him. I never saw a shell so near, and never without doing some damage, but luckily it fell over his head and just in front of him, so that he was behind it, which is, I believe, the best position to be in. The one that hit me at Delville was three times as far away.

It was one of the kind that you can hear go off perhaps six miles away, and then after a minute, just the faintest whirr before it bursts with a terrific crash.

The Germans seem to be behaving abominably; that is in keeping with their traditions apparently, but it makes me feel that they won't realise the war till they have had their own houses deliberately blown up by a number of insulting fiends. Losing colonies or navies doesn't affect the individuals at all closely, and though they mayn't have the guilt of their government, I think they have to bear the punishment of the crimes they commit to order.

Now I must stop as I am taking the coy. to get baths and hope to get one myself.

March 26.

I've just got a letter from you.

I don't think I should be like ———. But, of course, one has to remember that a good many people's nerves do go wrong in the war, and it won't be over for them even when peace is declared. That is one of the penalties of war, I suppose. You cannot go in and kill one another and then say suddenly—'We've had enough'; though, I dare say, for the majority the thing will be nothing but a dull memory.

27. I didn't get this letter off by yesterday's post owing to a beastje early parade combined with too much smoke in the eyes. We are too utterly foolish about these things. The Boches have standardised a small stove with funnel to take the smoke away, and have it in every dug-out (one of their jokes is to leave a bomb in the mouth of the stove-pipe when they retire),

whereas we, every time we go to a new camp, just hunt about for some expensive can, knock holes in it, burn wet wood in it, and sit with smoke in our eyes and the oily grease and soot spoiling everything in the place. The cost of the stove and pipe is probably less than the cost of every can we destroy. I think Chowser [26] is right and Picardy has the worst climate in Europe. It has snowed and sludged and sleeted for the last ten days, in spite of which I seem to keep remarkably fit.

I'm afraid I'm an Epicurean thrown among Stoics. It's rather crushing (and, no doubt, a form of Nemesis) when my stomach turns at some horrible dish to find them all smacking their lips over it. I have to be fastidious all by my lone!

You know how they say Tommies always grouse, and dismiss it cheerfully as a peculiarity of the Tommy. Personally, I think they grouse very little at the inevitable things and are as cheerful and patient as possible. What they grouse at is the unnecessary discomforts, and so do I. They can see as plainly as any one that to sit in the cold and wet with fuel all round you is absurd; to get a bath in two months when they might have one once a week, is somebody's mismanagement. And when they grouse, somebody ought to suffer instead of the matter being lightly dismissed as a humorous trait of the private soldier; or else, after the war, they will grouse in earnest at all the want of organisation for which they were not responsible, but somebody else was. Of course some things are well done, but a lot are not.

Post goes soon, and this is written in bed after breakfast. What luxury.

March 30.

I'm writing this in a tent in a camp in the middle of a sea of mud, near a small ruined French town, weather squally snow or rain but tent pretty dry. We sleep on very muddy scraps of board: with a Boche stove in the middle which keeps us pretty warm—a *Feld Ofen*. On the table is a Madonna of painted plaster—rather good—looted by one of the servants from . the ruins of the church, I suppose. We also have an armchair with a broken spring—very comfortable, and a cane chair—both collected from cellars. Very safe position so far as one can judge, but not a good place for writing letters. My servant went off

---

26. Mr Maurice Wilkinson, F.R. Hist. S., a friend from Oxford days.

three days ago to munitions, and I have instead an elderly gentleman (probably 35) of charming manners, who used to cook for us.

I have just been offered a musketry course, and think I have evaded it. Don't expect any letters at present.

March 31

Nothing has been doing today except hailstorms, and I've sat all day in the tent, mostly putting wood on the *Feld Ofen*. It's too horribly miry to want a walk: also it's not worth getting wet when one hasn't a change of clothes. I believe we move on a bit tomorrow, and I'm afraid letters will be sparse and long on the way, so you mustn't expect much in that line. It's not bad here at all: my main objection is that it's still too cold to sleep properly. One wakes up frizzed at intervals. But I suppose every day is a step further from winter, even if it isn't a step nearer summer. I don't think the men get so much of the cold as they are squeezed into tents like peas in a pod, and so warm one another even when wet through. Whether that makes for health, however, is doubtful, I should think. I would give a good deal for leave, but there seems not the slightest chance of it.

I return the Frenchman's letter: he certainly writes very well. It's the lack of self-consciousness, I imagine. Send him my congratulations on his *Croix de Guerre* when you write. I don't know what the attack was, but evidently a good deal east of where they were.

April 1. Bustling off for billets. 216

April 4.

Just another line to say very fitly. We are in another village—farm kitchen with ceiling but no roof, and a large brick fireplace on which we burn rafters and suchlike—the best fires I've seen in France. We sleep on boards slung halfway down the wall and the servants sleep underneath. The country ahead comparatively unspoilt; but every village bashed in completely—not a cottage left in places three times the size of Standon. Quite heavy snow last night, but the billet is nice and warm, unlike most places we've been in. Went for a walk with B. yesterday to see our front.

I've got your beautiful cake, and it's more than half eaten at the first go. It's very fine and good. Shortbread from Frdk. and a parcel from my mother arrived at same time, which is unusual but most useful, as we get further from our base of supplies. Haven't time to send more this time.

April 5.

It's quite a fine day and I believe we move up a bit. Edith's parcel has arrived, very good, please thank her very much for it; and the cheroots, also very good, as is the pipe and the sweets and the handkerchief which you sent with that particularly good cake, which vanished away within twenty four hours, large as it was.

Didn't you ask if I had had any conversation with the C.O.? Well, I haven't. Everyone seems to think him extremely competent. He strikes me as far more able than any one I have met yet.

I had a nice ride yesterday over country almost unshelled on the coy. horse, which has been clipped and goes like the wind on turf—quite a different beast from what it is on the road.

We have been most comfortable in this billet, with a fire almost too hot to sit by.

Yes, I got *The Sergeant*, [27] but haven't heard it sung yet.

Easter Sunday, April 8.

I suppose you have been to the Early Service, haven't you? And is it a fine day as it is here, after a beastje one yesterday?

We are in most luxurious quarters—more or less at the Front—a farm stables practically uninjured by the retiring Boches. It has not been clent for ages, but the 'nures' [manures] are nice and soft, and I have just slept on a spring mattress gathered in from the adjoining ruins. We also have tables and chairs dotted among the nure-heaps, and a small artificial Christmas tree, evidently left by the Boches.

Our last shelter was not so good, being the ruins of the Manse in another village. The snow and wind blew through it and the chimney beam caught fire and threatened to bring the chimbley on top of us, so we had to go cold—which it was. There is no exaggeration about the state these villages are left in. The Boches cut out a brick or two at intervals in every house wall,

---

27. A musical setting of his poem *The Sergeant*, by a stranger, Mr F. G. Ladds, who, having read the poem in the newspaper, had written asking to be allowed to set it to music.

insert explosives, and bring the whole thing down, so that often you can sit under the gables as they rest on the ground with the whole house and all the contents ground to dust below.

The advantage to us of this destruction is that everywhere now there is fuel—broken beams and laths and doors and chairs with which one can mostly keep big fires going. The military advantage to them is less than nothing.

I am glad America is coming in. I suppose there is no doubt now. If so, the Boches must feel themselves coming very close to the pit they digged for others, unless their submarines can work miracles.

Send your *téléphoniste* my congratulations on his *Croix de Guerre*. He has what every soldier must desire—the recognition of his valour.

I think it will be summer soon, and perhaps the war will end this year and I shall see my Pretty One again.

WAR OFFICE.

Deeply regret to inform you that 2nd Lieut. R. E. Vernède, Rifle Brigade, died of wounds, April ninth. The Army Council express their sympathy.—Secretary, War Office.

ALSO FROM LEONAUR
AVAILABLE IN SOFTCOVER OR HARDCOVER WITH DUST JACKET

THE WOMAN IN BATTLE by *Loreta Janeta Velazquez*—Soldier, Spy and Secret Service Agent for the Confederacy During the American Civil War.

BOOTS AND SADDLES by *Elizabeth B. Custer*—The experiences of General Custer's Wife on the Western Plains.

FANNIE BEERS' CIVIL WAR by *Fannie A. Beers*—A Confederate Lady's Experiences of Nursing During the Campaigns & Battles of the American Civil War.

LADY SALE'S AFGHANISTAN by *Florentia Sale*—An Indomitable Victorian Lady's Account of the Retreat from Kabul During the First Afghan War.

THE TWO WARS OF MRS DUBERLY by *Frances Isabella Duberly*—An Intrepid Victorian Lady's Experience of the Crimea and Indian Mutiny.

THE REBELLIOUS DUCHESS by *Paul F. S. Dermoncourt*—The Adventures of the Duchess of Berri and Her Attempt to Overthrow French Monarchy.

LADIES OF WATERLOO by *Charlotte A. Eaton, Magdalene de Lancey & Juana Smith*—The Experiences of Three Women During the Campaign of 1815: Waterloo Days by Charlotte A. Eaton, A Week at Waterloo by Magdalene de Lancey & Juana's Story by Juana Smith.

NURSE AND SPY IN THE UNION ARMY by *Sarah Emma Evelyn Edmonds*—During the American Civil War

WIFE NO. 19 by *Ann Eliza Young*—The Life & Ordeals of a Mormon Woman During the 19th Century

DIARY OF A NURSE IN SOUTH AFRICA by *Alice Bron*—With the Dutch-Belgian Red Cross During the Boer War

MARIE ANTOINETTE AND THE DOWNFALL OF ROYALTY by *Imbert de Saint-Amand*—The Queen of France and the French Revolution

THE MEMSAHIB & THE MUTINY by *R. M. Coopland*—An English lady's ordeals in Gwalior and Agra during the Indian Mutiny 1857

MY CAPTIVITY AMONG THE SIOUX INDIANS by *Fanny Kelly*—The ordeal of a pioneer woman crossing the Western Plains in 1864

WITH MAXIMILIAN IN MEXICO by *Sara Yorke Stevenson*—A Lady's experience of the French Adventure

AVAILABLE ONLINE AT **www.leonaur.com**
AND FROM ALL GOOD BOOK STORES

www.ingramcontent.com/pod-product-compliance
Lightning Source LLC
Chambersburg PA
CBHW030228170426
43201CB00006B/141